MODERN STATISTICAL THINKING

MODERN STATISTICAL THINKING

PRINCIPLES FOR THE DATA-DRIVEN ERA

Chloe Robinson
Chase Barrett

Kruger Brentt
Publishers

2026

Kruger Brentt Publishers UK. LTD.
Company Number 9728962

Regd. Office: 68 St Margarets Road, Edgware, Middlesex HA8 9UU

ISBN: 978-1-78715-654-8

For information on all our publications visit our website at http://krugerbrentt.com/

PREFACE

The rapid expansion of data across scientific, technological, and societal domains has ushered in a transformative era—one in which statistical thinking is no longer optional but foundational. Modern Statistical Thinking: Principles for the Data-Driven Era has been developed to equip learners, researchers, and practitioners with a comprehensive understanding of the conceptual frameworks and analytical tools that underpin evidence-based inquiry. In writing this text, our goal has been to bridge classical statistical principles with modern computational approaches, offering a coherent perspective that reflects the evolving landscape of data-centric disciplines.

This book emphasizes the essential role of reasoning, interpretation, and uncertainty, moving beyond procedural techniques to cultivate a deeper appreciation for how statistical insights are generated, validated, and applied. Integrating theory with real-world relevance, we highlight the ways in which statistical thinking informs decisions in science, industry, policy, healthcare, and the social sciences. Throughout, the focus remains on clarity, rigor, and the development of a critical mindset capable of navigating complex data environments.

We hope this volume serves as both a foundational guide and a forward-looking companion for students beginning their statistical journey as well as professionals seeking to strengthen their analytical capabilities. It is our aspiration that readers will not only gain technical proficiency but also develop the intellectual confidence to engage thoughtfully with the challenges and opportunities of a data-driven world.

Chloe Robinson

Chase Barrett

CONTENTS

Chapter-1

Introduction to Statistical Thinking

1.1 Statistical Thinking: An Overview

Statistical thinking is a method of comprehending a complicated world by articulating it in relatively simple terms that effectively encapsulate fundamental characteristics of its structure or function, while simultaneously conveying the degree of uncertainty associated with that knowledge. The principles of statistical thinking originate mostly from mathematics and statistics, as well as from computer science, psychology, and various other disciplines.

Statistical thinking can be differentiated from other cognitive approaches that are less likely to accurately represent reality. Human intuition frequently attempts to address the same inquiries that statistical reasoning can resolve, yet it often yields incorrect conclusions. In recent years, the majority of Americans have indicated that they perceive violent crime to be more severe than in the preceding year (Pew Research Center). Nevertheless, a statistical examination of the actual crime data indicates that violent crime has consistently diminished during the 1990s. Intuition is unreliable as it depends on heuristics, or educated guesses, which can frequently lead to errors. For instance, individuals frequently assess the frequency of certain events, such as violent crime, by an availability heuristic, which refers to the ease with which examples of violent crime come to mind. Consequently, our perceptions of rising crime rates may be more indicative of heightened media attention, notwithstanding a genuine decline in crime rates. Statistical reasoning equips us with the instruments to comprehend the world more precisely and mitigate the biases inherent in human judgment.

1.2 Statistics Anxiety

Numerous individuals approach their inaugural statistics lesson with considerable apprehension and concern, particularly upon learning that coding will be necessary for data analysis. I administer a survey to students before the initial session to assess their attitudes regarding statistics, requesting them to evaluate several items on a scale from 1 (strongly disagree) to 7 (strongly agree). One of the survey items is "The prospect of enrolling in a statistics course induces anxiety in me." In a recent session, about two-thirds of the students rated a five or above, while approximately one-fourth expressed strong agreement with the statement. If you experience apprehension around the commencement of statistics learning, you are not solitary in this sentiment.

Anxiety is unpleasant; but, psychological research indicates that this emotional arousal might enhance performance on many activities by sharpening our focus. If you begin to have anxiety regarding the content of this book, remember yourself that numerous other readers share similar feelings, and that this emotional arousal may enhance your comprehension of the subject, even if it appears otherwise.

1.3 What benefits can statistics provide us?

There are three primary applications of statistics:

- Describe: The world is complex and we often need to describe it in a simplified way that we can understand.
- Decide: We often need to make decisions based on data, usually in the face of uncertainty.
- Predict: We often wish to make predictions about new situations based on our knowledge of previous situations.

Let us examine an example of these principles in practice, focusing on an issue of widespread interest: How can we determine what constitutes a healthy diet? Numerous sources of information exist, including governmental dietary recommendations, nutrition literature, and online influencers, among others. Let us concentrate on a particular inquiry: Is the presence of saturated fat in our diet detrimental?

A potential approach to addressing this dilemma is through common sense. If we consume fat, it will directly convert into fat within our body, correct? We have all observed images of arteries obstructed by fat, suggesting that the consumption of fat will indeed obstruct our arteries, correct?

Alternatively, we could address this inquiry by heeding authoritative figures. The Dietary Guidelines from the US Food and Drug Administration include a Key Recommendation stating that "A healthy eating pattern limits saturated fats." One may anticipate that these guidelines are grounded in sound scientific principles; however, as Nina Teicholz elucidates in her book "Big Fat Surprise" (Teicholz 2014), this specific recommendation appears to be more influenced by the entrenched dogma of nutrition researchers than by empirical evidence.

Ultimately, we may examine empirical scientific research. We will begin by examining a substantial investigation known as the PURE project, which has analyzed dietary patterns and health outcomes, including mortality, in over 135,000 individuals across 18 different nations. In a 2017 analysis published in The Lancet by Dehghan et al., the PURE investigators examined the correlation between the consumption of different macronutrient categories, including saturated fats and carbohydrates, and the mortality risk during the follow-up period. Participants were monitored for a median duration of 7.4 years, indicating that half of the subjects were observed for less than this period, while the other half were observed for longer. Figure 1.1 illustrates data from the study (sourced from the paper), depicting the correlation between the consumption of saturated fats and carbs and the mortality risk from all causes.

This graph is derived from 10 numerical values. To derive these figures, the researchers divided the cohort of 135,335 study participants, referred to as the "sample," into five groups, or "quintiles," based on their nutrient intake. The first quintile comprises the lowest 20% of intake, while the fifth quintile encompasses the highest 20% of intake. The researchers subsequently calculated the mortality rates of individuals within each group during the observation period.

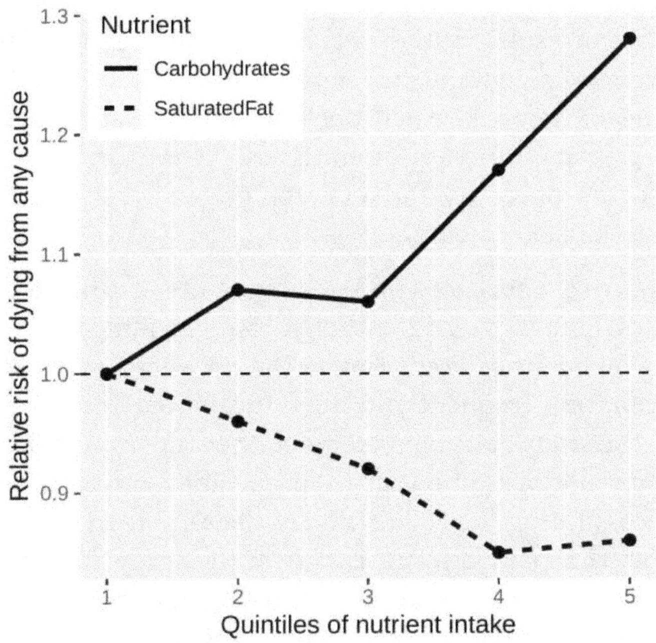

Figure 1.1: A graph from the PURE study illustrating the correlation between mortality from all causes and the relative consumption of saturated fats and carbohydrates.

The graphic articulates this in relation to the relative risk of mortality compared to the lowest quintile: If this value exceeds one, it indicates that individuals in the group have a higher mortality risk compared to those in the lowest quintile; conversely, if it is below one, it signifies that individuals in the group have a lower mortality risk. The data is unequivocal: Individuals who consumed greater amounts of saturated fat exhibited a reduced mortality rate throughout the research, with the lowest death rate observed among those in the fourth quintile (i.e., those who ingested more fat than the lowest 60% but less than the highest 20%). Conversely, an increase in carbohydrate consumption correlated with a higher likelihood of mortality during the research. This example illustrates how statistics can simplify a complex dataset into a more manageable set of numbers; examining the data from all study participants simultaneously would result in information overload, obscuring the patterns that become apparent through simpler descriptions.

Figure 1.1 indicates a correlation between decreased mortality and saturated fat consumption, alongside an increase in mortality with carbohydrate intake; however, the data is fraught with uncertainty, as some individuals who adhered to a low-carbohydrate diet experienced early mortality, while others with high carbohydrate consumption lived to an advanced age. Considering this heterogeneity, we aim to determine if the observed associations in the data are sufficiently substantial to suggest that they would not arise randomly in the absence of a genuine correlation between food and longevity. Statistics equip us with the means to make such decisions, and external observers frequently perceive this as the primary function of statistics. However, as will be demonstrated throughout the book, the necessity for dichotomous conclusions based on ambiguous evidence has frequently misled researchers.

We aim to forecast future events based on the facts. A life insurance company may utilize data regarding an individual's fat and carbohydrate consumption to forecast their life expectancy. A crucial element of prediction is the necessity to generalize from existing data to alternative scenarios, frequently in the future; if our results were confined to the unique individuals in the study at a given moment, the study would lack significant utility. Researchers must generally presume that their specific sample accurately represents a larger population, necessitating the acquisition of the sample in a manner that ensures an unbiased depiction of the population. If the PURE study had exclusively recruited volunteers from religious groups that adhere to vegetarianism, it would be inappropriate to extrapolate the findings to individuals with differing dietary practices.

1.4 The fundamental concepts of statistics

Several fundamental concepts permeate practically all facets of statistical reasoning. Stigler (2016) delineates several of these in his exemplary work "The Seven Pillars of Statistical Wisdom," which I have supplemented here.

1.4.1 Acquiring knowledge from data

Statistics can be regarded as a collection of instruments that facilitate the extraction of insights from data. In any circumstance, we commence with a collection of concepts or assumptions regarding potential realities. In the PURE investigation, the researchers likely commenced with the presumption that increased fat consumption would correlate with elevated mortality rates, considering the dominant negative doctrine of saturated fats. Subsequently in the course, we shall provide the concept of previous knowledge, intended to denote the understanding we contribute to a circumstance. The level of prior knowledge can fluctuate, typically influenced by the extent of our experience; for instance, upon visiting a restaurant for the first time, my expectations are likely to be weak, however after 10 visits to the same establishment, my expectations will be significantly stronger. Likewise, if I examine a restaurant review site and observe that a restaurant's average rating of four stars is derived from merely three reviews, my expectations will be diminished compared to if it were based on 300 reviews.

Statistics offers a methodology for optimizing the utilization of fresh data to refine our views, hence establishing profound connections between statistics and psychology. Numerous theories of human and animal learning in psychology are closely connected with those from the emerging science of machine learning. Machine learning is a discipline at the intersection of statistics and computer science that concentrates on developing algorithms capable of learning from experience. Although statistics and machine learning frequently address analogous issues, scholars from these disciplines typically adopt markedly divergent methodologies; the renowned statistician Leo Breiman famously termed them "The Two Cultures" to illustrate the extent of their differences (Breiman 2001). This book aims to integrate the two cultures, as both perspectives offer valuable methodologies for analyzing data.

1.4.2 Aggregation

Statistics might be conceptualized as "the science of discarding data". In the aforementioned PURE investigation, we synthesized over 100,000 data points into ten. This type of aggregation is a fundamental idea in statistics. This was groundbreaking when initially proposed: If we disregard all details concerning each participant, how can we ascertain that we are not overlooking something significant?

Statistics offers methods to delineate the structure of data aggregation, supported by theoretical foundations that elucidate its efficacy. Nonetheless, it is crucial to recognize that aggregation can be excessive, and subsequently, we will face instances when a summary may present a highly deceptive representation of the data being aggregated.

1.4.3 Uncertainty

The world is an unpredictable environment. Cigarette smoking is now established as a cause of lung cancer; nevertheless, this relationship is probabilistic. A 68-year-old guy, who has smoked two packs daily for the past 50 years and persists in smoking, has a 15% (1 in 7) probability of developing lung cancer, significantly exceeding the risk for nonsmokers. Nonetheless, this implies that some individuals may smoke throughout their lives without ever developing lung cancer. Statistics equips us with the means to delineate uncertainty, facilitate decision-making among uncertainty, and generate predictions for which we can quantify the uncertainty.

The world is an erratic environment. Cigarette smoking is now recognized as a causative factor for lung cancer; nevertheless, this association is probabilistic. A 68-year-old man, who has smoked two packs daily for the previous 50 years and continues to smoke, has a 15% (1 in 7) likelihood of acquiring lung cancer, markedly higher than the risk for nonsmokers. Nevertheless, this suggests that certain individuals may smoke for their entire lives without ever contracting lung cancer. Statistics provides the tools to clarify ambiguity, aid decision-making under uncertainty, and produce forecasts that allow for the quantification of that uncertainty.

1.4.4 Population sampling

The notion of aggregation suggests that valuable insights can be derived by consolidating data; but, what is the requisite volume of data? The concept of sampling posits that an entire population can be represented by a limited number of samples, provided that these samples are collected appropriately. The PURE project enlisted approximately 135,000 individuals, aiming to yield insights applicable to the billions of persons constituting the broader population from whom the sample was drawn. The method of obtaining the study sample is crucial, as it dictates the extent to which we may generalize the results. A crucial understanding of sampling is that although larger samples enhance the accuracy of population representation, the benefits decline as the sample size increases. The rate at which the advantage of larger samples diminishes adheres to a straightforward mathematical principle, increasing with the square root of the sample size; hence, to double the precision of our estimate, we must quadruple the sample size.

1.5 Causality and statistics

The PURE study appeared to offer compelling evidence for a favorable correlation between saturated fat consumption and longevity; nevertheless, it does not address the critical question: Does increased saturated fat intake directly result in a longer lifespan? This is due to our uncertainty regarding a direct causal association between the consumption of saturated fat and longevity. The findings support this association, although they also align with the possibility of an alternative cause contributing to both increased saturated fat and extended lifespan. For instance, one might presume that wealthier individuals consume greater amounts of saturated fat and that affluent individuals generally have longer lifespans; however, their extended longevity may not be attributable to fat consumption, but rather to superior healthcare, diminished psychological stress, enhanced food quality, or numerous other variables. The PURE study authors attempted to control for these characteristics; nevertheless, we cannot ascertain that their efforts entirely eliminated the influence of other variables. The possibility that additional factors may elucidate the link between saturated fat consumption and mortality exemplifies the principle commonly taught in beginning statistics that "correlation does not imply causation," although the esteemed data visualization authority Edward Tufte has remarked, "but it certainly suggests."

While observational research, such as the PURE study, cannot definitively establish causal relationships, it is widely accepted that causation can be proven through studies that experimentally control and change specific variables. In the field of medicine, this type of investigation is known as a randomized controlled trial (RCT). Suppose we aim to conduct a randomized controlled trial to investigate whether an increase in saturated fat consumption extends lifespan. We will choose a cohort of individuals and allocate them to either a treatment group, instructed to augment their saturated fat consumption, or a control group, directed to maintain their previous dietary habits. It is imperative that we allocate the individuals to these groups at random. Alternatively, individuals selecting the therapy may differ in certain aspects from those opting for the control group; for instance, they may exhibit a greater propensity for engaging in additional healthful activities. Subsequently, we would monitor the participants longitudinally to ascertain the mortality rates within each group. Due to the random assignment of participants to treatment or control groups, we can be fairly assured that no confounding differences exist between the groups affecting the treatment effect; nonetheless, certainty is elusive as randomization may occasionally result in treatment and control groups differing in significant ways. Researchers frequently attempt to mitigate these confounds by statistical studies;

nevertheless, eliminating a confound's influence from the data can prove exceedingly challenging.

Several randomized controlled trials have investigated whether alterations in saturated fat consumption lead to improved health and longevity. These experiments have concentrated on diminishing saturated fat intake due to the prevailing belief among nutrition researchers that saturated fat is harmful; many of these academics would likely contend that it is unethical to encourage increased consumption of saturated fat. Nevertheless, the randomized controlled trials have demonstrated a similar trend: There is no significant impact on mortality rates from decreasing saturated fat consumption.

Chapter-2

Working with Data

2.1 Data

The primary point regarding data is that it is plural, notwithstanding some differing opinions on this matter. You may also question the pronunciation of "data" - I articulate it as "day-tah", although I am aware of other individuals who pronounce it as "dah-tah", and I have maintained amicable relations with them regardless of this divergence. If I heard them state "the data is," that would constitute a more significant concern.

2.1.1 Qualitative data

Data consist of variables, each representing a distinct measurement or quantity. Certain variables are qualitative, indicating that they characterize a quality rather than a numerical value. In my statistics course, I typically administer an introduction survey to gather data for class usage and to gain insights into the students. I inquire, "What is your favorite food?" Responses have included blueberries, chocolate, tamales, pasta, pizza, and mango. The data are not inherently numerical; we might assign numerical values to each item (1 = blueberries, 2 = chocolate, etc.), but these numbers would merely serve as labels rather than true numerical values. This also limits our actions regarding those numbers; for instance, calculating their average would be illogical. However, we will often code qualitative data using numbers in order to make them easier to work with, as you will see later.

Table 2.1: Counts of the prevalence of different responses to the question "Why are you taking this class?"

Why are you taking this class?	Number of students
It fulfills a degree plan requirement	105
It fulfills a General Education Breadth Requirement	32
It is not required but I am interested in the topic	11
Other	4

2.1.2 Quantitative data

In statistics, we predominantly engage with quantitative data, which refers to numerical information. Table 2.1 presents the findings from an additional question posed in my introductory class: "Why are you taking this class?"

It is important to note that the students' responses were qualitative; nonetheless, we produced a quantitative summary by tallying the number of students who provided each answer.

2.1.2.1 Different Types of numbers

In statistics, we utilize many categories of numbers. Understanding these distinctions is crucial, partly because statistical analysis languages, such as R, frequently differentiate between them. Binary numerals. The most fundamental are binary numbers, which consist just of zero and one. Binary numbers are frequently employed to denote the veracity or falsity of a statement, or the presence or absence of an entity. I may inquire of 10 individuals whether they have ever encountered a migraine headache, documenting their responses as "Yes" or "No". Utilizing logical values, which represent either TRUE or FALSE, is frequently advantageous. This is particularly advantageous when utilizing computer languages such as R for data analysis, as these languages inherently comprehend the ideas of TRUE and FALSE. Most computer languages equivalently treat truth values and binary numbers. The numeral 1 corresponds to the logical value TRUE, while the numeral 0 corresponds to the logical value FALSE.

Whole numbers. Integers are complete numbers devoid of fractional or decimal components. Integers are frequently seen in counting, but they also commonly appear in psychological measuring. In my introductory survey, I provide a series of questions regarding attitudes towards statistics (e.g., "Statistics appears quite enigmatic to me."), to which students react with a numerical value ranging from 1 ("Disagree strongly") to 7 ("Agree strongly").

Real numbers. In statistics, we predominantly utilize real numbers, which possess a fractional or decimal component. For instance, an individual's weight can be quantified with several degrees of precision, ranging from kilograms to micrograms.

2.2 Discrete and continuous measurements

A discrete measurement is one that assumes a certain value from a finite number of distinct options. These may represent qualitative attributes (such as various dog breeds) or quantitative metrics (such as the number of friends on Facebook). Significantly, there exists no intermediary between the measurements; it is illogical to assert that one possesses 33.7 pals.

A continuous measurement is characterized by its definition as a real number. The value may reside within a specific range, however our measurement instruments typically constrain the precision of our measurements; for instance, a floor scale may quantify weight to the nearest kilogram, despite the theoretical possibility of measuring weight with more accuracy.

Statistics courses typically provide an in-depth examination of several "scales" of measurement, elaborated further in the Appendix of this chapter. The primary conclusion is that certain statistical methods are inapplicable to specific types of data. For instance, consider the collection of postal Zip Code data from several persons. The numbers are portrayed as integers; nevertheless, they do not correspond to a numeric scale, as each zip code functions merely as a designation for a distinct location. Consequently, discussing the average zip code would be illogical.

2.3 What constitutes an effective measurement?

In many fields such as psychology, the thing that we are measuring is not a physical feature, but instead is an unobservable theoretical concept, which we usually refer to as a construct. For example, let's say that I want to test how well you understand the distinction between the different types of numbers described above. I could give you a pop quiz that would ask you several questions about these concepts and count how many you got right. This test might or might not be a good measurement of the construct of your actual knowledge - for example, if I were to write the test in a confusing way or use language that you don't understand, then the test might suggest you don't understand the concepts when really you do. On the other hand, if I give a multiple choice test with very obvious wrong answers, then you might be able to perform well on the test even if you don't actually understand the material.

It is usually impossible to measure a construct without some amount of error. In the example above, you might know the answer, but you might mis-read the question and get it wrong. In other cases, there is error intrinsic to the thing being measured, such as when we measure how long it takes a person to respond on a simple reaction time test, which will vary from trial to trial for many reasons. We generally want our measurement error to be as low as possible, which we can achieve either by improving the quality of the measurement (for example, using a better time to measure reaction time), or by averaging over a larger number of indvidiual measurements.

Sometimes there is a standard against which other measurements can be tested, which we might refer to as a "gold standard" - for example, measurement of sleep can be done using many different devices (such as devices that measure movement in bed), but they are generally considered inferior to the gold standard of polysomnography (which uses measurement of brain waves to quantify the amount of time a person spends in each stage of sleep). Often the gold standard is more difficult or expensive to perform, and the cheaper method is used even though it might have greater error.

When we think about what makes a good measurement, we usually distinguish two different aspects of a good measurement: it should be reliable, and it should be valid.

2.3.1 What is Reliability?

Reliability signifies the uniformity of our measurements. Test-retest reliability is a common measure of consistency that evaluates the stability of measurements when the identical assessment is administered multiple times. For example, I could distribute a questionnaire assessing your views on statistics today, replicate it tomorrow, and evaluate your responses from both days; we would expect them to be similar, barring any intervening events that might shift your perception of statistics (such as reading this book!). A different approach to assess dependability occurs when the data includes subjective evaluations. A researcher seeks to determine if a treatment modifies an autistic child's interactions with peers, evaluated by specialists witnessing the child's engagements with other children. In this situation, we seek to guarantee that the responses remain unaffected by the specific evaluator, hence attaining superior inter-rater reliability. This can be assessed by utilizing numerous evaluators, followed by a comparison of their ratings to ensure a high level of agreement. Dependability is essential for measurement comparison, as the correlation between two distinct variables cannot surpass the dependability of either variable in isolation. An unreliable measure can never develop a strong statistical association with any other measure. Consequently, researchers developing a new measurement instrument, such as a survey, often invest significant effort to establish and improve its reliability.

2.3.2 What is Validity?

While reliability is crucial, it is insufficient in isolation. Ultimately, I could establish a wholly dependable measurement on a personality assessment by reassigning every response with the identical numeral, irrespective of the individual's actual answers. We desire our measurements to be valid; specifically, we aim to ensure that we are accurately measuring the construct we intend to assess (Figure 2.1). Numerous sorts of validity are frequently examined; we will concentrate on three of them.

Face validity. Does the measurement make sense on its face?

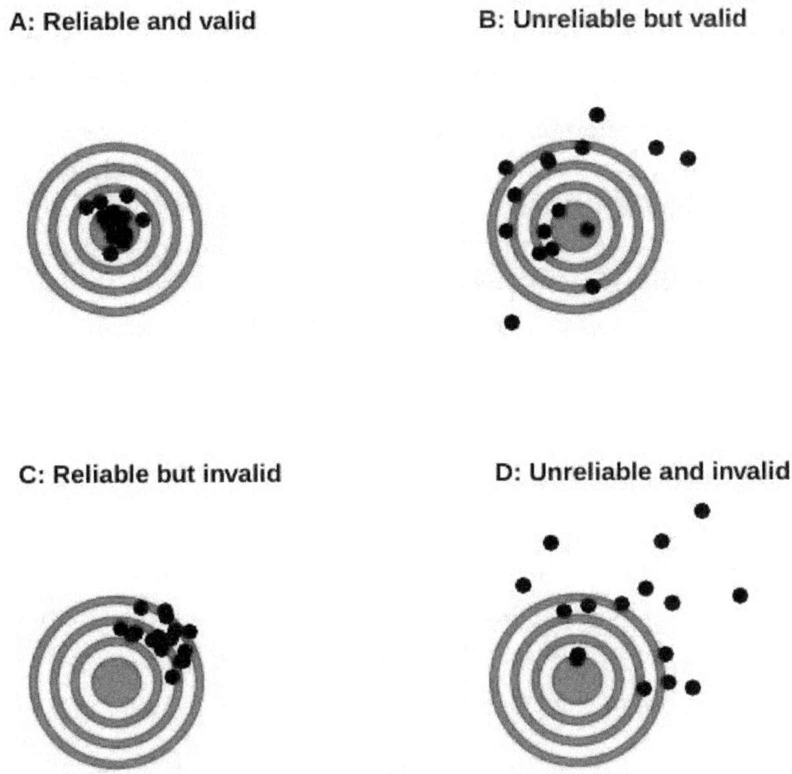

Figure 2.1: A figure demonstrating the distinction between reliability and validity, using shots at a bullseye. Reliability refers to the consistency of location of shots, and validity refers to the accuracy of the shots with respect to the center of the bullseye.

If I were to tell you that I was going to measure a person's blood pressure by looking at the color of their tongue, you would probably think that this was not a valid measure on its face. On the other hand, using a blood pressure cuff would have face validity. This is usually a first reality check before we dive into more complicated aspects of validity.

Construct validity. Is the measurement related to other measurements in an appropriate way? This is often subdivided into two aspects. Convergent validity means that the measurement should be closely related to other measures that are thought to reflect the same construct. Let's say that I am interested in measuring how extroverted a person is using either a questionnaire or an interview. Convergent validity would be demonstrated if both of these different measurements are closely related to one another. On the other hand, measurements thought to reflect different constructs should be unrelated, known as divergent validity. If my theory of personality says that extraversion and conscientiousness are two distinct constructs, then I should also see that my measurements of extraversion are unrelated to measurements of conscientiousness.

Predictive validity. If our metrics are genuinely valid, they should also predict other outcomes. For instance, consider the hypothesis that the psychological attribute of sensation seeking, defined as the pursuit of novel experiences, correlates with real-world risk-taking behavior. To evaluate the predictive validity of a sensation-seeking measurement, we would assess the extent to which test scores forecast results on an alternative survey that gauges real-world risk-taking behavior.

2.4 Appendix

2.4.1 Scales of measurement

All variables must assume a minimum of two distinct values; otherwise, they would be classified as constants rather than variables. However, varying values of the variable might interrelate in diverse manners, which we denote as scales of measurement. There are four methods by which the various values of a variable can differ.

- Identity: Each value of the variable has a unique meaning.
- Magnitude: The values of the variable reflect different magnitudes and have an ordered relationship to one another - that is, some values are larger and some are smaller.
- Equal intervals: Units along the scale of measurement are equal to one another. This means, for example, that the difference between 1 and 2 would be equal in its magnitude to the difference between 19 and 20 .
- Absolute zero: The scale has a true meaningful zero point. For example, for many measurements of physical quantities such as height or weight, this is the complete absence of the thing being measured.

There are four different scales of measurement that go along with these different ways that values of a variable can differ.

Nominal scale. A nominal variable satisfies the criterion of identity, such that each value of the variable represents something different, but the numbers simply serve as qualitative labels as discussed above. For example, we might ask people for their political party affiliation, and then code those as numbers: 1 = "Republican", 2 = "Democrat", 3 =

"Libertarian", and so on. However, the different numbers do not have any ordered relationship with one another.

Ordinal scale: An ordinal variable meets the conditions of identity and magnitude, allowing for the values to be arranged according to their magnitude. For instance, we may request an individual with chronic pain to fill out a daily form evaluating the severity of their pain on a number scale from 1 to 7. It is important to recognize that although an individual likely experiences greater pain on a day rated as 6 compared to a day rated as 3, it is inaccurate to assert that the pain on the former day is twice as severe as on the latter. The ordinal scale provides insight into relative intensity, yet the disparities between values are not necessarily uniform in magnitude.

Interval scale: An interval scale possesses all characteristics of an ordinal scale, with the added distinction that the intervals between units on the measuring scale are considered equal. A typical illustration is physical temperature quantified in Celsius or Fahrenheit; the physical disparity between 10 and 20 degrees is equivalent to that between 90 and 100 degrees, however each scale can also encompass negative numbers.

Ratio scale: A ratio scale variable possesses all four characteristics: identity, magnitude, equal intervals, and absolute zero. A ratio scale variable differs from an interval scale variable in that it possesses a genuine zero point. Instances of ratio scale variables encompass physical height and weight, as well as temperature quantified in Kelvin.

There are two important reasons that we must pay attention to the scale of measurement of a variable. First, the scale determines what kind of mathematical operations we can apply to the data (see Table 2.2). A nominal variable can only be compared for equality; that is, do two observations on that variable have the same numeric value? It would not make sense to apply other mathematical operations to a nominal variable, since they don't really function as numbers in a nominal variable, but rather as labels. With ordinal variables, we can also test whether one value is greater or lesser than another, but we can't do any arithmetic. Interval and ratio variables allow us to perform arithmetic; with interval variables we can only add or subtract values, whereas with ratio variables we can also multiply and divide values.

Table 2.2: Different scales of measurement admit different types of numeric operations

	Equal/not equal	>/<	+/−	Multiply/divide
Nominal	OK			
Ordinal	OK	OK		
Interval	OK	OK	OK	
Ratio	OK	OK	OK	OK

These limitations indicate that specific types of statistics can be calculated for each category of variable. Statistics that entail the enumeration of various values, such as the mode, can be computed for any type of variable. Other statistics rely on the ordering or ranking of values (such as the median, which represents the central value when all values are arranged by magnitude), necessitating that the values be at least on an ordinal scale. Ultimately, statistical calculations that entail summing values, such as the average or mean, necessitate that the variables be at a minimum on an interval scale. It is important to acknowledge that researchers frequently calculate the mean of ordinal variables, such as responses on personality assessments; yet, this practice can occasionally provide complications.

Chapter-3

Data Summarizing

3.1 What is the purpose of data summarization?

Summarizing data in statistics is the process of converting large, often overwhelming sets of raw information into clear, digestible insights that reveal the underlying structure of the data. It plays a crucial role in helping researchers, analysts, and decision-makers understand what the data is truly saying without getting lost in individual values. Through numerical summaries such as measures of central tendency (mean, median, mode) and measures of variability (range, variance, standard deviation), statisticians can describe the typical behavior of a dataset and the extent to which values differ from one another. Visual tools like bar charts, histograms, box plots, and scatterplots further enhance understanding by presenting patterns, trends, and relationships in an intuitive, easily interpretable form. Summarizing data also allows for quick comparisons between groups, identification of outliers, and detection of anomalies that may require deeper investigation. Moreover, it provides a solid foundation for advanced statistical methods, supporting hypothesis testing, predictive modeling, and informed decision-making. In essence, effective data summarization transforms raw numbers into meaningful knowledge, making it an essential first step in any statistical analysis.

Summarizing data inherently results in the loss of information, which may be a valid point of contention. For instance, let us revisit the PURE study mentioned in Chapter 1. Should we not consider that every aspect regarding each individual is significant, beyond what is encapsulated in the dataset? What are the precise details of the data collection, including the time of day and the participant's mood? All of these particulars are obscured when we condense the data.

One rationale for summarizing data is that it enables us to generalize, allowing for broad conclusions that transcend particular findings. The significance of generalization was emphasized by the author Jorge Luis Borges in his short story "Funes the Memorious," which depicts a character who forfeits the capacity to forget. Borges emphasizes the connection between generalization, which involves discarding material, and cognition: "To think is to forget a difference, to generalize, to abstract." In the excessively saturated realm of Funes, only details existed.

Psychologists have extensively examined the pivotal role of generalization in cognitive processes. An illustration of categorization is our ability to readily identify several instances of the category "birds," despite the significant differences in their superficial characteristics, such as those of an ostrich, a robin, and a chicken. Significantly, generalization enables us to forecast characteristics of these individuals; for instance, in the context of birds, we can anticipate their ability to fly and consume seeds, while inferring that they are unlikely to operate a vehicle or communicate in English. Although these forecasts may not always be accurate, they frequently possess sufficient use in practical applications.

3.1.1 Summarizing data using tables

A simple way to summarize data is to generate a table representing counts of various types of observations. This type of table has been used for thousands of years (see Figure 3.1).

Figure 3.1: A Sumerian tablet from the Louvre, showing a sales contract for a house and field. Public domain, via Wikimedia Commons.

Let's look at some examples of the use of tables, using a more realistic dataset. Throughout this book we will use the National Health and Nutrition Examination Survey (NHANES) dataset. This is an ongoing study that assesses the health and nutrition status of a sample of individuals from the United States on many different variables. We will use a version of the dataset that is available for the R statistical software package.

Table 3.1: Frequency distribution for PhysActive variable

PhysActive	AbsoluteFrequency
No	2473
Yes	2972
NA	1334

For this example, we will look at a simple variable, called PhysActive in the dataset. This variable contains one of three different values: "Yes" or "No" (indicating whether or not the person reports doing "moderate or vigorous-intensity sports, fitness or recreational activities"), or "NA" if the data are missing for that individual. There are different reasons that the data might be missing; for example, this question was not asked of children younger than 12 years of age, while in other cases an adult may have declined to answer the question during the interview, or the interviewer's recording of the answer on their form might be unreadable.

3.1.1 Frequency distributions

A distribution delineates the allocation of data over various potential values. This example examines the distribution of individuals across several physical activity categories.

Table 3.1 presents the frequency of various responses: 2473 participants answered "No," 2972 answered "Yes," and 1334 provided no response. This is termed a frequency distribution as it indicates the prevalence of each potential value within our sample.

This illustrates the absolute frequency of the two responses among all individuals who provided a response. This indicates that the number of individuals affirming "Yes" exceeds those responding "No"; nevertheless, discerning the magnitude of this difference in relative terms from absolute figures can be challenging. For this reason, we often would rather present the data using relative frequency, which is obtained by dividing each frequency by the sum of all frequencies:

$$\text{relative frequency}_i = \frac{\text{absolute frequency}}{\sum_{j=1}^{N} \text{absolute}_i \text{ frequency}_j}$$

Table 3.2: Absolute and relative frequencies and percentages for PhysActive variable

PhysActive	AbsoluteFrequency	RelativeFrequency	Percentage
No	2473	0.45	45
Yes	2972	0.55	55

The relative frequency offers a more accessible means to assess the magnitude of the imbalance. The relative frequencies can be expressed as percentages by multiplying them by 100. In this instance, we will eliminate the NA values to facilitate the interpretation of the relative frequencies of active versus inactive individuals. For this to be coherent, we must presume that the NA values are absent "at random," indicating that their occurrence or non-occurrence is unrelated to the actual value of the variable for that individual. If inactive participants are more inclined to decline answering the question compared to active participants, this might skew our estimate of physical activity frequency, resulting in a discrepancy between our estimate and the actual value.

Table 3.2 lets us see that 45.4 percent of the individuals in the NHANES sample said "No" and 54.6 percent said "Yes".

3.1.3 Cumulative distributions

The PhysActive variable analyzed previously had only two potential values; nevertheless, we frequently seek to summarize data with a greater range of possible values. When the values are quantitative, a beneficial method of summarization is through a cumulative frequency representation: instead of inquiring about the number of observations at a certain value, we consider how many observations possess a value equal to or less than a specified value.

We will examine another variable in the NHANES dataset, termed SleepHrsNight, which documents the number of hours participants report sleeping on typical weekdays. Table 3.3 presents a frequency table generated as previously described, subsequent to the exclusion of individuals having incomplete data for this question. The statistics can be summarized by examining the table; for instance, it indicates that the majority of individuals report sleeping between 6 and 8 hours.

Table 3.3: Frequency distribution for number of hours of sleep per night in the NHANES dataset

SleepHrsNight	AbsoluteFrequency	RelativeFrequency	Percentage
2	9	0.00	0.18
3	49	0.01	0.97
4	200	0.04	3.97

5	406	0.08	8.06
6	1172	0.23	23.28
7	1394	0.28	27.69
8	1405	0.28	27.90
9	271	0.05	5.38
10	97	0.02	1.93
11	15	0.00	0.30
12	17	0.00	0.34

To see this even more clearly, we can plot a histogram which shows the number of cases having each of the different values; see left panel of Figure 3.2. We can also plot the relative frequencies, which we will often refer to as densities - see the right panel of Figure 3.2.

What if we want to know how many people report sleeping 5 hours or less? To find this, we can compute a cumulative distribution. To compute the cumulative frequency for some value j , we add up the frequencies for all of the values up to and including j :

$$\text{cumulative frequency}_j = \sum_{i=1}^{j} \text{absolute frequency}_i$$

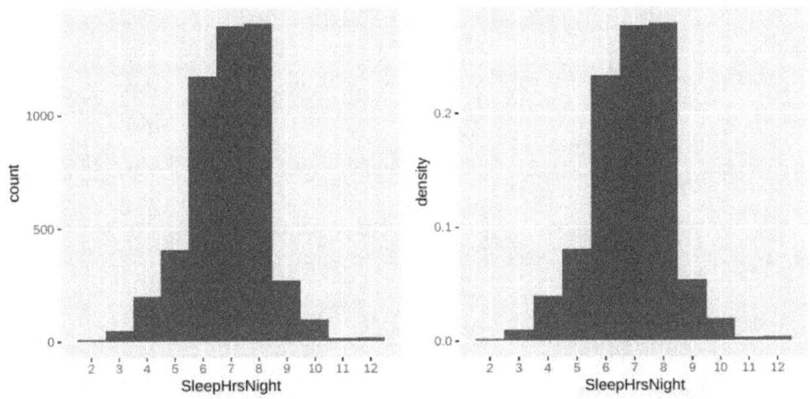

Figure 3.2: Left: Histogram showing the number (left) and proportion (right) of people reporting each possible value of the SleepHrsNight variable.

Let's calculate the absolute and cumulative frequency for our sleep variable. In the left panel of Figure 3.3, we illustrate the data; absolute frequency values are represented by solid lines, while cumulative frequencies are depicted by dashed lines. The cumulative frequency exhibits a monotonically increasing trend; it can only rise or remain constant, but it cannot decline. Typically, we consider relative frequencies to be more advantageous than absolute frequencies; these are seen in the right panel of Figure 3.3. The relative frequency plot has an identical structure to that of the absolute frequency plot; only the magnitude of the data has altered.

3.1.3 Constructing histograms

The variables we analyzed previously were rather straightforward, possessing only a limited number of potential values. Let us now examine a more intricate variable: Age. Initially, we will graph the Age variable for all individuals in the NHANES dataset (refer to the left panel of Figure 3.4). What do you observe in that location? Initially, it is important to observe that the population within each age cohort is diminishing with time. This is logical as the population is randomly sampled, resulting in a decline in individuals within the older age brackets due to mortality over time. Secondly, you may observe a significant increase in the graph at the age of 80. What do you think that's about? If were were to look up the information about the NHANES dataset, we would see the following definition for the Age variable: "Age in years at screening of study participant.

Table 3.4: Absolute and cumulative frequency distributions for SleepHrsNight variable

SleepHrsNight	AbsoluteFrequency	CumulativeFrequency
2	9	9
3	49	58
4	200	258
5	406	664
6	1172	1836
7	1394	3230
8	1405	4635
9	271	4906
10	97	5003
11	15	5018
12	17	5035

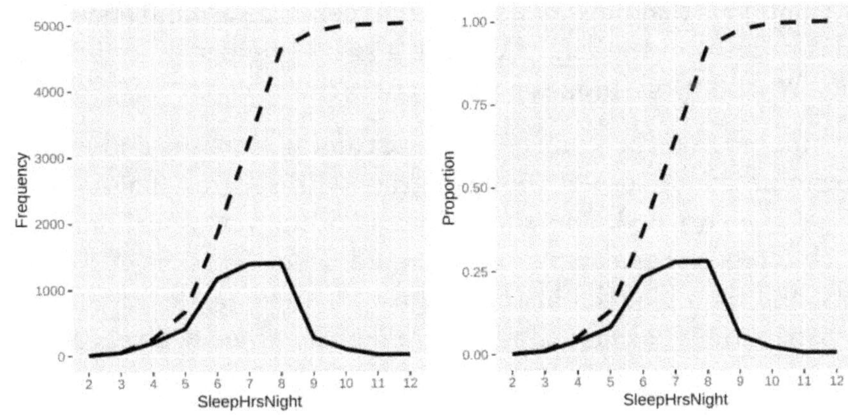

Figure 3.3: A plot of the relative (solid) and cumulative relative (dashed) values for frequency (left) and proportion (right) for the possible values of SleepHrsNight.

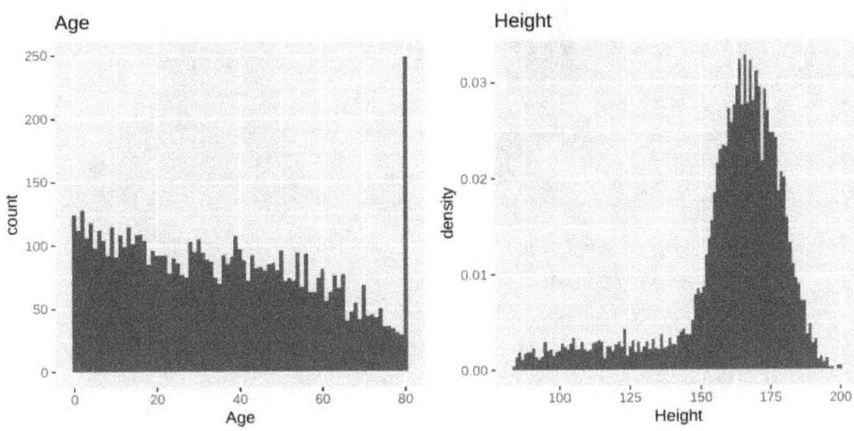

Figure 3.4: A histogram of the Age (left) and Height (right) variables in NHANES.

Note: Subjects 80 years or older were recorded as 80 ." The reason for this is that the relatively small number of individuals with very high ages would make it potentially easier to identify the specific person in the dataset if you knew their exact age; researchers generally promise their participants to keep their identity confidential, and this is one of the things they can do to help protect their research subjects. This also highlights the fact that it's always important to know where one's data have come from and how they have been processed; otherwise we might interpret them improperly, thinking that 80 -year-olds had been somehow overrepresented in the sample.

Let's look at another more complex variable in the NHANES dataset: Height. The histogram of height values is plotted in the right panel of Figure 3.4. The first thing you should notice about this distribution is that most of its density is centered around about 170 cm , but the distribution has a "tail" on the left; there are a small number of individuals with much smaller heights. What do you think is going on here?

You may have intuited that the small heights are coming from the children in the dataset. One way to examine this is to plot the histogram with separate colors for children and adults (left panel of Figure 3.5). This shows that all of the very short heights were indeed coming from children in the sample. Let's create a new version of NHANES that only includes adults, and then plot the histogram just for them (right panel of Figure 3.5). In that plot the distribution looks much more symmetric. As we will see later, this is a nice example of a normal (or Gaussian) distribution.

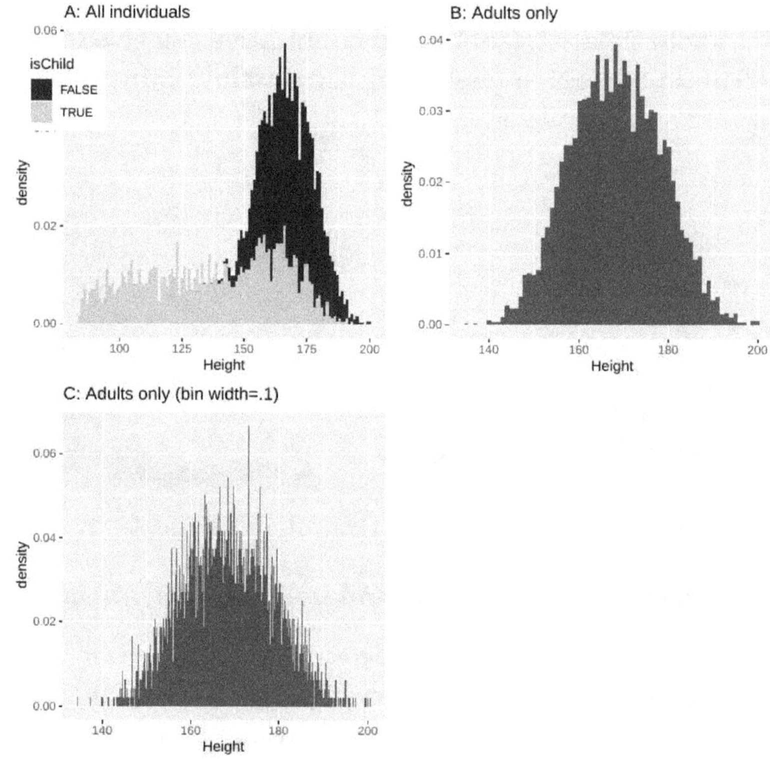

Figure 3.5: Histogram of heights for NHANES. A: values plotted separately for children (gray) and adults (black). B: values for adults only. C: Same as B , but with bin width $= 0.1$

3.1.4 Histogram bins

In the last example about the sleep variable, the data were presented as integers, and we merely enumerated the individuals who reported each potential value. Nevertheless, an examination of select values of the Height variable in NHANES (as illustrated in Table 3.5) reveals that it was recorded in centimeters to the first decimal place.

Table 3.5: A few values of Height from the NHANES data frame.

Height
169.6
169.8
167.5
155.2
173.8
174.5

Panel C of Figure 3.5 shows a histogram that counts the density of each possible value down the first decimal place. That histogram looks really jagged, which is because of the variability in specific decimal place values. For example, the value 173.2 occurs 32 times, while the value 173.3 only occurs 15 times. We probably don't think that there is really such a big difference between the prevalence of these two heights; more likely this is just due to random variability in our sample of people.

In general, when we create a histogram of data that are continuous or where there are many possible values, we will bin the values so that instead of counting and plotting the frequency of every specific value, we count and plot the frequency of values falling within specific ranges. That's why the plot looked less jagged above in Panel B of 3.5; in this panel we set the bin width to 1 , which means that the histogram is computed by combining values within bins with a width of one; thus, the values 1.3,1.5, and 1.6 would all count toward the frequency of the same bin, which would span from values equal to one up through values less than 2 .

Note that once the bin size has been selected, then the number of bins is determined by the data:

$$\text{number of bins} = \frac{\text{range of scores}}{\text{bin width}}$$

There is no definitive guideline for selecting the ideal bin width. At times, the solution may be apparent (such as when only a limited number of values exist), although in numerous others, it necessitates a process of trial and error. There exist techniques that aim to determine an appropriate bin size automatically, such as the Freedman-Diaconis method, which we shall employ in subsequent cases.

3.2 Optimized depictions of distributions

Datasets are like snowflakes, in that every one is different, but nonetheless there are patterns that one often sees in different types of data. This allows us to use idealized representations of the data to further summarize them. Let's take the adult height data plotted in 3.5, and plot them alongside a very different variable: pulse rate (heartbeats per minute), also measured in NHANES (see Figure 3.6).

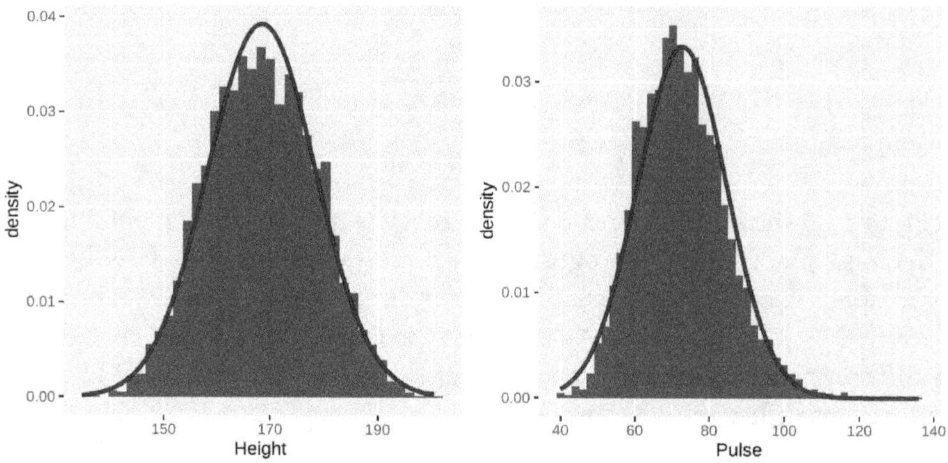

Figure 3.6: Histograms for height (left) and pulse (right) in the NHANES dataset, with the normal distribution overlaid for each dataset.

While these plots certainly don't look exactly the same, both have the general characteristic of being relatively symmetric around a rounded peak in the middle. This shape is in fact one of the commonly observed shapes of distributions when we collect data, which we call the normal (or Gaussian) distribution. This distribution is defined in terms of two values (which we call parameters of the distribution): the location of the center peak (which we call the mean) and the width of the distribution (which is described in terms of a parameter called the standard deviation). Figure 3.6 shows the appropriate normal distribution plotted on top of each of the histrograms. You can see that although the curves don't fit the data exactly, they do a pretty good job of characterizing the distribution - with just two numbers! Subsequently, when we examine the central limit theorem, we will uncover a profound mathematical rationale explaining why numerous variables in the environment manifest a normal distribution.

3.3.1 Skewness

The examples in Figure 3.6 followed the normal distribution fairly well, but in many cases the data will deviate in a systematic way from the normal distribution. One way in which the data can deviate is when they are asymmetric, such that one tail of the distribution is more dense than the other. We refer to this as "skewness". Skewness commonly occurs when the measurement is constrained to be non-negative, such as when we are counting things or measuring elapsed times (and thus the variable can't take on negative values).

An example of relatively mild skewness can be seen in the average waiting times at the airport security lines at San Francisco International Airport, plotted in the left panel of Figure 3.7. You can see that while most wait times are less than 20 minutes, there are a number of cases where they are much longer, over 60 minutes! This is an example of a "right-skewed" distribution, where the right tail is longer than the left; these are common when looking at counts or measured times, which can't be less than zero. It's less common to see "left-skewed" distributions, but they can occur, for example when looking at fractional values that can't take a value greater than one.

3.3.2 Long-tailed distributions

Traditionally, statistics has predominantly concentrated on data that conform to a normal distribution; nevertheless, other data types exhibit characteristics that diverge significantly from this distribution. Many real-world distributions are characterized as "long-tailed," indicating that the right tail extends much beyond the most typical elements of the distribution; thus, they exhibit considerable skewness. One of the most interesting types of data where long-tailed distributions occur arises from the analysis of social networks. For an example, let's look at the Facebook friend data from the Stanford Large Network Database and plot the histogram of number of friends across the 3,663 people in the database (see right panel of Figure 3.7). As we can see, this distribution has a very long right tail the average person has 24.09 friends, while the person with the most friends (denoted by the blue dot) has 1043 !

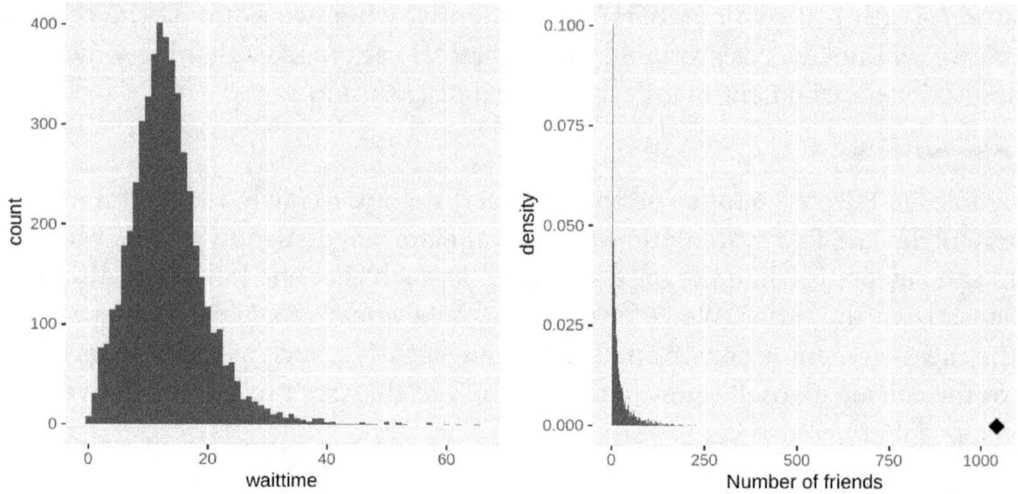

Figure 3.7: Examples of right-skewed and long-tailed distributions. Left: Average wait times for security at SFO Terminal A (Jan-Oct 2017), obtained from https://awt.cbp.gov/ . Right: A histogram of the number of Facebook friends amongst 3,663 individuals, obtained from the Stanford Large Network Database. The person with the maximum number of friends is indicated by the diamond.

Long-tailed distributions are increasingly being recognized in the real world. In particular, many features of complex systems are characterized by these distributions, from the frequency of words in text, to the number of flights in and out of different airports, to the connectivity of brain networks. There are a number of different ways that long-tailed distributions can come about, but a common one occurs in cases of the so-called "Matthew effect" from the Christian Bible:

For to every one who has will more be given, and he will have abundance; but from him who has not, even what he has will be taken away. - Matthew 25:29, Revised Standard Version.

This is often paraphrased as "the rich get richer". In these situations, advantages compound, such that those with more friends have access to even more new friends, and those with more money have the ability to do things that increase their riches even more.

Throughout the course, we will encounter numerous instances of long-tailed distributions, and it is essential to remember that many statistical approaches may be ineffective when addressing long-tailed data. Nassim Nicholas Taleb elucidated in "The Black Swan" that long-tailed distributions significantly contributed to the 2008 financial crisis, as numerous financial models employed by traders erroneously presumed that financial systems adhered to a normal distribution, whereas they evidently did not.

Chapter-4

Data Visualization

On January 28, 1986, the Space Shuttle Challenger detonated 73 seconds post-launch, resulting in the fatalities of all 7 personnel aboard. An official inquiry was conducted following the incident, revealing that a leaking O-ring connecting two portions of the solid rocket booster caused the joint failure and subsequent explosion of the massive liquid fuel tank. (see figure 4.1).

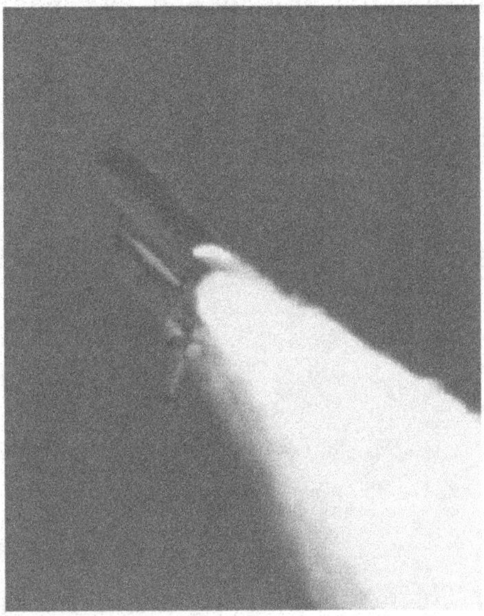

Figure 4.1: An image of the solid rocket booster leaking fuel, seconds before the explosion. The small flame visible on the side of the rocket is the site of the O-ring failure. By NASA (Great Images in NASA Description) [Public domain], via Wikimedia Commons.

The study revealed numerous deficiencies in NASA's decision-making process, particularly highlighting a meeting between NASA personnel and engineers from Morton Thiokol, the contractor responsible for constructing the solid rocket boosters. The engineers were especially apprehensive due to the expectation of extremely low temperatures on the morning of the launch, coupled with historical data indicating that the performance of the O-rings deteriorated at reduced temperatures. During a conference the evening prior to the launch, the engineers presented their data to the NASA managers but failed to persuade them to delay the launch. Their evidence consisted of a collection of handwritten slides displaying figures from multiple previous launches.

Edward Tufte, a visualization expert, contends that an appropriate presentation of the data may have significantly enhanced the engineers' persuasiveness. Specifically, they could have presented a graphic akin to that in graphic 4.2, which underscores two significant truths. The extent of O-ring damage, characterized by the erosion and soot present outside the rings following the retrieval of solid rocket boosters from the ocean in prior missions, was closely correlated with the temperature during launch. Secondly, it indicates that the projected temperature range for the morning of January 28 (depicted in the shaded area) significantly exceeded the range of all prior launches. Although certainty is unattainable, it appears possible that this could have been more compelling.

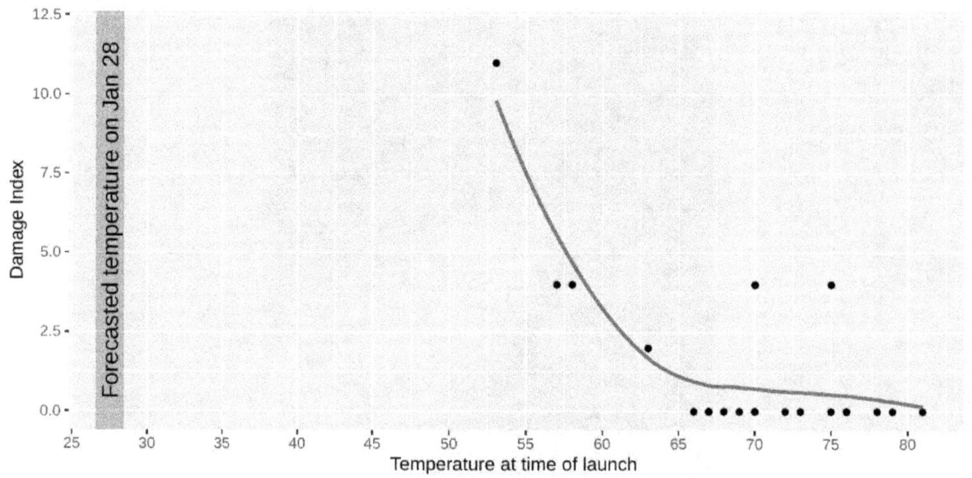

Figure 4.2: A replotting of Tufte's damage index data. The line shows the trend in the data, and the shaded patch shows the projected temperatures for the morning of the launch.

4.1 Anatomy and types of a plot

The purpose of data visualization is to present a summary of a dataset in a two-dimensional (or occasionally three-dimensional) manner. The dimensions are known as axes; the horizontal axis is labeled the X-axis, and the vertical axis is referred to as the Y-axis. We can arrange the data along the axes to highlight the data values. These values may be categorized as either continuous or categorical.

Diverse types of plots exist, each with unique advantages and disadvantages. We aim to delineate the height differential between men and women in the NHANES dataset. Figure 4.3 depicts four unique techniques for viewing this data.

1. The bar graph in panel A shows the difference in means, but doesn't show us how much spread there is in the data around these means and as we will see later, knowing this is essential to determine whether we think the difference between the groups is large enough to be important.

2. The second plot shows the bars with all of the data points overlaid this makes it a bit clearer that the distributions of height for men and women are overlapping, but it's still hard to see due to the large number of data points.

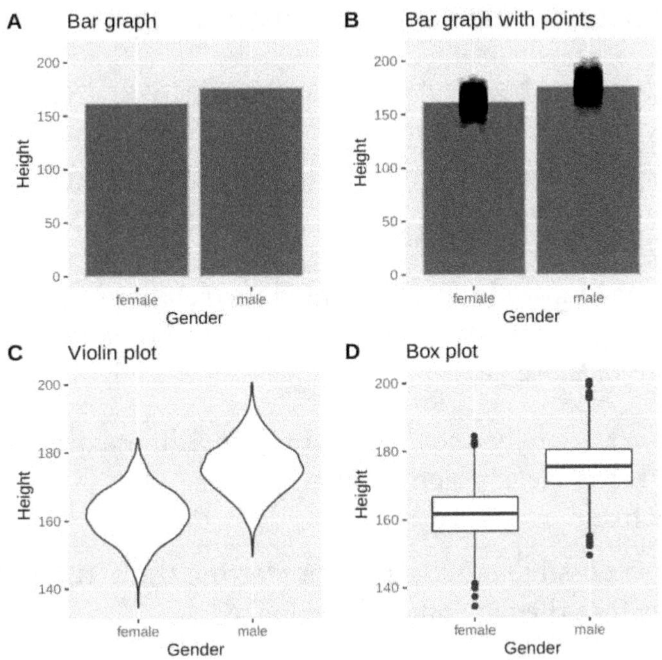

Figure 4.3: Four different ways of plotting the difference in height between men and women in the NHANES dataset. Panel A plots the means of the two groups, which gives no way to assess the relative overlap of the two distributions. Panel B shows the same bars, but also overlays the data points, jittering them so that we can see their overall distribution. Panel C shows a violin plot, which shows the distribution of the datasets for each group. Panel D shows a box plot, which highlights the spread of the distribution along with any outliers (which are shown as individual points).

In general we prefer using a plotting technique that provides a clearer view of the distribution of the data points.

3. In panel C , we see one example of a violin plot, which plots the distribution of data in each condition (after smoothing it out a bit).

4. Another option is the box plot shown in panel D , which shows the median (central line), a measure of variability (the width of the box, which is based on a measure called the interquartile range), and any outliers (noted by the points at the ends of the lines). These are both effective ways to show data that provide a good feel for the distribution of the data.

4.2 Fundamentals of effective visualizing

A multitude of literature has been authored on the effective visualization of data. Some principles are widely accepted by these authors, while others remain disputed. Here, we delineate some fundamental principles.

4.2.1 Present the data prominently

Let's say that I performed a study that examined the relationship between dental health and time spent flossing, and I would like to visualize my data. Figure 4.4 shows four possible presentations of these data.

1. In panel A, we don't actually show the data, just a line expressing the relationship between the data. This is clearly not optimal, because we can't actually see what the underlying data look like.

Panels B-D show three possible outcomes from plotting the actual data, where each plot shows a different way that the data might have looked.

2. If we saw the plot in Panel B, we would probably be suspicious - rarely would real data follow such a precise pattern.

3. The data in Panel C, on the other hand, look like real data - they show a general trend, but they are messy, as data in the world usually are.

4. The data in Panel D show us that the apparent relationship between the two variables is solely caused by one individual, who we would refer to as an outlier because they fall so far outside of the pattern of the rest of the group. It should be clear that we probably don't want to conclude very much from an effect that is driven by one data point. This figure

highlights why it is always important to look at the raw data before putting too much faith in any summary of the data.

4.2.2 Maximize the data/ink ratio

Edward Tufte has proposed an idea called the data/ink ratio:

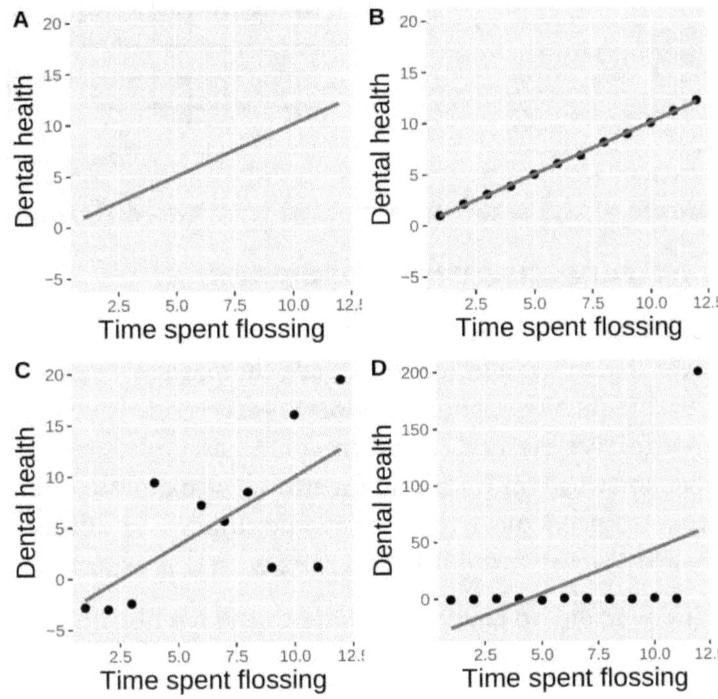

Figure 4.4: Four different possible presentations of data for the dental health example. Each point in the scatter plot represents one data point in the dataset, and the line in each plot represents the linear trend in the data.

$$\text{data/ink ratio} = \frac{\text{amount of ink used on data}}{\text{total amount of ink}}$$

The point of this is to minimize visual clutter and let the data show through. For example, take the two presentations of the dental health data in Figure 4.5. Both panels show the same data, but panel A is much easier to apprehend, because of its relatively higher data/ink ratio.

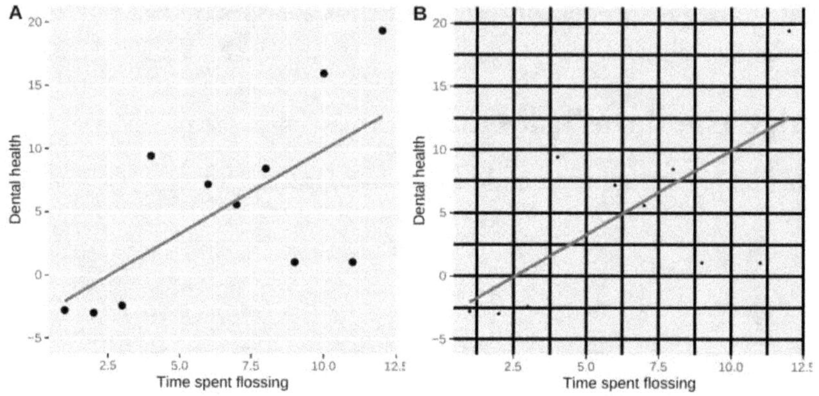

Figure 4.5: An example of the same data plotted with two different data/ink ratios.

4.2.3 Eliminate extraneous graphical elements

It is particularly prevalent to encounter data presentations in mainstream media embellished with several graphic elements that are thematically pertinent to the text yet irrelevant to the actual facts. This phenomenon is referred to as chartjunk and must be eschewed entirely. A effective method to circumvent chartjunk is to refrain from utilizing prevalent spreadsheet software for data visualization. For example, the chart in Figure 4.6 (created using Microsoft Excel) plots the relative popularity of different religions in the United States. There are at least three things wrong with this figure:

- it has graphics overlaid on each of the bars that have nothing to do with the actual data
- it has a distracting background texture
- it uses three-dimensional bars, which distort the data

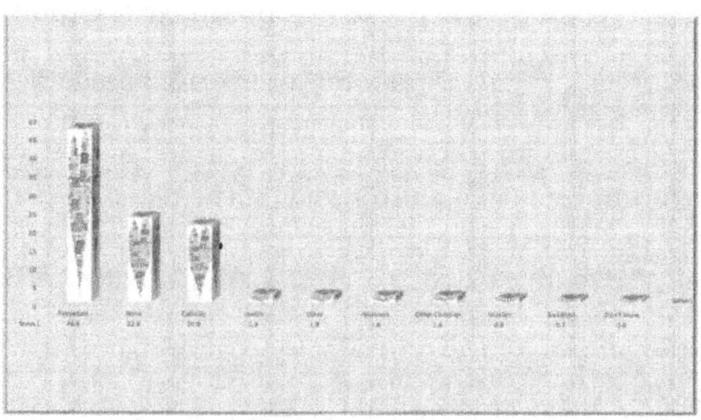

Figure 4.6: An example of chart junk.

4.2.4 Avoid distorting the data

It's often possible to use visualization to distort the message of a dataset. A very common one is use of different axis scaling to either exaggerate or hide a pattern of data. For example, let's say that we are interested in seeing whether rates of violent crime have changed in the US. In Figure 4.7, we can see these data plotted in ways that either make it look like crime has remained constant, or that it has plummeted. The same data can tell two very different stories!

One of the major controversies in statistical data visualization is how to choose the Y axis, and in particular whether it should always include zero. In his famous book "How to lie with statistics", Darrell Huff argued strongly that one should always include the zero point in the Y axis. On the other hand, Edward Tufte has argued against this: "In general, in a time-series, use a baseline that shows the data not the zero point; don't spend a lot of empty vertical space trying

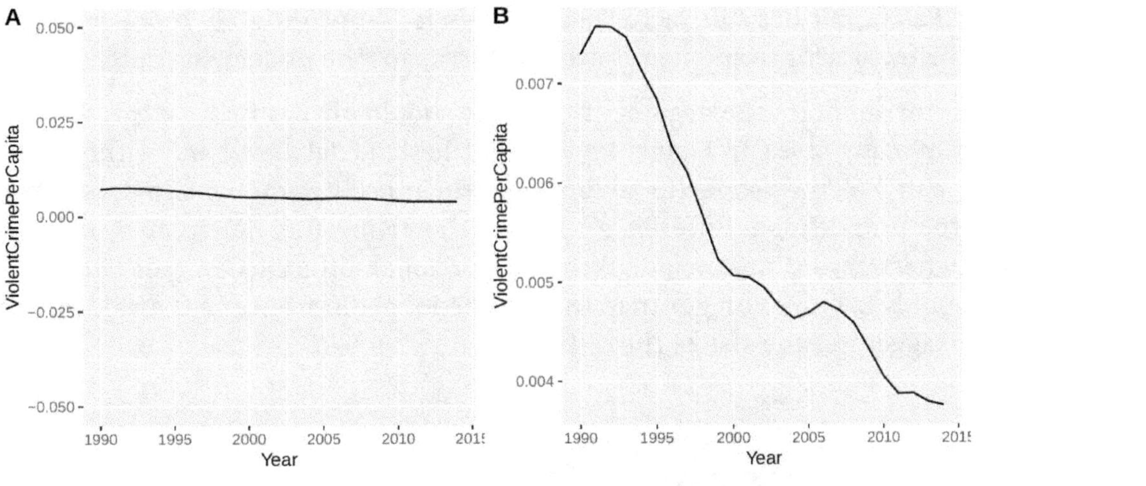

Figure 4.7: Crime data from 1990 to 2014 plotted over time. Panels *A* and *B* show the same data, but with different ranges of values along the Y axis.

There are certainly cases where using the zero point makes no sense at all. Let's say that we are interested in plotting body temperature for an individual over time. In Figure 4.8 we plot the same (simulated) data with or without zero in the Y axis. It should be obvious that by plotting these data with zero in the Y axis (Panel A) we are wasting a lot of space in the figure, given that body temperature of a living person could never go to zero! By including zero, we are also making the apparent jump in temperature during days 21-30 much less evident. In general, my inclination for line plots and scatterplots is to use all of the space in the graph, unless the zero point is truly important to highlight.

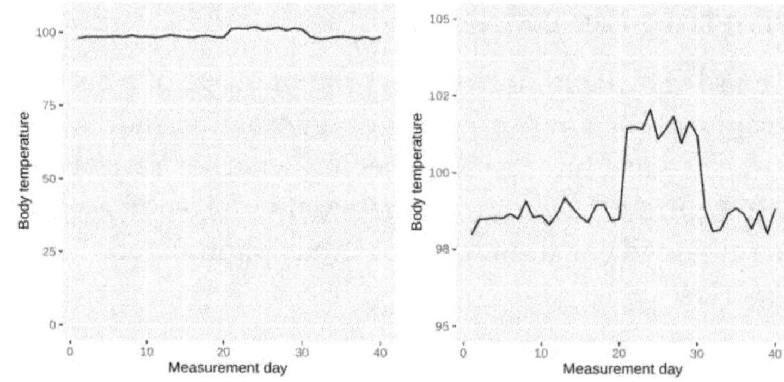

Figure 4.8: Body temperature over time, plotted with or without the zero point in the Y axis.

Edward Tufte introduced the concept of the lie factor to describe the degree to which physical differences in a visualization correspond to the magnitude of the differences in the data. If a graphic has a lie factor near 1 , then it is appropriately representing the data, whereas lie factors far from one reflect a distortion of the underlying data.

The lie factor supports the argument that one should always include the zero point in a bar chart in many cases. In Figure 4.9 we plot the same data with and without zero in the Y axis. In panel A , the proportional difference in area between the two bars is exactly the same as the proportional difference between the values (i.e. lie factor = 1), whereas in Panel B (where zero is not included) the proportional difference in area between the two bars is roughly 2.8 times bigger than the proportional difference in the values, and thus it visually exaggerates the size of the difference.

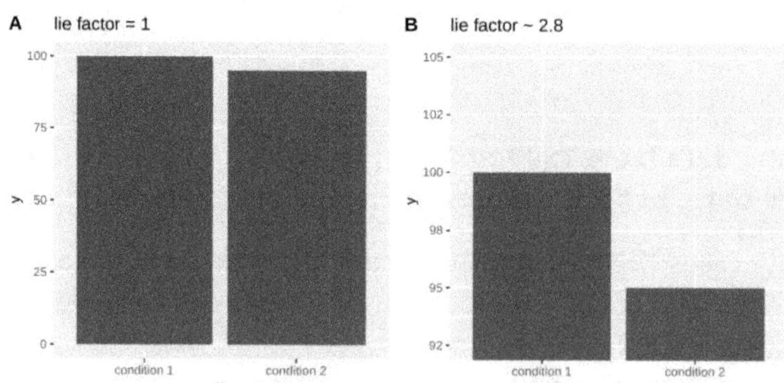

Figure 4.9: Two bar charts with associated lie factors.

4.3 Accommodating human constraints

Humans possess perceptual and cognitive constraints that can render certain visuals exceedingly challenging to comprehend. It is essential to consider these factors when constructing a visualization.

4.3.1 Perceptual limitations

One important perceptual limitation that many people (including myself) suffer from is color blindness. This can make it very difficult to perceive the information in a figure (like the one in Figure 4.10) where there is only color contrast between the elements but no brightness contrast. It is always helpful to use graph elements that differ substantially in brightness and/or texture, in addition to color. There are also "colorblind-friendly" palettes available for use with many visualization tools.

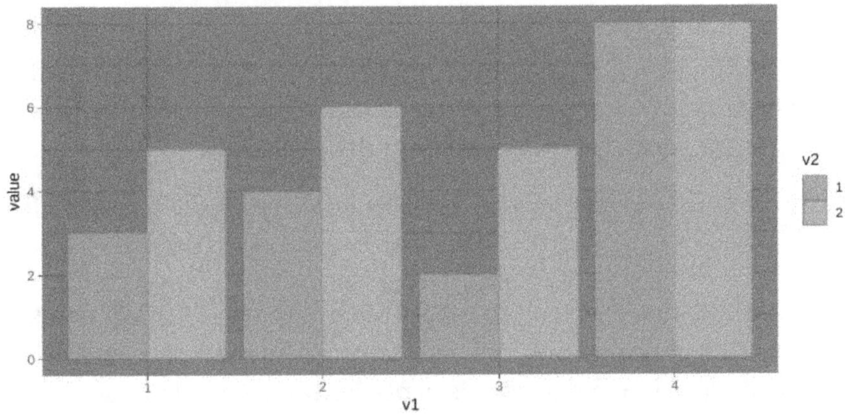

Figure 4.10: Example of a bad figure that relies solely on color contrast.

Even for people with perfect color vision, there are perceptual limitations that can make some plots ineffective. This is one reason why statisticians never use pie charts: It can be very difficult for humans to accurately perceive differences in the volume of shapes. The pie chart in Figure 4.11 (presenting the same data on religious affiliation that we showed above) shows how tricky this can be.

This plot is terrible for several reasons. First, it requires distinguishing a large number of colors from very small patches at the bottom of the figure. Second, the visual perspective distorts the relative numbers, such that the pie wedge for Catholic appears much larger than the pie wedge for None, when in fact the number for None is slightly larger (22.8 vs 20.8 percent), as was evident in Figure 4.6. Third, by separating the legend from the graphic, it requires the viewer to hold information in their working memory in order to map between the graphic and legend and to conduct many "table look-ups" in order to continuously match the legend labels to the visualization.

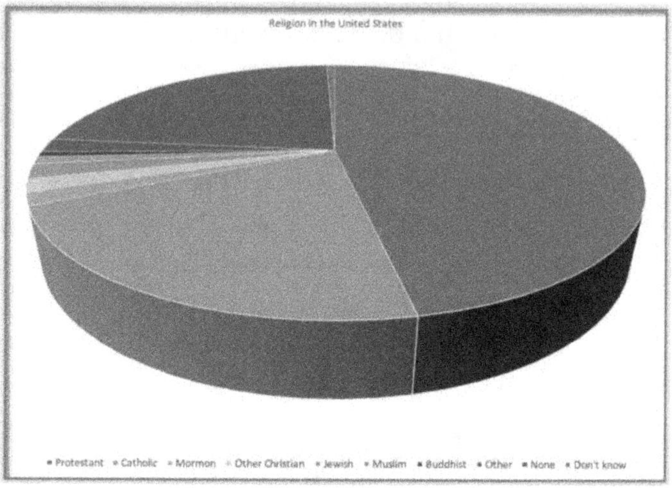

Figure 4.11: An example of a pie chart, highlighting the difficulty in apprehending the relative volume of the different pie slices.

And finally, it uses text that is far too small, making it impossible to read without zooming in.

Plotting the data using a more reasonable approach (Figure 4.12), we can see the pattern much more clearly. This plot may not look as flashy as the pie chart generated using Excel, but it's a much more effective and accurate representation of the data.

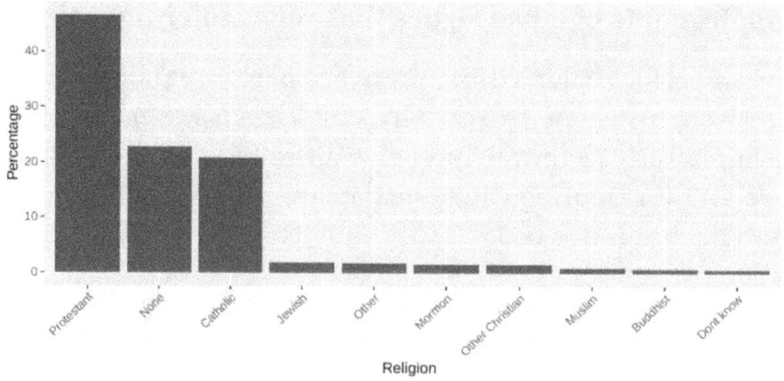

Figure 4.12: A clearer presentation of the religious affiliation data (obtained from http://www.pewforum.org/religious-landscape-study/).

This plot allows the viewer to make comparisons based on the the length of the bars along a common scale (the y -axis). Humans tend to be more accurate when decoding differences based on these perceptual elements than based on area or color.

4.4 Adjusting for additional variables

Often we are interested in plotting data where the variable of interest is affected by other factors than the one we are interested in. For example, let's say that we want to understand how the price of gasoline has changed over time. Figure 4.13 shows historical gas price data, plotted either with or without adjustment for inflation. Whereas the unadjusted data show a huge increase, the adjusted data show that this is mostly just reflective of inflation. Other examples where one needs to adjust data for other factors include population size and data collected across different seasons.

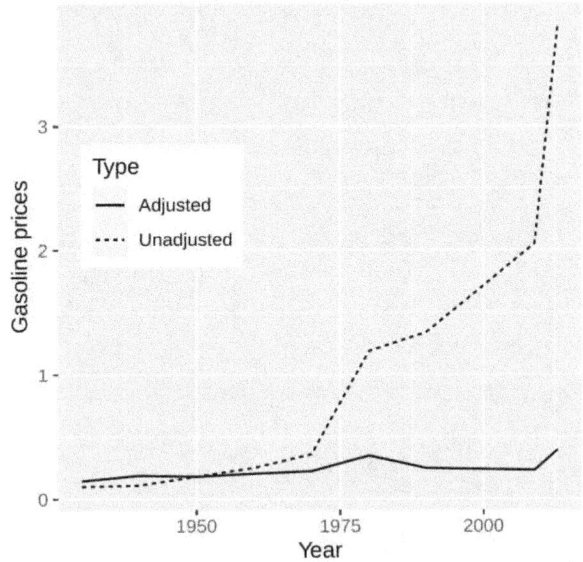

Figure 4.13: The price of gasoline in the US from 1930 to 2013 (obtained from http://www.thepeoplehistory.com/70yearsofpricechange.html) with or without correction for inflation (based on Consumer Price Index).

4.5 Learning objectives

Having read this chapter, you should be able to:

- Describe the principles that distinguish between good and bad graphs, and use them to identify good versus bad graphs.

- Understand the human limitations that must be accommodated in order to make effective graphs.
- Promise to never create a pie chart. Ever.

4.6 Suggested readings and videos

- Fundamentals of Data Visualization, by Claus Wilke
- Visual Explanations, by Edward Tufte
- Visualizing Data, by William S. Cleveland
- Graph Design for the Eye and Mind, by Stephen M. Kosslyn
- How Humans See Data, by John Rauser

Chapter-5

Fitting Models to Data

One of the fundamental activities in statistics is creating models that can summarize data using a small set of numbers, thus providing a compact description of the data. In this chapter we will discuss the concept of a statistical model and how it can be used to describe data.

5.1 What is a model?

In the physical world, "models" are generally simplifications of things in the real world that nonetheless convey the essence of the thing being modeled. A model of a building conveys the structure of the building while being small and light enough to pick up with one's hands; a model of a cell in biology is much larger than the actual thing, but again conveys the major parts of the cell and their relationships.

In statistics, a model is meant to provide a similarly condensed description, but for data rather than for a physical structure. Like physical models, a statistical model is generally much simpler than the data being described; it is meant to capture the structure of the data as simply as possible. In both cases, we realize that the model is a convenient fiction that necessarily glosses over some of the details of the actual thing being modeled. As the statistician George Box famously said: "All models are wrong but some are useful." It can also be useful to think of a statistical model as a theory of how the observed data were generated; our goal then becomes to find the model that most efficiently and accurately summarizes the way in which the data were actually generated. But as we will see below, the desires of efficiency and accuracy will often be diametrically opposed to one another.

The basic structure of a statistical model is:

$$\text{data} = \text{model} + \text{error}$$

This expresses the idea that the data can be broken into two portions: one portion that is described by a statistical model, which expresses the values that we expect the data to take given our knowledge, and another portion that we refer to as the error that reflects the difference between the model's predictions and the observed data.

In essence we would like to use our model to predict the value of the data for any given observation. We would write the equation like this:

$$\widehat{\text{data}_i} = \text{model}_i$$

The "hat" over the data denotes that it's our prediction rather than the actual value of the data. This means that the predicted value of the data for observation i is equal to the value of the model for that observation. Once we have a prediction from the model, we can then compute the error:

$$\text{error}_i = \text{data}_i - \widehat{\text{data}}_i$$

That is, the error for any observation is the difference between the observed value of the data and the predicted value of the data from the model.

5.2 Statistical modeling: An example

Let's look at an example of building a model for data, using the data from NHANES. In particular, we will try to build a model of the height of children in the NHANES sample. First let's load the data and plot them (see Figure 5.1).

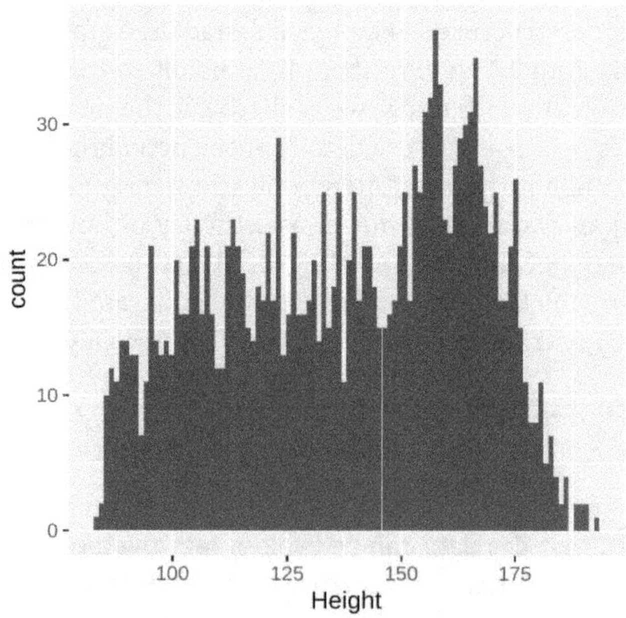

Figure 5.1: Histogram of height of children in NHANES.

Remember that we want to describe the data as simply as possible while still capturing their important features. The simplest model that we can imagine would involve only a single number; that is, the model would predict the same value for each observation, regardless of what else we might know about those observations. We generally describe a model in terms of its parameters, which are values that we can change in order to modify the predictions of the model. Throughout the book we will refer to these using the Greek letter beta (β); when the model has more than one parameter, we will use subscripted numbers to denote the different betas (e.g. β_1). It's also customary to refer to the values of the data using the letter y, and to use a subscripted version y_i to refer to the individual observations.

We generally don't know the true values of the parameters, so we have to estimate them from the data. For this reason, we will generally put a "hat" over the β symbol to denote that we are using an estimate of the parameter value rather than its true value (which we generally don't know). Thus, our simple model for height using a single parameter would be:

$$y_i = \beta + \epsilon$$

The subscript i doesn't appear on the right side of the equation, which means that the prediction of the model doesn't depend on which observation we are looking at - it's the same for all of them. The question then becomes: how do we estimate the best values of the parameter(s) in the model? In this particular case, what single value is the best estimate for β ? And, more importantly, how do we even define best?

One very simple estimator that we might imagine is the mode, which is simply the most common value in the dataset. This redescribes the entire set of 1691 children in terms of a single number. If we wanted to predict the height of any new children, then our predicted value would be the same number:

$$\hat{y}_i = 166.5$$

The error for each individual would then be the difference between the predicted value ($\hat{y}_i$) and their actual height (y_i):

$$\text{error}_i = y_i - \hat{y}_i$$

How good of a model is this? In general we define the goodness of a model in terms of the magnitude of the error, which represents the degree to which the data diverge from the model's predictions; all things being equal, the model that produces lower error is the better model. (Though as we will see later, all things are usually not equal...) What we find in this case is that the average individual has a fairly large error of -28.8 centimeters when we use the mode as our estimator for β, which doesn't seem very good on its face.

How might we find a better estimator for our model parameter? We might start by trying to find an estimator that gives us an average error of zero. One good candidate is the arithmetic mean (that is, the average, often denoted by a bar over the variable, such as $\bar{X}$), computed as the sum of all of the values divided by the number of values. Mathematically, we express this as:

$$\bar{X} = \frac{\sum_{i=1}^{n} x_i}{n}$$

It turns out that if we use the arithmetic mean as our estimator then the average error will indeed be zero (see the simple proof at the end of the chapter if you are interested). Even though the average of errors from the mean is zero, we can see from the histogram in Figure 5.2 that each individual still has some degree of error; some are positive and some are negative, and those cancel each other out to give an average error of zero.

The fact that the negative and positive errors cancel each other out means that two different models could have errors of very different magnitude in absolute terms, but would still have the same average error. This is exactly why the average error is not a good criterion for our estimator; we want a criterion that tries to minimize the overall error regardless of its direction. For this reason, we generally summarize errors in terms of some kind of measure that counts both positive and negative errors as bad. We could use the absolute value of each error value, but it's more common to use the squared errors, for reasons that we will see later in the book.

There are several common ways to summarize the squared error that you will encounter at various points in this book, so it's important to understand how they relate to one another. First, we could simply add them up; this is referred to as the sum of squared errors. The reason we don't usually use this is that its magnitude depends on the number of data points, so it can be difficult to interpret unless we are looking at the same number of observations.

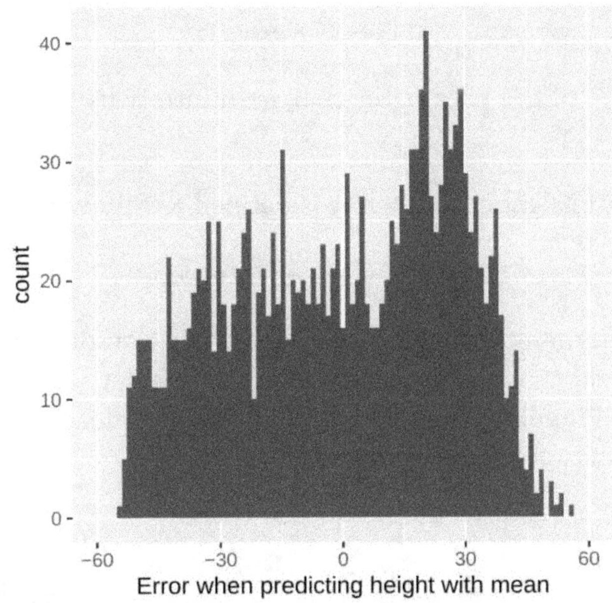

Figure 5.2: Distribution of errors from the mean.

Second, we could take the mean of the squared error values, which is referred to as the mean squared error (MSE). However, because we squared the values before averaging, they are not on the same scale as the original data; they are in centimeters ^{2}. For this reason, it's also common to take the square root of the MSE, which we refer to as the root mean squared error (RMSE), so that the error is measured in the same units as the original values (in this example, centimeters).

The mean has a pretty substantial amount of error - any individual data point will be about 27 cm from the mean on average - but it's still much better than the mode, which has a root mean squared error of about 39 cm .

5.2.1 Improving our model

Can we imagine a better model? Remember that these data are from all children in the NHANES sample, who vary from 2 to 17 years of age. Given this wide age range, we might expect that our model of height should also include age. Let's plot the data for height against age, to see if this relationship really exists.

The black points in Panel A of Figure 5.3 show individuals in the dataset, and there seems to be a strong relationship between height and age, as we would expect. Thus, we might build a model that relates height to age:

$$\hat{y}_i = \hat{\beta} * age_i$$

where $\hat{\beta}$ is our estimate of the parameter that we multiply by age to generate the model prediction.

You may remember from algebra that a line is defined as follows:

$$y = \text{slope} * x + \text{intercept}$$

If age is the X variable, then that means that our prediction of height from age will be a line with a slope of β and an intercept of zero - to see this, let's plot the best fitting line in blue on top of the data (Panel B in Figure 5.3). Something is clearly wrong with this model, as the line doesn't seem to follow the data very well.

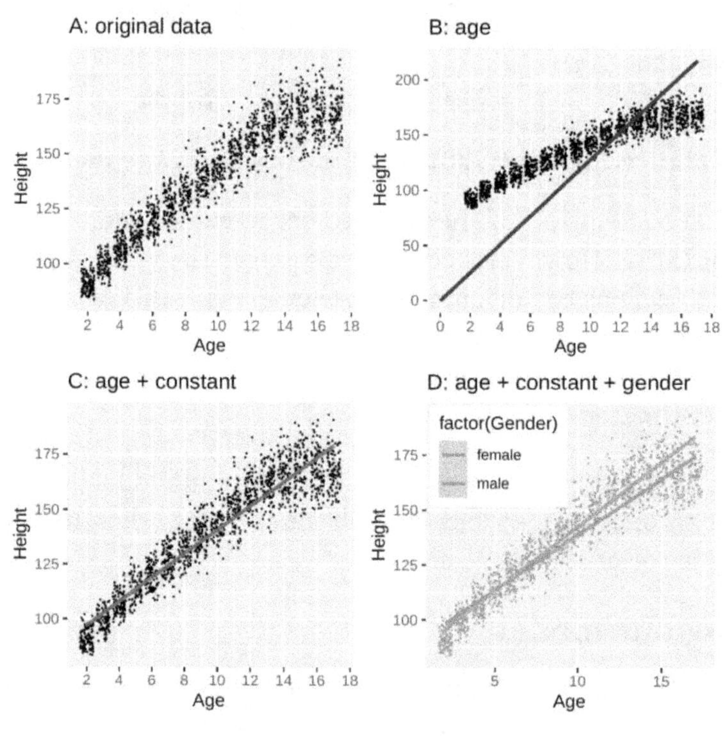

Figure 5.3: Height of children in NHANES, plotted without a model (A), with a linear model including only age (B) or age and a constant (C), and with a linear model that fits separate effects of age for males and females (D).

In fact, the RMSE for this model (39.16) is actually higher than the model that only includes the mean! The problem comes from the fact that our model only includes age, which means that the predicted value of height from the model must take on a value of zero when age is zero. Even though the data do not include any children with an age of zero, the line is mathematically required to have a y -value of zero when x is zero, which explains why the line is pulled down below the younger datapoints. We can fix this by including an intercept in our model, which basically represents the estimated height when age is equal to zero; even though an age of zero is not plausible in this dataset, this is a mathematical trick that will allow the model to account for the overall magnitude of the data. The model is:

$$\hat{y}_i = \hat{\beta}_0 + \hat{\beta}_1 * age_i$$

where $\hat{\beta}_0$ is our estimate for the intercept, which is a constant value added to the prediction for each individual; we call it the intercept because it maps onto the intercept in the equation for a straight line. We will learn later how it is that we actually estimate these parameter values for a particular dataset; for now, we will use our statistical software to estimate the parameter values that give us the smallest error for these particular data. Panel C in Figure 5.3 shows this model applied to the NHANES data, where we see that the line matches the data much better than the one without a constant.

Our error is much smaller using this model - only 8.36 centimeters on average. Can you think of other variables that might also be related to height? What about gender? In Panel D of Figure 5.3 we plot the data with lines fitted separately for males and females. From the plot, it seems that there is a difference between males and females, but it is relatively small and only emerges after the age of puberty. In Figure 5.4 we plot the root mean squared error values across the different models, including one with an additional parameter that models the effect of gender. From this we see that the model got a little bit better going from mode to mean, much better going from mean to mean + age, and only very slightly better by including gender as well.

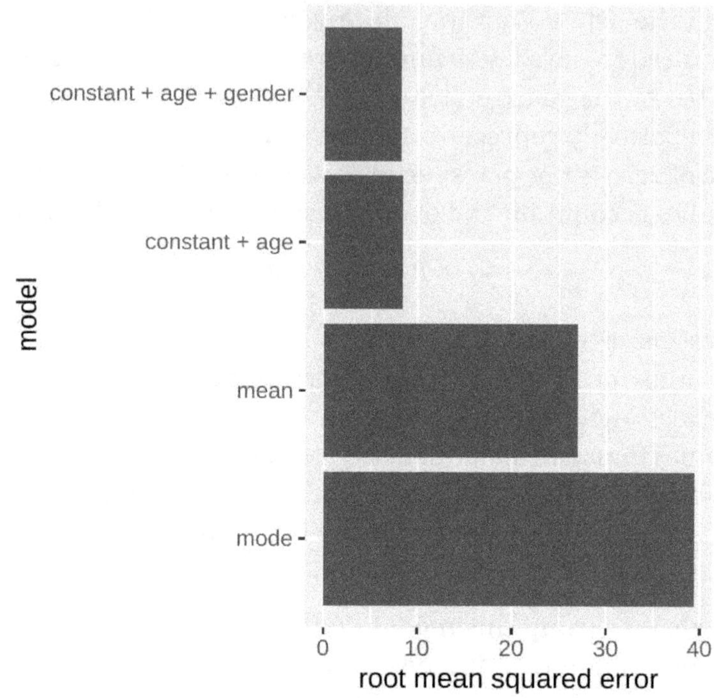

Figure 5.4: Mean squared error plotted for each of the models tested above.

5.3 What constitutes a "good" model?

Typically, there are two distinct objectives we seek from our statistical model. Initially, we want for it to accurately represent our data; specifically, we seek to minimize the error in modeling our data. Secondly, we aim for it to generalize effectively to novel datasets; specifically, we like its error to be minimized when applied to a new dataset for predictive purposes. These two traits frequently conflict with one another.

To comprehend this, let us consider the origins of error. Initially, this may transpire if our model is erroneous; for instance, if we incorrectly assert that height diminishes with age rather than increases, our mistake will exceed that of the proper model. Likewise, the omission of a significant variable from our model would exacerbate our inaccuracy, as evidenced by the exclusion of age from the height model. Nonetheless, inaccuracies may arise even when the model is accurate, attributable to random fluctuations in the data, sometimes termed "measurement error" or "noise". Occasionally, this is attributable to inaccuracies in our measures, particularly when they depend on human intervention, such as utilizing a stopwatch to record elapsed time in a footrace. In certain instances, our measurement apparatus exhibits exceptional precision (such as a digital scale for assessing body weight), however the subject of measurement is influenced by numerous factors that induce variability. While knowledge of all these aspects would enable the construction of a more precise model, such comprehensive understanding is never attainable in practice.

Let me illustrate this with an example. Instead of utilizing actual data, we will create simulated data for the example through a computer simulation, which will be further upon in subsequent chapters. We aim to comprehend the correlation between an individual's blood alcohol concentration (BAC) and their reaction time during a simulated driving assessment. We can produce simulated data and illustrate the correlation (refer to Panel A of Figure 5.5).

In this instance, reaction time increases predictably with blood alcohol content; the line represents the optimal fitting model, and the minimal error is apparent as all points are closely aligned with the line.

We could also imagine data that show the same linear relationship, but have much more error, as in Panel B of Figure 5.5. Here we see that there is still a systematic increase of reaction time with BAC, but it's much more variable across individuals.

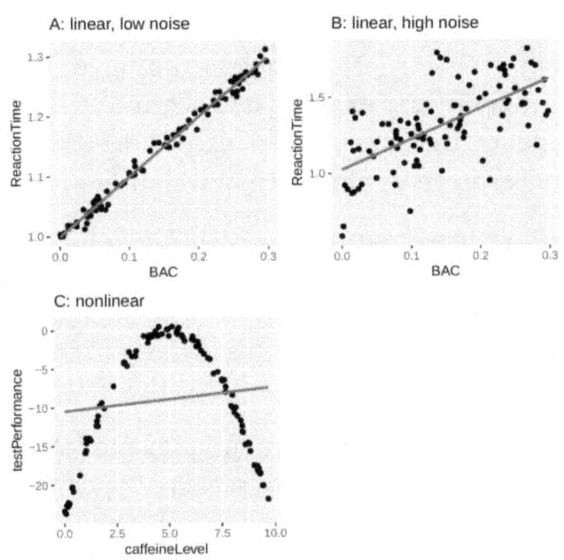

Figure 5.5: Simulated relationship between blood alcohol content and reaction time on a driving test, with best-fitting linear model represented by the line. A: linear relationship with low measurement error. B: linear relationship with higher measurement error. C: Nonlinear relationship with low measurement error and (incorrect) linear model

These were both examples where the relationship between the two variables appears to be linear, and the error reflects noise in our measurement. On the other hand, there are other situations where the relationship between the variables is not linear, and error will be increased because the model is not properly specified. Let's say that we are interested in the relationship between caffeine intake and performance on a test. The relation between stimulants like caffeine and test performance is often nonlinear - that is, it doesn't follow a straight line. This is because performance goes up with smaller amounts of caffeine (as the person becomes more alert), but then starts to decline with larger amounts (as the person becomes nervous and jittery). We can simulate data of this form, and then fit a linear model to the data (see Panel C of Figure 5.5). The blue line shows the straight line that best fits these data; clearly, there is a high degree of error. Although there is a very lawful relation between test performance and caffeine intake, it follows a curve rather than a straight line. The model that assumes a linear relationship has high error because it's the wrong model for these data.

5.4 Can a model exhibit excessive proficiency?

Error is generally perceived negatively, and typically, a model with reduced error is favored over one with higher error. Nonetheless, we have noted a tension between a model's capacity to accurately fit the existing dataset and its proficiency in generalizing to novel datasets; it appears that the model exhibiting the lowest error frequently performs significantly poorer in generalizing to new datasets.

To see this, let's once again generate some data so that we know the true relation between the variables. We will create two simulated datasets, which are generated in exactly the same way - they just have different random noise added to them. That is, the equation for both of them is $y = \beta * X + \epsilon$; the only difference is that different random noise was used for ϵ in each case.

The left panel in Figure 5.6 shows that the more complex model (in red) fits the data better than the simpler model (in blue). However, we see the opposite when the same model is applied to a new dataset generated in the same way - here we see that the simpler model fits the new data better than the more complex model. Intuitively, we can see that the more complex model is influenced heavily by the specific data points in the first dataset; since the exact position of these data points was driven by random noise, this leads the more complex model to fit badly on the new dataset.

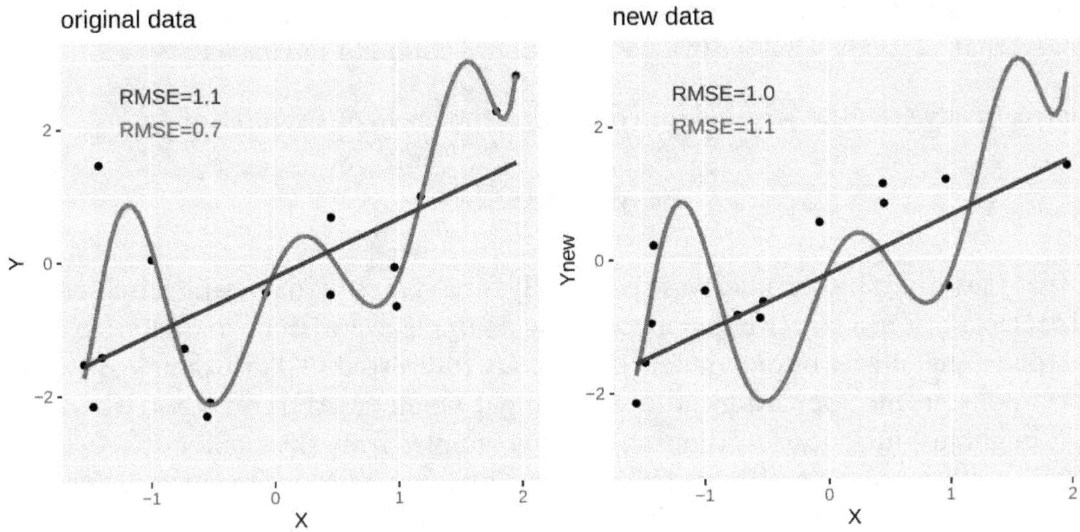

Figure 5.6: An example of overfitting. Both datasets were generated using the same model, with different random noise added to generate each set. The left panel shows the data used to fit the model, with a simple linear fit in blue and a complex (8th order polynomial) fit in red. The root mean square error (RMSE) values for each model are shown in the figure; in this case, the complex model has a lower RMSE than the simple model. The right panel shows the second dataset, with the same model overlaid on it and the RMSE values computed using the model obtained from the first dataset. Here we see that the simpler model actually fits the new dataset better than the more complex model, which was overfitted to the first dataset.

This is a phenomenon that we call overfitting. For now it's simply important to keep in mind that our model fit needs to be good, but not too good. As Albert Einstein (1933) said: "It can scarcely be denied that the supreme goal of all theory is to make the irreducible basic elements as simple and as few as possible without having to surrender the adequate representation of a single datum of experience." Which is often paraphrased as: "Everything should be as simple as it can be, but not simpler."

5.5 Data summarization by the mean

We have already encountered the mean (or average) above, and in fact most people know about the average even if they have never taken a statistics class. It is commonly used to describe what we call the "central tendency" of a dataset - that is, what value are the data centered around? Most people don't think of computing a mean as fitting a model to data. However, that's exactly what we are doing when we compute the mean.

We have already seen the formula for computing the mean of a sample of data:

$$\bar{X} = \frac{\sum_{i=1}^{n} x_i}{n}$$

Note that I said that this formula was specifically for a sample of data, which is a set of data points selected from a larger population. Using a sample, we wish to characterize a larger population - the full set of individuals that we are interested in. For example, if we are a political pollster our population of interest might be all registered voters, whereas our sample might just include a few thousand people sampled from this population. In Chapter 7 we will talk in more detail about sampling, but for now the important point is that statisticians generally like to use different symbols to differentiate statistics that describe values for a sample from parameters that describe the true values for a population; in this case, the formula for the population mean (denoted as μ) is:

$$\mu = \frac{\sum_{i=1}^{N} x_i}{N}$$

where N is the size of the entire population.

We have already seen that the mean is the estimator that is guaranteed to give us an average error of zero, but we also learned that the average error is not the best criterion; instead, we want an estimator that gives us the lowest sum of squared errors (SSE), which the mean also does. We could prove this using calculus, but instead we will demonstrate it graphically in Figure 5.7.

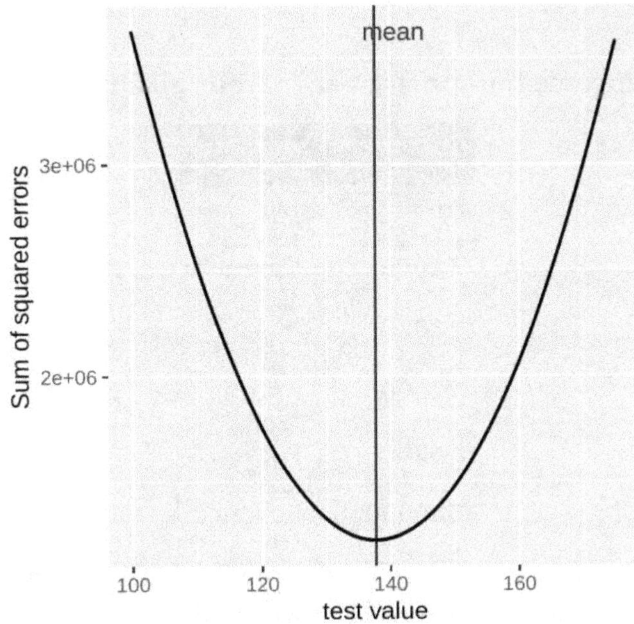

Figure 5.7: A demonstration of the mean as the statistic that minimizes the sum of squared errors. Using the NHANES child height data, we compute the mean (denoted by the blue bar). Then, we test a range of possible parameter estimates, and for each one we compute the sum of squared errors for each data point from that value, which are denoted by the black curve. We see that the mean falls at the minimum of the squared error plot.

This minimization of SSE is a good feature, and it's why the mean is the most commonly used statistic to summarize data. However, the mean also has a dark side. Let's say that five people are in a bar, and we examine each person's income (Table 5.1):

Table 5.1: Income for our five bar patrons

income	person
48000	Joe
64000	Karen
58000	Mark
72000	Andrea
66000	Pat

Table 5.2: Income for our five bar patrons plus Beyoncé Knowles.

income	person
48000	Joe
64000	Karen
58000	Mark
72000	Andrea
66000	Pat
54000000	Beyonce

The mean (61600.00) seems to be a pretty good summary of the income of those five people. Now let's look at what happens if Beyoncé Knowles walks into the bar (Table 5.2).

The average is currently about 10 million dollars, which does not accurately reflect the individuals in the bar, particularly due to the significant influence of the outlier value represented by Beyoncé. The mean is particularly susceptible to outliers, making it essential to verify the absence of extreme values when utilizing the mean for data summarization.

5.5.1 Robustly summarizing facts through the median

If we want to summarize the data in a way that is less sensitive to outliers, we can use another statistic called the median. If we were to sort all of the values in order of their magnitude, then the median is the value in the middle.

If there is an even number of values then there will be two values tied for the middle place, in which case we take the mean (i.e. the halfway point) of those two numbers.

Let's look at an example. Say we want to summarize the following values:

$$8 \quad 6 \quad 3 \quad 14 \quad 12 \quad 7 \quad 6 \quad 4 \quad 9$$

If we sort those values:

$$3 \quad 4 \quad 6 \quad 6 \quad 7 \quad 8 \quad 9 \quad 12 \quad 14$$

Then the median is the middle value - in this case, the 5th of the 9 values.

Whereas the mean minimizes the sum of squared errors, the median minimizes a slighty different quantity: The sum of the absolute value of errors. This explains why it is less sensitive to outliers - squaring is going to exacerbate the effect of large errors compared to taking the absolute value. We can see this in the case of the income example: The median income ($65,000) is much more representative of the group as a whole than the mean ($9,051,333), and less sensitive to the one large outlier.

In light of this, what rationale exists for utilizing the mean? As will be discussed in a subsequent chapter, the mean is the most effective estimator, as it exhibits less variability across different samples compared to alternative estimators. It is our responsibility to determine if the sensitivity to prospective outliers is justified; statistics fundamentally involves trade-offs.

5.6 The mode

Sometimes we wish to describe the central tendency of a dataset that is not numeric. For example, let's say that we want to know which models of iPhone are most commonly used. To test this, we could ask a large group of iPhone users which model each person owns. If we were to take the average of these values, we might see that the mean iPhone model is 9.51 , which is clearly nonsensical, since the iPhone model numbers are not meant to be quantitative measurements. In this case, a more appropriate measure of central tendency is the mode, which is the most common value in the dataset, as we discussed above.

5.7 Variability: How well does the mean fit the data?

Once we have described the central tendency of the data, we often also want to describe how variable the data are - this is sometimes also referred to as "dispersion", reflecting the fact that it describes how widely dispersed the data are.

We have already encountered the sum of squared errors above, which is the basis for the most commonly used measures of variability: the variance and the standard deviation. The variance for a population (referred to as σ^2) is simply the sum of squared errors divided by the number of observations that is, it is exactly the same as the mean squared error that you encountered earlier:

$$\sigma^2 = \frac{SSE}{N} = \frac{\sum_{i=1}^{n} (x_i - \mu)^2}{N}$$

where μ is the population mean. The population standard deviation is simply the square root of this - that is, the root mean squared error that we saw before. The standard deviation is useful because the errors are in the same units as the original data (undoing the squaring that we applied to the errors).

We usually don't have access to the entire population, so we have to compute the variance using a sample, which we refer to as $\hat{\sigma}^2$, with the "hat" representing the fact that this is an estimate based on a sample. The equation for $\hat{\sigma}^2$ is similar to the one for σ^2 :

$$\hat{\sigma}^2 = \frac{\sum_{i=1}^{n} (x_i - \bar{X})^2}{n-1}$$

The only difference between the two equations is that we divide by $n-1$ instead of N . This relates to a fundamental statistical concept: degrees of freedom. Remember that in order to compute the sample variance, we first had to estimate the sample mean $\bar{X}$. Having estimated this, one value in the data is no longer free to vary. For example, let's say we have the following data points for a variable x : [3,5,7,9,11], the mean of which is 7.

Table 5.3: Variance estimates using n versus $n-1$; the estimate using $n-1$ is closer to the population value

Estimate	Value
Population variance	725
Variance estimate using n	710
Variance estimate using n-1	725

Because we know that the mean of this dataset is 7 , we can compute what any specific value would be if it were missing. For example, let's say we were to obscure the first value (3). Having done this, we still know that its value must be 3 , because the mean of 7 implies that the sum of all of the values is $7 * n = 35$ and $35 - (5 + 7 + 9 + 11) = 3$.

So when we say that we have "lost" a degree of freedom, it means that there is a value that is not free to vary after fitting the model. In the context of the sample variance, if we don't account for the lost degree of freedom, then our estimate of the sample variance will be biased, causing us to underestimate the uncertainty of our estimate of the mean.

5.8 Employing simulations to comprehend statistics

I firmly advocate for the utilization of computer simulations to comprehend statistical ideas, and subsequent chapters will explore their application in greater depth. This section will explore the necessity of subtracting 1 from the sample size when calculating the sample variance.

We will consider the complete sample of children from the NHANES data as our "population" and evaluate the accuracy of sample variance calculations using either n or n-1 in the denominator in estimating the population variance across numerous simulated random samples from the data. We will revisit the specifics of this process in a subsequent chapter.

The findings in 5.3 indicate that the aforementioned theory is accurate: The variance estimate utilizing n-1 as the denominator closely approximates the variance calculated from the complete dataset (i.e., the population), but the variance computed with n as the denominator is biased (underestimated) relative to the true value.

5.9 Z-scores

Having characterized a distribution in terms of its central tendency and variability, it is often useful to express the individual scores in terms of where they sit with respect to the overall distribution. Let's say that we are interested in characterizing the relative level of crimes across different states, in order to determine whether California is a particularly dangerous place.

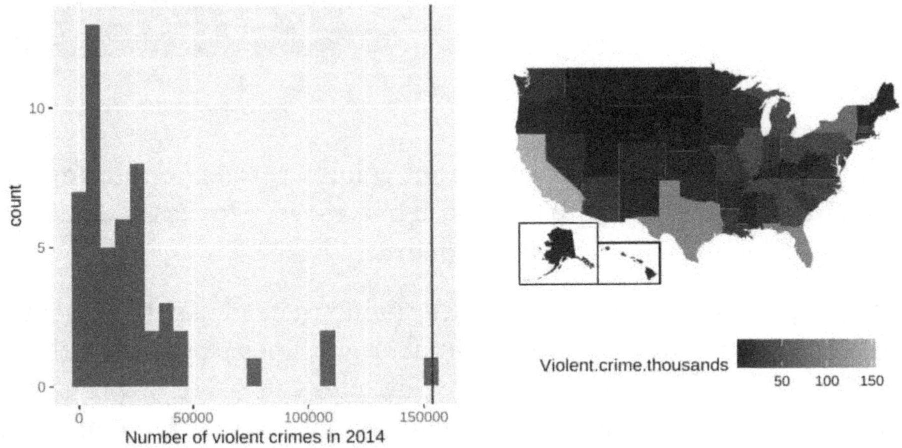

Figure 5.8: Left: Histogram of the number of violent crimes. The value for CA is plotted in blue. Right: A map of the same data, with number of crimes (in thousands) plotted for each state in color.

We can ask this question using data for 2014 from the FBI's Uniform Crime Reporting site. The left panel of Figure 5.8 shows a histogram of the number of violent crimes per state, highlighting the value for California. Looking at these data, it seems like California is terribly dangerous, with 153709 crimes in that year. We can visualize these data by generating a map showing the distribution of a variable across states, which is presented in the right panel of Figure 5.8.

It may have occurred to you, however, that CA also has the largest population of any state in the US, so it's reasonable that it will also have a larger number of crimes. If we plot the number of crimes against one the population of each state (see left panel of Figure 5.9), we see that there is a direct relationship between two variables.

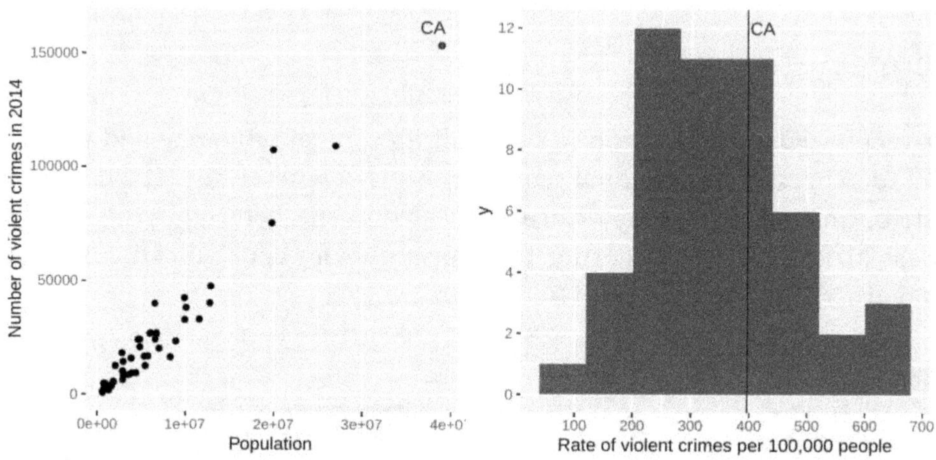

Figure 5.9: Left: A plot of number of violent crimes versus population by state. Right: A histogram of per capita violent crime rates, expressed as crimes per 100,000 people.

Instead of using the raw numbers of crimes, we should instead use the violent crime rate per capita, which we obtain by dividing the number of crimes per state by the population of each state. The dataset from the FBI already includes this value (expressed as rate per 100,000 people). Looking at the right panel of Figure 5.9, we see that California is not so dangerous after all - its crime rate of 396.10 per 100,000 people is a bit above the mean across states of 346.81, but well within the range of many other states. But what if we want to get a clearer view of how far it is from the rest of the distribution?

The Z-score allows us to express data in a way that provides more insight into each data point's relationship to the overall distribution. The formula to compute a Z -score for an individual data point given that we know the value of the population mean μ and standard deviation σ is:

$$Z(x) = \frac{x - \mu}{\sigma}$$

Intuitively, you can think of a Z-score as telling you how far away any data point is from the mean, in units of standard deviation. We can compute this for the crime rate data, as shown in Figure 5.10, which plots the Z-scores against the original scores.

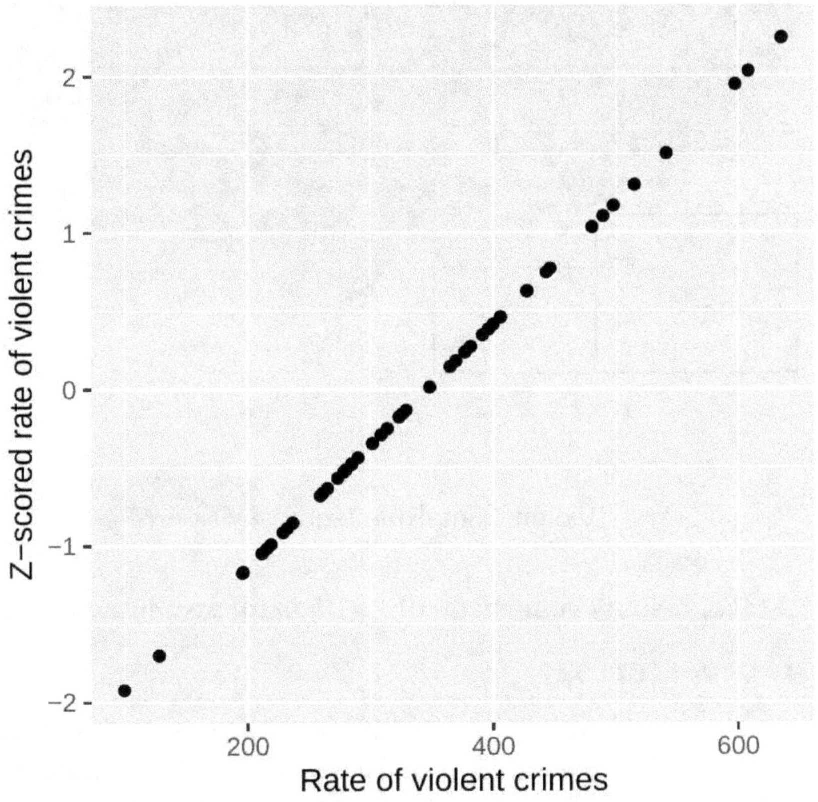

Figure 5.10: Scatterplot of original crime rate data against Z-scored data.

The scatterplot shows us that the process of Z-scoring doesn't change the relative distribution of the data points (visible in the fact that the orginal data and Z-scored data fall on a straight line when plotted against each other) - it just shifts them to have a mean of zero and a standard deviation of one. Figure 5.11 shows the Z-scored crime data using the geographical view.

This provides us with a slightly more interpretable view of the data. For example, we can see that Nevada, Tennessee, and New Mexico all have crime rates that are roughly two standard deviations above the mean.

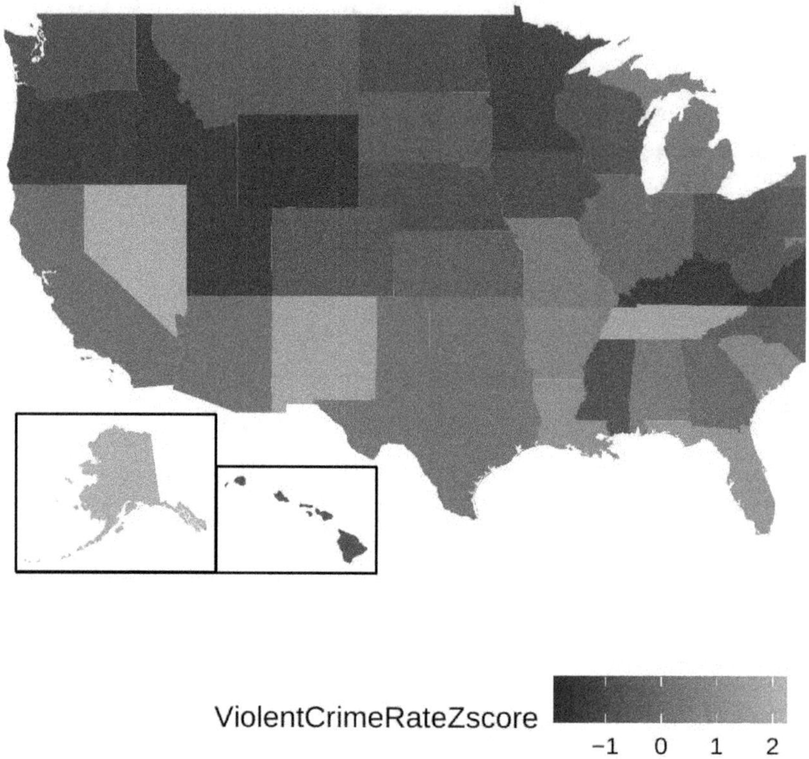

Figure 5.11: Crime data rendered onto a US map, presented as Z-scores.

5.9.1 Analysis of Z-scores

The "Z" in "Z-score" originates from the designation of the standard normal distribution, characterized by a mean of zero and a standard deviation of one, commonly known as the "Z" distribution. The standard normal distribution aids in interpreting the significance of certain Z scores in relation to the overall distribution of data points.

The upper panel in Figure 5.12 shows that we expect about 16% of values to fall in $Z \geq 1$, and the same proportion to fall in $Z \leq -1$.

Figure 5.13 shows the same plot for two standard deviations. Here we see that only about 2.3% of values fall in $Z \leq -2$ and the same in $Z \geq 2$. Thus, if we know the Z-score for a particular data point, we can estimate how likely or unlikely we would be to find a value at least as extreme as that value, which lets us put values into better context. In the case of crime rates, we see that California has a Z-score of 0.38 for its violent crime rate per capita, showing that it is quite near the mean of other states, with about 35% of states having higher rates and 65% of states having lower rates.

5.9.2 Standardized scores

Let's say that instead of Z-scores, we wanted to generate standardized crime scores with a mean of 100 and standard deviation of 10 . This is similar to the standardization that is done with scores from intelligence tests to generate the intelligence quotient (IQ). We can do this by simply multiplying the Z-scores by 10 and then adding 100 .

5.9.2.1 Using Z-scores to compare distributions

One useful application of Z-scores is to compare distributions of different variables. Let's say that we want to compare the distributions of violent crimes and property crimes across states. In the left panel of Figure 5.15 we plot those against one another, with CA plotted in blue. As you can see, the raw rates of property crimes are far higher than the raw rates of violent crimes, so we can't just compare the numbers directly. However, we can plot the Z-scores for these data against one another (right panel of Figure 5.15)here again we see that the distribution of the data does not change. Having put the data into Z-scores for each variable makes them comparable, and lets us see that California is actually right in the middle of the distribution in terms of both violent crime and property crime.

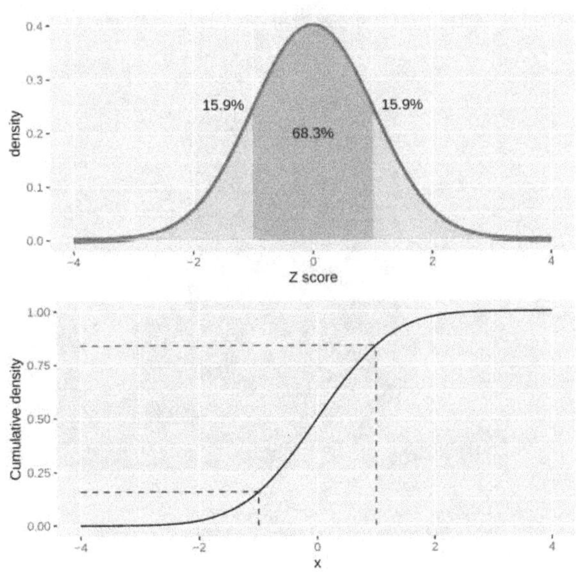

Figure 5.12: Density (top) and cumulative distribution (bottom) of a standard normal distribution, with cutoffs at one standard deviation above/below the mean.

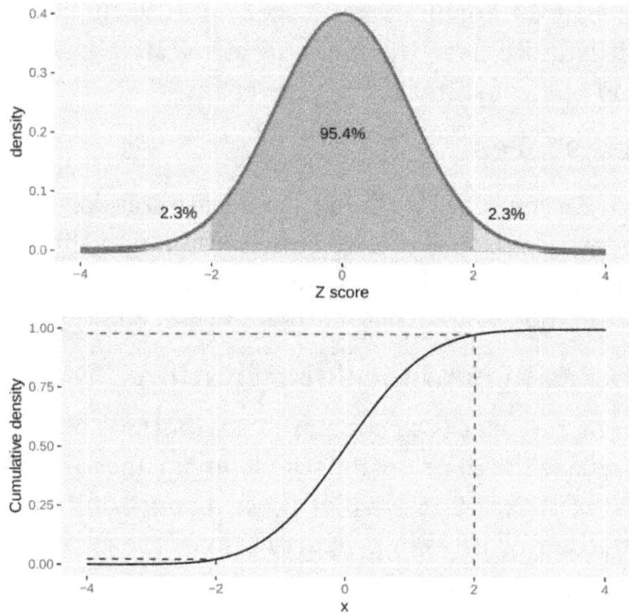

Figure 5.13: Density (top) and cumulative distribution (bottom) of a standard normal distribution, with cutoffs at two standard deviations above/below the mean

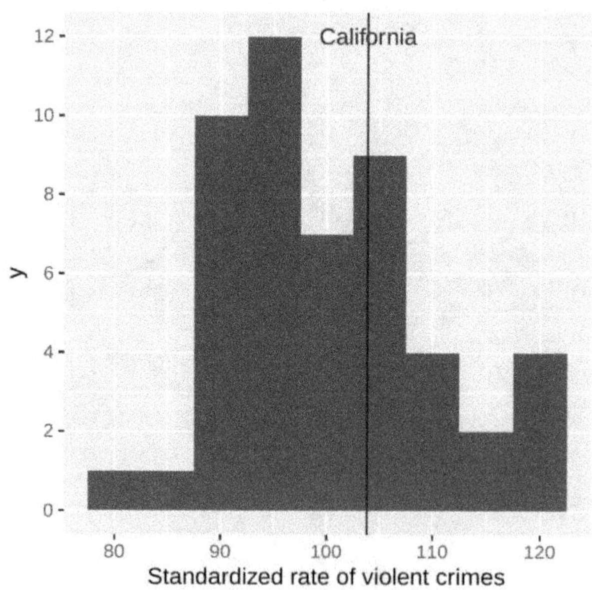

Figure 5.14: Crime data presented as standardized scores with mean of 100 and standard deviation of 10 .

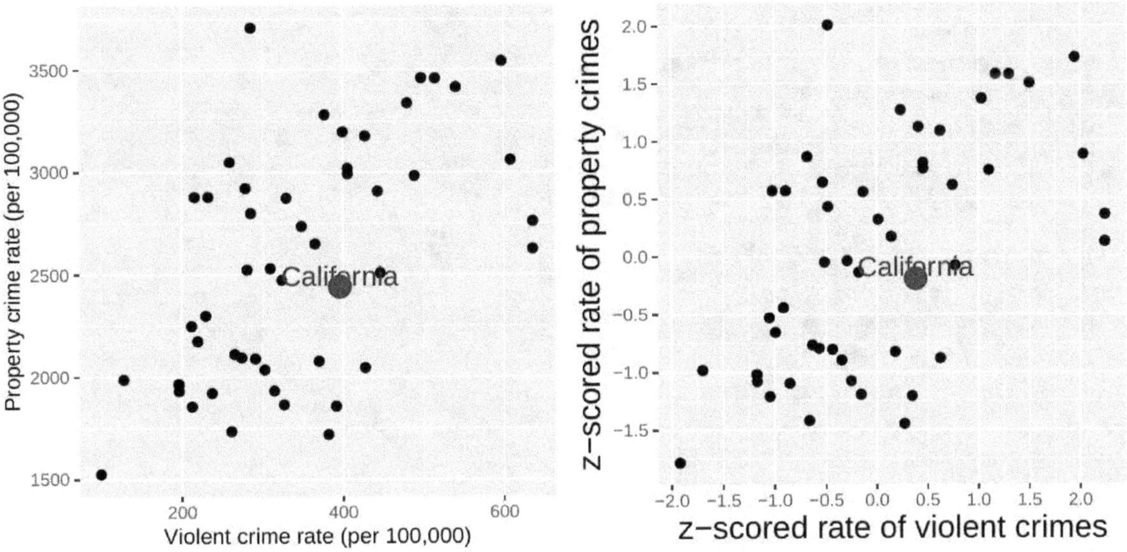

Figure 5.15: Plot of violent vs. property crime rates (left) and Z-scored rates (right).

Let's add one more factor to the plot: Population. In the left panel of Figure 5.16 we show this using the size of the plotting symbol, which is often a useful way to add information to a plot.

Because Z-scores are directly comparable, we can also compute a difference score that expresses the relative rate of violent to non-violent (property) crimes across states. We can then plot those scores against population (see right panel of Figure 5.16). This shows how we can use Z -scores to bring different variables together on a common scale.

It is worth noting that the smallest states appear to have the largest differences in both directions. While it might be tempting to look at each state and try to determine why it has a high or low difference score, this probably reflects the fact that the estimates obtained from smaller samples are necessarily going to be more variable, as we will discuss in Chapter 7.

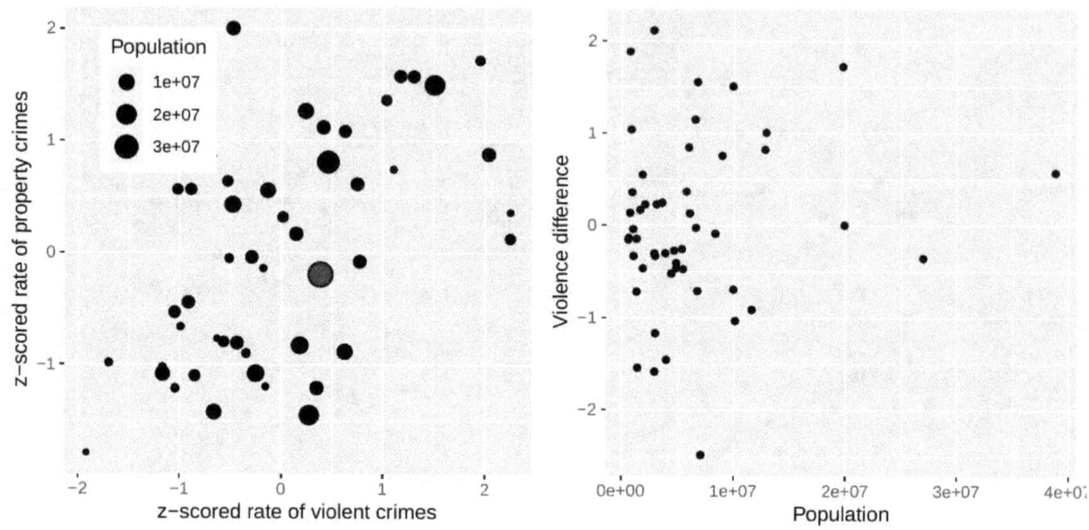

Figure 5.16: Left: Plot of violent vs. property crime rates, with population size presented through the size of the plotting symbol; California is presented in blue. Right: Difference scores for violent vs. property crime, plotted against population.

5.10 Appendix

5.10.1 Proof that the sum of errors from the Mean is zero

$$\text{error} = \sum_{i=1}^{n} (x_i - \bar{X}) = 0$$

$$\sum_{i=1}^{n} x_i - \sum_{i=1}^{n} \bar{X} = 0$$

$$\sum_{i=1}^{n} x_i = \sum_{i=1}^{n} \bar{X}$$

$$\sum_{i=1}^{n} x_i = n\bar{X}$$

$$\sum_{i=1}^{n} x_i = \sum_{i=1}^{n} x_i$$

Chapter-6

Probability

Probability is a branch of mathematics that deals with measuring uncertainty and predicting the likelihood of events. It helps us understand how likely an outcome is to occur in any given situation, whether in everyday life or scientific study. Originally developed through the analysis of gambling and games of chance, probability has now become an essential tool in science, economics, engineering, and data analysis. It provides a systematic way to quantify risk and uncertainty by assigning numerical values between 0 and 1 to different outcomes. A probability of 0 means an event is impossible, while a probability of 1 means it will definitely occur; values in between represent varying levels of likelihood. Probability theory introduces important ideas such as random experiments, sample spaces, events, conditional probability, and independence, all of which help in solving problems that involve uncertainty. Probability distributions—such as the binomial, normal, and Poisson distributions—describe how outcomes are spread out and play a key role in advanced analysis. Today, probability forms the foundation of statistics and supports data-driven decision-making in almost every field. By using probability, we can make informed predictions and better understand the randomness present in the world around us.

Probability theory is the mathematical discipline that addresses chance and uncertainty. It constitutes a crucial component of the foundation for statistics, as it furnishes the mathematical instruments necessary to characterize uncertain events. The study of probability emerged partly from the need to comprehend games of chance, such as cards and dice. These games exemplify numerous statistical concepts, as the probability of various outcomes largely remains consistent with repetition.

6.1 Probability

Probability is commonly understood as a numerical representation of the likelihood of an event occurring, ranging from zero (impossibility) to one (certainty). Probabilities may also be conveyed as percentages, ranging from zero to one hundred, exemplified by a weather forecast indicating a twenty percent likelihood of rain today. In each instance, these figures denote the probability of a specific event occurring, spanning from utterly impossible to unequivocally certain. To formalize probability theory, we first need to define a few terms:

- An experiment is any activity that produces or observes an outcome.

Examples are flipping a coin, rolling a 6 -sided die, or trying a new route to work to see if it's faster than the old route.

- The sample space is the set of possible outcomes for an experiment. We represent these by listing them within a set of squiggly brackets. For a coin flip, the sample space is { heads, tails }. For a six-sided die, the sample space is each of the possible numbers that can appear: {1,2,3,4,5,6}. For the amount of time it takes to get to work, the sample space is all possible real numbers greater than zero (since it can't take a negative amount of time to get somewhere, at least not yet). We won't bother trying to write out all of those numbers within the brackets.
- An event is a subset of the sample space. In principle it could be one or more of possible outcomes in the sample space, but here we will focus primarily on elementary events which consist of exactly one possible outcome. For example, this could be obtaining heads in a single coin flip, rolling a 4 on a throw of the die, or taking 21 minutes to get home by the new route.

Now that we have those definitions, we can outline the formal features of a probability, which were first defined by the Russian mathematician Andrei Kolmogorov. These are the features that a value has to have if it is going to be a probability. Let's say that we have a sample space defined by N independent events, $E_1, E_2, \ldots, E_N$, and X is a random variable denoting which of the events has occurred. $P(X = E_i)$ is the probability of event i :

- Probability cannot be negative: $P(X = E_i) \geq 0$
- The total probability of all outcomes in the sample space is 1 ; that is, if the, if we take the probability of each Ei and add them up, they must sum to 1 . We can express this using the summation symbol $\sum$:

$$\sum_{i=1}^{N} P(X = E_i) = P(X = E_1) + P(X = E_2) + \cdots + P(X = E_N) = 1$$

This is interpreted as saying "Take all of the N elementary events, which we have labeled from 1 to N , and add up their probabilities. These must sum to one."

- The probability of any individual event cannot be greater than one: $P(X = E_i) \leq 1$. This is implied by the previous point; since they must sum to one, and they can't be negative, then any particular probability cannot exceed one.

6.2 What methods are employed to ascertain probabilities?

Now that we know what a probability is, how do we actually figure out what the probability is for any particular event?

6.2.1 Personal belief

What would be the chance of Bernie Sanders winning the 2016 presidential election had he been the Democratic nominee instead of Hillary Clinton? We are unable to conduct the experiment to determine the outcome. Nonetheless, the majority of individuals well-versed in American politics would likely be inclined to provide an estimate of the likelihood of this occurrence. In several instances, personal knowledge and/or opinion serves as the sole criterion for assessing the likelihood of an event, although this approach lacks scientific rigor.

6.2.2 Empirical frequency

Another method to ascertain the probability of an event is to do the experiment repeatedly and tally the frequency of each occurrence. By analyzing the relative frequency of various events, we may calculate the probability of each outcome. For instance, we seek to ascertain the probability of precipitation in San Francisco. Initially, we must delineate the experiment; for instance, we will analyze the National Weather Service data for each day in 2017 to ascertain the occurrence of precipitation at the downtown San Francisco weather station. Data indicates that there were 73 rainy days in 2017. To calculate the likelihood of precipitation in San Francisco, we divide the number of wet days by the total number of days (365), resulting in P(rain in SF in 2017) = 0.2.

What is the basis for asserting that empirical probability yields accurate results? The response to this inquiry derives from the law of big numbers, which demonstrates that empirical probability converges to the real probability as the sample size expands. This can be observed by simulating numerous coin flips and examining our probability estimate of heads following each flip. We will allocate additional time to the discussion of simulation in a subsequent chapter; for the present, simply accept that we possess a computational method to produce a random result for each coin flip.

The left panel of Figure 6.1 illustrates that when the sample size (i.e., coin flip trials) rises, the estimated probability of heads approaches the true value of 0.5. Nevertheless, be aware that the estimations may significantly deviate from the actual value when the sample sizes are limited. An illustrative instance of this occurred during the 2017 special election for the US Senate in Alabama, featuring Republican Roy Moore opposing Democrat Doug Jones. The right panel of Figure 6.1 illustrates the proportion of votes recorded for each contender throughout the evening, as an escalating number of ballots were tabulated. In the early evening, the vote counts exhibited significant volatility, initially favoring Jones, then shifting to a prolonged advantage for Moore, before Jones ultimately regained the lead to secure victory in the contest.

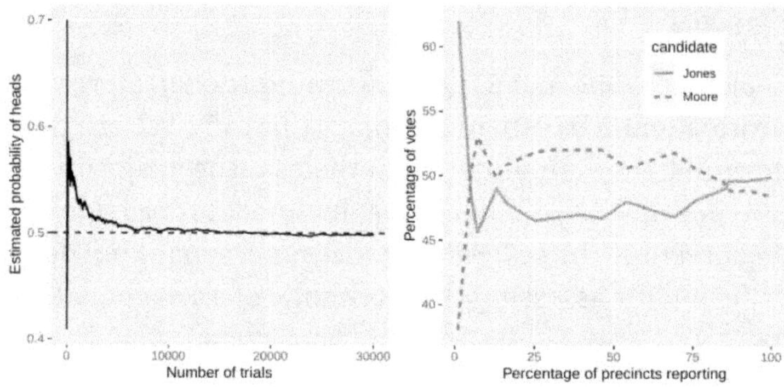

Figure 6.1: Left: A demonstration of the law of large numbers. A coin was flipped 30,000 times, and after each flip the probability of heads was computed based on the number of heads and tail collected up to that point. It takes about 15,000 flips for the probability to settle at the true probability of 0.5 . Right: Relative proportion of the vote in the Dec 12, 2017 special election for the US Senate seat in Alabama, as a function of the percentage of precincts reporting. These data were transcribed from https://www.ajc.com/news/national/alabama-senate-race-live-updates-roy-moore-doug-jones/KPRfkdaweoiXICW3FHjXqI/

These two instances illustrate that although big samples will eventually align with the correct probability, the outcomes derived from small samples may significantly deviate. Regrettably, numerous individuals neglect this and excessively interpret findings from limited samples. This phenomenon is termed the law of small numbers by psychologists Danny Kahneman and Amos Tversky, who demonstrated that individuals, including professional researchers, frequently act as though the law of large numbers is applicable to tiny samples, so attributing excessive significance to outcomes derived from limited datasets. This course will illustrate how unstable statistical results can be when derived from tiny samples.

6.2.3 Classical probability

Although it is improbable that any of us has flipped a coin tens of thousands of times, we are nevertheless inclined to accept that the probability of landing heads is 0.5. This illustrates the application of an additional method for calculating probabilities, known as classical probability. This method involves calculating the likelihood directly from our understanding of the circumstances.

Classical probability originated from the examination of games of chance, including dice and cards. An illustrious instance emerged from a dilemma faced by a French gambler known as Chevalier de Méré. de Méré participated in two distinct dice games: In the first instance, he wagered on the probability of obtaining at least one six in four rolls of a six-sided die, whereas in the second instance, he wagered on the probability of achieving at least one double-six in 24 rolls of two dice. He anticipated profiting from both gambles; nevertheless, he discovered that, on average, he gained from the first gamble but incurred losses on the second gamble after multiple plays. To comprehend this, he consulted his friend, the mathematician Blaise Pascal, who is now acknowledged as a pioneer of probability theory.

How can we understand this question using probability theory? In classical probability, we start with the assumption that all of the elementary events in the sample space are equally likely; that is, when you roll a die, each of the possible outcomes ({1,2,3,4,5,6}) is equally likely to occur. (No loaded dice allowed!) Given this, we can compute the probability of any individual outcome as one divided by the number of possible outcomes:

$$P(\text{ outcome }_i) = \frac{1}{\text{number of possible outcomes}}$$

For the six-sided die, the probability of each individual outcome is 1/6.

This is nice, but de Méré was interested in more complex events, like what happens on multiple dice throws. How do we compute the probability of a complex event (which is a union of single events), like rolling a six on the first or the second throw? We represent the union of events mathematically using the ∪ symbol: for example, if the probability of rolling a six on the first throw is referred to as $P(\text{Roll6}_{\text{throw 1}})$ and the probability of rolling a six on the second throw is $P(\text{Roll6}_{\text{throw 2}})$, then the union is referred to as $P(\text{Roll6}_{\text{throw 1}} \cup \text{Roll6}_{\text{throw 2}})$.

de Méré thought (incorrectly, as we will see below) that he could simply add together the probabilities of the individual events to compute the probability of the combined event, meaning that the probability of rolling a six on the first or second roll would be computed as follows:

$$P(\text{Roll}_{\text{throw 1}}) = 1/6$$
$$P(\text{Roll}_{\text{throw 2}}) = 1/6$$

deMéré's error :

$P(\text{Roll6}_{\text{throw 1}} \cup \text{Roll6}_{\text{throw 2}}) = P(\text{Roll6}_{\text{throw 1}}) + P(\text{Roll6}_{\text{throw 2}}) = 1/6 + 1/6 = 1/3$

de Méré reasoned based on this incorrect assumption that the probability of at least one six in four rolls was the sum of the probabilities on each of the individual throws: $4 * \frac{1}{6} = \frac{2}{3}$. Similarly, he reasoned that since the probability of a double-six when throwing two dice is 1/36, then the probability of at least one double-six on 24 rolls of two dice would be $24 * \frac{1}{36} = \frac{2}{3}$. Yet, while he consistently won money on the first bet, he lost money on the second bet. What gives?

To understand de Méré's error, we need to introduce some of the rules of probability theory. The first is the rule of subtraction, which says that the probability of some event A not happening is one minus the probability of the event happening:

$$P(\neg A) = 1 - P(A)$$

where $\neg A$ means "not A ". This rule derives directly from the axioms that we discussed above; because A and $\neg A$ are the only possible outcomes, then their total probability must sum to 1 . For example, if the probability of rolling a one in a single throw is $\frac{1}{6}$, then the probability of rolling anything other than a one is $\frac{5}{6}$.

A second rule tells us how to compute the probability of a conjoint event - that is, the probability that both of two events will occur. We refer to this as an intersection, which is signified by the $\cap$ symbol; thus, $P(A \cap B)$ means the probability that both A and B will occur. We will focus on a version of the rule that tells us how to compute this quantity in the special case when the two events are independent from one another; we will learn later exactly what the concept of independence means, but for now we can just take it for granted that the two die throws are independent events. We compute the probability of the intersection of two independent events by simply multiplying the probabilities of the individual events:

$$P(A \cap B) = P(A) * P(B) \text{ if and only if A and B are independent}$$

Thus, the probability of throwing a six on both of two rolls is $\frac{1}{6} * \frac{1}{6} = \frac{1}{36}$.

The third rule tells us how to add together probabilities - and it is here that we see the source of de Méré's error. The addition rule tells us that to obtain the probability of either of two events occurring, we add together the individual probabilities, but then subtract the likelihood of both occurring together:

$$P(A \cup B) = P(A) + P(B) - P(A \cap B)$$

In a sense, this prevents us from counting those instances twice, and that's what distinguishes the rule from de Méré's incorrect computation. Let's say that we want to find the probability of rolling 6 on either of two throws. According to our rules:

$$P(\text{Roll}_{\text{throw1}} \cup \text{Roll}_{\text{throw2}}) = P(\text{Roll}_{\text{throw1}}) + P(\text{Roll}_{\text{throw2}}) - P(\text{Roll}_{\text{throw1}} \cap \text{Roll}_{\text{throw2}})$$
$$= \frac{1}{6} + \frac{1}{6} - \frac{1}{36} = \frac{11}{36}$$

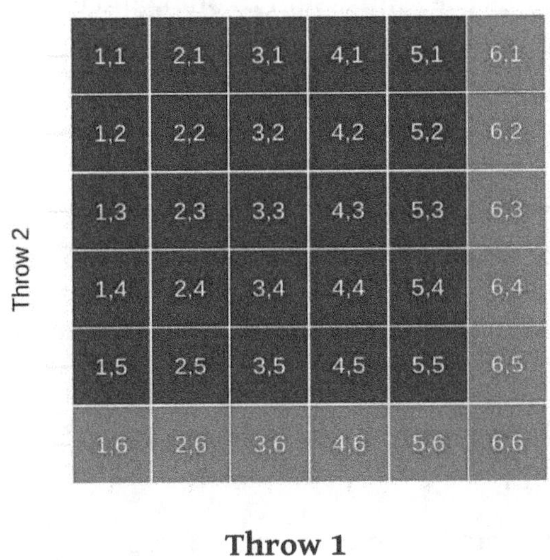

Figure 6.2: Each cell in this matrix represents one outcome of two throws of a die, with the columns representing the first throw and the rows representing the second throw. Cells shown in red represent the cells with a six in either the first or second throw; the rest are shown in blue.

Let's use a graphical depiction to get a different view of this rule. Figure 6.2 shows a matrix representing all possible combinations of results across two throws, and highlights the cells that involve a six on either the first or second throw. If you count up the cells in red you will see that there are 11 such cells. This shows why the addition rule gives a different answer from de Méré's; if we were to simply add together the probabilities for the two throws as he did, then we would count (6,6) towards both, when it should really only be counted once.

6.2.4 Solving de Méré's problem

Blaise Pascal used the rules of probability to come up with a solution to de Méré's problem. First, he realized that computing the probability of at least one event out of a combination was tricky, whereas computing the probability that something does not occur across several events is relatively easy - it's just the product of the probabilities of the individual events. Thus, rather than computing the probability of at least one six in four rolls, he instead computed the probability of no sixes across all rolls:

$$P(\text{ no sixes in four rolls }) = \frac{5}{6} * \frac{5}{6} * \frac{5}{6} * \frac{5}{6} = \left(\frac{5}{6}\right)^4 = 0.482$$

He then used the fact that the probability of no sixes in four rolls is the complement of at least one six in four rolls (thus they must sum to one), and used the rule of subtraction to compute the probability of interest:

$$P(\text{ at least one six in four rolls }) = 1 - \left(\frac{5}{6}\right)^4 = 0.517$$

de Méré's gamble that he would throw at least one six in four rolls has a probability of greater than 0.5 , explaning why de Méré made money on this bet on average.

But what about de Méré's second bet? Pascal used the same trick:

$$P(\text{ no double six in 24 rolls }) = \left(\frac{35}{36}\right)^{24} = 0.509$$

$$P(\text{ at least one double six in 24 rolls }) = 1 - \left(\frac{35}{36}\right)^{24} = 0.491$$

The probability of this outcome was slightly below 0.5 , showing why de Méré lost money on average on this bet.

6.3 Probability distributions

A probability distribution describes the probability of all of the possible outcomes in an experiment. For example, on Jan 20 2018, the basketball player Steph Curry hit only 2 out of 4 free throws in a game against the Houston Rockets. We know that Curry's overall probability of hitting free throws across the entire season was 0.91 , so it seems pretty unlikely that he would hit only 50% of his free throws in a game, but exactly how unlikely is it? We can determine this using a theoretical probability distribution; throughout this book we will encounter a number of these probability distributions, each of which is appropriate to describe different types of data. In this case, we use the binomial distribution, which provides a way to compute the probability of some number of successes out of a number of trials on which there is either success or failure and nothing in between (known as "Bernoulli trials"), given some known probability of success on each trial. This distribution is defined as:

$$P(k; n, p) = P(X = k) = \binom{n}{k} p^k (1-p)^{n-k}$$

This refers to the probability of k successes on n trials when the probability of success is p. You may not be familiar with $\binom{n}{k}$, which is referred to as the binomial coefficient. The binomial coefficient is also referred to as "n-choose-k" because it describes the number of different ways that one can choose k items out of n total items. The binomial coefficient is computed as:

$$\binom{n}{k} = \frac{n!}{k!\,(n-k)!}$$

where the exclamation point (!) refers to the factorial of the number:

$$n! = \prod_{i=1}^{n} i = n * (n-1) * \ldots * 2 * 1$$

The product operator Π is similar to the summation operator Σ , except that it multiplies instead of adds. In this case, it is multiplying together all numbers from one to n.

In the example of Steph Curry's free throws:

$$P(2; 4{,}0.91) = \binom{4}{2} 0.91^2 (1-0.91)^{4-2} = 0.040$$

This shows that given Curry's overall free throw percentage, it is very unlikely that he would hit only 2 out of 4 free throws. Which just goes to show that unlikely things do actually happen in the real world.

6.3.1 Cumulative probability distributions

Often we want to know not just how likely a specific value is, but how likely it is to find a value that is as extreme or more than a particular value; this will become very important when we discuss hypothesis testing in Chapter 9. To answer this question, we can use a cumulative probability distribution; whereas a standard probability distribution tells us the probability of some specific value, the cumulative distribution tells us the probability of a value as large or larger (or as small or smaller) than some specific value.

In the free throw example, we might want to know: What is the probability that Steph Curry hits 2 or fewer free throws out of four, given his overall free throw probability of 0.91 . To determine this, we could simply use the the binomial probability equation and plug in all of the possible values of k and add them together:

$$P(k \leq 2) = P(k = 2) + P(k = 1) + P(k = 0) = 6e^{-5} + .002 + .040 = .043$$

In many cases the number of possible outcomes would be too large for us to compute the cumulative probability by enumerating all possible values;

Table 6.1: Simple and cumulative probability distributions for number of successful free throws by Steph Curry in 4 attempts.

numSuccesses	Probability	CumulativeProbability
0	0.000	0.000
1	0.003	0.003
2	0.040	0.043
3	0.271	0.314
4	0.686	1.000

fortunately, it can be computed directly for any theoretical probability distribution. Table 6.1 shows the cumulative probability of each possible number of successful free throws in the example from above, from which we can see that the probability of Curry landing 2 or fewer free throws out of 4 attempts is 0.043.

6.4 Conditional probability

Thus far, we have confined our analysis to elementary probabilities, specifically the likelihood of an individual event or a set of events. We frequently want to ascertain the chance of an event contingent upon the occurrence of another event, referred to as conditional probabilities. Let's take the 2016 US Presidential election as an example. There are two simple probabilities that we could use to describe the electorate. First, we know the probability that a voter in the US is affiliated with the Republican party: $p(\text{Republican}) = 0.44$. We also know the probability that a voter cast their vote in favor of Donald Trump: $p(\text{Trumpvoter}) = 0.46$. However, let's say that we want to know the following: What is the probability that a person cast their vote for Donald Trump, given that they are a Republican?

To compute the conditional probability of A given B (which we write as $P(A \mid B)$, "probability of A , given B "), we need to know the joint probability (that is, the probability of both A and B occurring) as well as the overall probability of B :

$$P(A \mid B) = \frac{P(A \cap B)}{P(B)}$$

That is, we want to know the probability that both things are true, given that the one being conditioned upon is true.

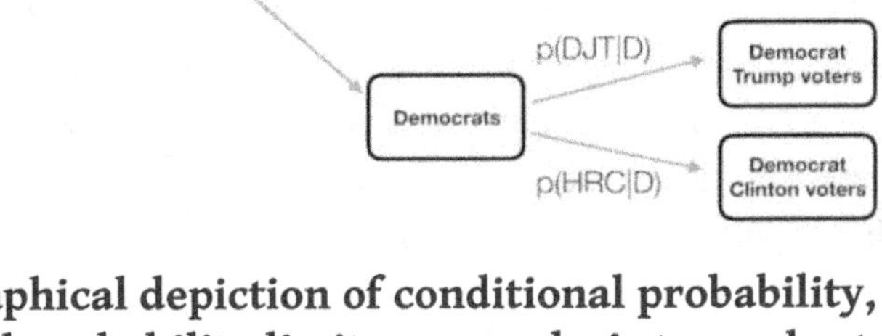

Figure 6.3: A graphical depiction of conditional probability, showing how the conditional probability limits our analysis to a subset of the data.

It can be useful to think of this graphically. Figure 6.3 shows a flow chart depicting how the full population of voters breaks down into Republicans and Democrats, and how the conditional probability (conditioning on party) further breaks down the members of each party according to their vote.

Table 6.2: Summary data for diabetes and physical activity

Answer	N_diabetes	P_diabetes	N_PhysActive	P_PhysActive
No	4893	0.9	2472	0.45
Yes	550	0.1	2971	0.55

Table 6.3: Joint probabilities for Diabetes and PhysActive variables.

Diabetes	PhysActive	n	prob
No	No	2123	0.39
No	Yes	2770	0.51
Yes	No	349	0.06
Yes	Yes	201	0.04

6.5 Computing conditional probabilities from data

We can also compute conditional probabilities directly from data. Let's say that we are interested in the following question: What is the probability that someone has diabetes, given that they are not physically active? that is, P (diabetes|inactive). The NHANES dataset includes two variables that address the two parts of this question. The first (Diabetes) asks whether the person has ever been told that they have diabetes, and the second (PhysActive) records whether the person engages in sports, fitness, or recreational activities that are at least of moderate intensity. Let's first compute the simple probabilities, which are shown in Table 6.2. The table shows that the probability that someone in the NHANES dataset has diabetes is .1 , and the probability that someone is inactive is .45 .

To compute P (diabetes | inactive) we would also need to know the joint probability of being diabetic and inactive, in addition to the simple probabilities of each. These are shown in Table 6.3. Based on these joint probabilities, we can compute P (diabetes|inactive). One way to do this in a computer program is to first determine the whether the PhysActive variable was equal to "No" for each indivdual, and then take the mean of those truth values. Since TRUE/FALSE values are treated as 1/0 respectively by most programming languages (including R and Python), this allows us to easily identify the probability of a simple event by simply taking the mean of a logical variable representing its truth value. We then use that value to compute the conditional probability, where we find that the probability of someone having diabetes given that they are physically inactive is 0.141 .

6.6 Independence

The term "independent" has a very specific meaning in statistics, which is somewhat different from the common usage of the term. Statistical independence between two variables means that knowing the value of one variable doesn't tell us anything about the value of the other. This can be expressed as:

$$P(A \mid B) = P(A)$$

That is, the probability of A given some value of B is just the same as the overall probability of A. Looking at it this way, we see that many cases of what we would call "independence" in the real world are not actually statistically independent. For example, there is currently a move by a small group of California citizens to declare a new independent state called Jefferson, which would comprise a number of counties in northern California and Oregon. If this were to happen, then the probability that a current California resident would now live in the state of Jefferson would be $P(\text{ Jeffersonian }) = 0.014$, whereas the probability that they would remain a California resident would be $P(\text{ Californian }) = 0.986$. The new states might be politically independent, but they would not be statistically independent, because if we know that a person is Jeffersonian, then we can be sure that they are not Californian! That is, while independence in common language often refers to sets that are exclusive, statistical independence refers to the case where one cannot predict anything about one variable from the value of another variable. For example, knowing a person's hair color is unlikely to tell you whether they prefer chocolate or strawberry ice cream.

Let's look at another example, using the NHANES data: Are physical health and mental health independent of one another? NHANES includes two relevant questions: PhysActive, which asks whether the individual is physically active, and DaysMentHlthBad, which asks how many days out of the last 30 that the individual experienced bad mental health.

Table 6.4: Summary of absolute frequency data for mental health and physical activity.

PhysActive	Bad Mental Health	Good Mental Health	Total
No	414	1664	2078
Yes	292	1926	2218
Total	706	3590	4296

Table 6.5: Summary of relative frequency data for mental health and physical activity.

PhysActive	Bad Mental Health	Good Mental Health	Total
No	0.10	0.39	0.48
Yes	0.07	0.45	0.52
Total	0.16	0.84	1.00

Let's consider anyone who had more than 7 days of bad mental health in the last month to be in bad mental health. Based on this, we can define a new variable called badMentalHealth as a logical variable telling whether each person had more than 7 days of bad mental health or not. We can first summarize the data to show how many individuals fall into each combination of the two variables (shown in Table 6.4), and then divide by the total number of observations to create a table of proportions (shown in Table 6.5):

This shows us the proportion of all observations that fall into each cell. However, what we want to know here is the conditional probability of bad mental health, depending on whether one is physically active or not. To compute this, we divide each physical activity group by its total number of observations, so that each row now sums to one (shown in Table 6.6). Here we see the conditional probabilities of bad or good mental health for each physical activity group (in the top two rows) along with the overall probability of good or bad mental health in the third row. To determine whether mental health and physical activity are independent, we would compare the simple probability of bad mental health (in the third row) to the conditional probability of bad mental health given that one is physically active (in the second row).

Table 6.6: Summary of conditional probabilities for mental health given physical activity.

PhysActive	Bad Mental Health	Good Mental Health	Total
No	0.20	0.80	1
Yes	0.13	0.87	1
Total	0.16	0.84	1

The overall probability of poor mental health P(bad mental health) is 0.16, but the conditional probability P(bad mental health|physically active) is 0.13. Consequently, the conditional probability appears to be marginally less than the overall probability, indicating a lack of independence; nevertheless, this conclusion cannot be definitively drawn only from the data, as the figures may vary due to random sampling variability. Subsequently in the book, we will examine statistical instruments that enable us to directly assess the independence of two variables.

6.7 Inverting a conditional probability: Bayes' theorem

In many cases, we know $P(A \mid B)$ but we really want to know $P(B \mid A)$. This commonly occurs in medical screening, where we know P (positive test result | disease) but what we want to know is P (disease positive test result). For example, some doctors recommend that men over the age of 50 undergo screening using a test called prostate specific antigen (PSA) to screen for possible prostate cancer. Before a test is approved for use in medical practice, the manufacturer needs to test two aspects of the test's performance. First, they need to show how sensitive it is - that is, how likely is it to find the disease when it is present: sensitivity = P (positive test | disease). They also need to show how specific it is: that is, how likely is it to give a negative result when there is no disease present: specificity = P (negative test | no disease). For the PSA test, we know that sensitivity is about 80% and specificity is about 70%. However, these don't answer the question that the physician wants to answer for any particular patient: what is the likelihood that they actually have cancer, given that the test comes back positive? This requires that we reverse the conditional probability that defines sensitivity: instead of

$P($ positive test | disease $)$ we want to know $P($ disease | positive test $)$.

In order to reverse a conditional probability, we can use Bayes' rule:

$$P(B \mid A) = \frac{P(A \mid B) * P(B)}{P(A)}$$

Bayes' rule is fairly easy to derive, based on the rules of probability that we learned earlier in the chapter (see the Appendix for this derivation).

If we have only two outcomes, we can express Bayes' rule in a somewhat clearer way, using the sum rule to redefine $P(A)$:

$$P(A) = P(A \mid B) * P(B) + P(A \mid \neg B) * P(\neg B)$$

Using this, we can redefine Bayes's rule:

$$P(B \mid A) = \frac{P(A \mid B) * P(B)}{P(A \mid B) * P(B) + P(A \mid \neg B) * P(\neg B)}$$

We can plug the relevant numbers into this equation to determine the likelihood that an individual with a positive PSA result actually has cancer - but note that in order to do this, we also need to know the overall probability of cancer for that person, which we often refer to as the base rate. Let's take a 60 year old man, for whom the probability of prostate cancer in the next 10 years is $P(\text{ cancer }) = 0.058$. Using the sensitivity and specificity values that we outlined above, we can compute the individual's likelihood of having cancer given a positive test:

$$P(\text{ cancer } \mid \text{ test }) = \frac{P(\text{ test } \mid \text{ cancer }) * P(\text{ cancer })}{P(\text{ test } \mid \text{ cancer }) * P(\text{ cancer }) + P(\text{ test } \mid \neg \text{ cancer }) * P(\neg \text{ cancer })}$$
$$= \frac{0.8 * 0.058}{0.8 * 0.058 + 0.3 * 0.942} = 0.14$$

That's pretty small - do you find that surprising? Many people do, and in fact there is a substantial psychological literature showing that people systematically neglect base rates (i.e. overall prevalence) in their judgments.

6.8 Learning from data

Another way to think of Bayes' rule is as a way to update our beliefs on the basis of data - that is, learning about the world using data. Let's look at Bayes' rule again:

$$P(B \mid A) = \frac{P(A \mid B) * P(B)}{P(A)}$$

The different parts of Bayes' rule have specific names, that relate to their role in using Bayes' rule to update our beliefs. We start out with an initial guess about the probability of B($P(B)$), which we refer to as the prior probability. In the PSA example we used the base rate as our prior, since it was our best guess as to the individual's chance of cancer before we knew the test result. We then collect some data, which in our example was the test result. The degree to which the data A are consistent with outcome B is given by $P(A \mid B)$, which we refer to as the likelihood. You can think of this as how likely the data are, given that the particular hypothesis being tested is true. In our example, the hypothesis being tested was whether the individual had cancer, and the likelihood was based on our knowledge about the sensitivity of the test (that is, the probability of a positive test outcome given cancer is present). The denominator ($P(A)$) is referred to as the marginal likelihood, because it expresses the overall likelihood of the data, averaged across all of the possible values of B (which in our example were disease present and disease absent). The outcome to the left ($P(B \mid A)$) is referred to as the posterior - because it's what comes out the back end of the computation.

There is another way of writing Bayes rule that makes this a bit clearer:

$$P(B \mid A) = \frac{P(A \mid B)}{P(A)} * P(B)$$

The part on the left $\left(\frac{P(A|B)}{P(A)}\right)$ tells us how much more or less likely the data A are given B , relative to the overall (marginal) likelihood of the data, while the part on the right side ($P(B)$) tells us how likely we thought B was before we knew anything about the data. This makes it clearer that the role of Bayes theorem is to update our prior knowledge based on the degree to which the data are more likely given B than they would be overall. If the hypothesis is more likely given the data than it would be in general, then we increase our belief in the hypothesis; if it's less likely given the data, then we decrease our belief.

6.9 Odds and odds ratios

The result in the last section showed that the likelihood that the individual has cancer based on a positive PSA test result is still fairly low, even though it's more than twice as big as it was before we knew the test result. We would often like to quantify the relation between probabilities more directly, which we can do by converting them into odds which express the relative likelihood of something happening or not:

$$\text{odds of A} = \frac{P(A)}{P(\neg A)}$$

In our PSA example, the odds of having cancer (given the positive test) are:

$$\text{odds of cancer } = \frac{P(\text{ cancer })}{P(\neg \text{ cancer })} = \frac{0.14}{1 - 0.14} = 0.16$$

This tells us that the that the odds are fairly low of having cancer, even though the test was positive. For comparison, the odds of rolling a 6 in a single dice throw are:

$$\text{odds of } 6 = \frac{1}{5} = 0.2$$

As an aside, this is a reason why many medical researchers have become increasingly wary of the use of widespread screening tests for relatively uncommon conditions; most positive results will turn out to be false positives, resulting in unneccessary followup tests with possible complications, not to mention added stress for the patient.

We can also use odds to compare different probabilities, by computing what is called an odds ratio - which is exactly what it sounds like. For example, let's say that we want to know how much the positive test increases the individual's odds of having cancer. We can first compute the prior odds that is, the odds before we knew that the person had tested positively. These are computed using the base rate:

$$\text{prior odds } = \frac{P(\text{ cancer })}{P(\neg \text{ cancer })} = \frac{0.058}{1 - 0.058} = 0.061$$

We can then compare these with the posterior odds, which are computed using the posterior probability:

$$\text{odds ratio } = \frac{\text{posterior odds}}{\text{prior odds}} = \frac{0.16}{0.061} = 2.62$$

This tells us that the odds of having cancer are increased by 2.62 times given the positive test result. An odds ratio is an example of what we will later call an effect size, which is a way of quantifying how relatively large any particular statistical effect is.

6.10 What is the significance of probabilities?

It might strike you that it is a bit odd to talk about the probability of a person having cancer depending on a test result; after all, the person either has cancer or they don't. Historically, there have been two different ways that probabilities have been interpreted.

The first (known as the frequentist interpretation) interprets probabilities in terms of long-run frequencies. For example, in the case of a coin flip, it would reflect the relative frequencies of heads in the long run after a large number of flips. While this interpretation might make sense for events that can be repeated many times like a coin flip, it makes less sense for events that will only happen once, like an individual person's life or a particular presidential election; and as the economist John Maynard Keynes famously said, "In the long run, we are all dead."

The other interpretation of probablities (known as the Bayesian interpretation) is as a degree of belief in a particular proposition. If I were to ask you "How likely is it that the US will return to the moon by 2040 ", you can provide an answer to this question based on your knowledge and beliefs, even though there are no relevant frequencies to compute a frequentist probability. One way that we often frame subjective probabilities is in terms of one's willingness to accept a particular gamble. For example, if you think that the probability of the US landing on the moon by 2040 is 0.1 (i.e. odds of 9 to 1), then that means that you should be willing to accept a gamble that would pay off with anything more than 9 to 1 odds if the event occurs.

The two distinct definitions of probability are pertinent to the divergent approaches statisticians employ in evaluating statistical hypotheses, which we will explore in subsequent chapters.

6.11 Appendix

6.11 .1 Derivation of Bayes' rule

First, remember the rule for computing a conditional probability:

$$P(A \mid B)=\frac{P(A \cap B)}{P(B)}$$

We can rearrange this to get the formula to compute the joint probability using the conditional:

$$P(A \cap B)=P(A \mid B) * P(B)$$

Using this we can compute the inverse probability:

$$P(B \mid A)=\frac{P(A \cap B)}{P(A)}=\frac{P(A \mid B) * P(B)}{P(A)}$$

Chapter-7

Sampling

Sampling in statistics is a fundamental process used to select a subset of individuals, items, or observations from a larger population. It allows researchers to gather meaningful information without studying the entire population. This approach saves time, reduces cost, and makes data collection more manageable. A well-designed sample can accurately represent the characteristics of the whole group. Sampling is essential when the population is too large or inaccessible. It helps statisticians draw conclusions and make predictions efficiently. Different sampling methods are used depending on the research goals. These include probability and non-probability sampling techniques.

Probability sampling ensures every member has a known chance of selection. non-probability sampling relies on non-random selection based on convenience or judgment. A good sampling method reduces bias and increases reliability.

It also improves the validity of statistical analysis. Sampling techniques are widely used in surveys, experiments, and social research. They play a key role in fields such as economics, medicine, education, and marketing. Accurate sampling ensures better decision-making and policy formulation. It forms the backbone of data-driven studies in many disciplines. Researchers must carefully plan how samples are chosen. Clear sampling procedures strengthen the credibility of findings. Thus, sampling is a critical tool in modern statistical practice. It bridges the gap between limited data and meaningful conclusions.

One of the foundational ideas in statistics is that we can make inferences about an entire population based on a relatively small sample of individuals from that population. In this chapter we will introduce the concept of statistical sampling and discuss why it works.

Anyone living in the United States will be familiar with the concept of sampling from the political polls that have become a central part of our electoral process. In some cases, these polls can be incredibly accurate at predicting the outcomes of elections. The best known example comes from the 2008 and 2012 US Presidential elections, when the pollster Nate Silver correctly predicted electoral outcomes for 49/50 states in 2008 and for all 50 states in 2012. Silver did this by combining data from 21 different polls, which vary in the degree to which they tend to lean towards either the Republican or Democratic side. Each of these polls included data from about 1000 likely voters - meaning that Silver was able to almost perfectly predict the pattern of votes of more than 125 million voters using data from only about 21,000 people, along with other knowledge (such as how those states have voted in the past).

7.1 What is our sampling methodology?

Our goal in sampling is to determine the value of a statistic for an entire population of interest, using just a small subset of the population. We do this primarily to save time and effort - why go to the trouble of measuring every individual in the population when just a small sample is sufficient to accurately estimate the statistic of interest?

In the election example, the population is all registered voters in the region being polled, and the sample is the set of 1000 individuals selected by the polling organization. The way in which we select the sample is critical to ensuring that the sample is representative of the entire population, which is a main goal of statistical sampling. It's easy to imagine a non-representative sample; if a pollster only called individuals whose names they had received from the local Democratic party, then it would be unlikely that the results of the poll would be representative of the population as a whole. In general, we would define a representative poll as being one in which every member of the population has an equal chance of being selected. When this fails, then we have to worry about whether the statistic that we compute on the sample is biased - that is, whether its value is systematically different from the population value (which we refer to as a parameter). Keep in mind that we generally don't know this population parameter, because if we did then we wouldn't need to sample! But we will use examples where we have access to the entire population, in order to explain some of the key ideas.

It's important to also distinguish between two different ways of sampling: with replacement versus without replacement. In sampling with replacement, after a member of the population has been sampled, they are put back into the pool so that they can potentially be sampled again. In sampling without replacement, once a member has been sampled they are not eligible to be sampled again. It's most common to use sampling without replacement, but there will be some contexts in which we will use sampling with replacement, as when we discuss a technique called bootstrapping in Chapter 8.

7.2 Sampling error

Regardless of how representative our sample is, it's likely that the statistic that we compute from the sample is going to differ at least slightly from the population parameter. We refer to this as sampling error. If we take multiple samples, the value of our statistical estimate will also vary from sample to sample; we refer to this distribution of our statistic across samples as the sampling distribution.

Table 7.1: Example means and standard deviations for several samples of Height variable from NHANES.

sampleMean	sampleSD
167	9.1
171	8.3
170	10.6
166	9.5
168	9.5

Sampling error is directly related to the quality of our measurement of the population. Clearly we want the estimates obtained from our sample to be as close as possible to the true value of the population parameter. However, even if our statistic is unbiased (that is, we expect it to have the same value as the population parameter), the value for any particular estimate will differ from the population value, and those differences will be greater when the sampling error is greater. Thus, reducing sampling error is an important step towards better measurement.

We will use the NHANES dataset as an example; we are going to assume that the NHANES dataset is the entire population of interest, and then we will draw random samples from this population. We will have more to say in the next chapter about exactly how the generation of "random" samples works in a computer.

In this example, we know the adult population mean (168.35) and standard deviation (10.16) for height because we are assuming that the NHANES dataset is the population. Table 7.1 shows the statistics computed from a few samples of 50 individuals from the NHANES population.

The sample mean and standard deviation are similar but not exactly equal to the population values. Now let's take a large number of samples of 50 individuals, compute the mean for each sample, and look at the resulting sampling distribution of means. We have to decide how many samples to take in order to do a good job of estimating the sampling distribution - in this case we will take 5000 samples so that we are very confident in the answer. Note that simulations like this one can sometimes take a few minutes to run, and might make your computer huff and puff. The histogram in Figure 7.1

shows that the means estimated for each of the samples of 50 individuals vary somewhat, but that overall they are centered around the population mean. The average of the 5000 sample means (168.3463) is very close to the true population mean (168.3497).

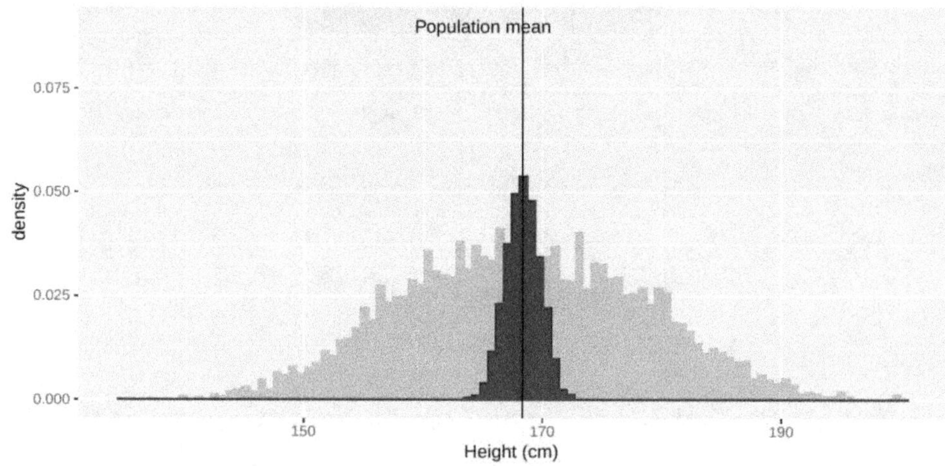

Figure 7.1: The blue histogram shows the sampling distribution of the mean over 5000 random samples from the NHANES dataset. The histogram for the full dataset is shown in gray for reference.

7.3 Standard error of the mean

Later in the book it will become essential to be able to characterize how variable our samples are, in order to make inferences about the sample statistics. For the mean, we do this using a quantity called the standard error of the mean (SEM), which one can think of as the standard deviation of the sampling distribution of the mean. To compute the standard error of the mean for our sample, we divide the estimated standard deviation by the square root of the sample size:

$$SEM = \frac{\hat{\sigma}}{\sqrt{n}}$$

Note that we have to be careful about computing SEM using the estimated standard deviation if our sample is small (less than about 30).

Because we have many samples from the NHANES population and we actually know the population SEM (which we compute by dividing the population standard deviation by the size of the population), we can confirm that the SEM computed using the population parameter (1.44) is very close to the observed standard deviation of the means for the samples that we took from the NHANES dataset (1.43).

The formula for the standard error of the mean implies that the quality of our measurement involves two quantities: the population variability, and the size of our sample. Because the sample size is the denominator in the formula for SEM, a larger sample size will yield a smaller SEM when holding the population variability constant. We have no control over the population variability, but we do have control over the sample size. Thus, if we wish to improve our sample statistics (by reducing their sampling variability) then we should use larger samples. However, the formula also tells us something very fundamental about statistical sampling - namely, that the utility of larger samples diminishes with the square root of the sample size. This means that doubling the sample size will not double the quality of the statistics; rather, it will improve it by a factor of $\sqrt{2}$. In Section 10.3 we will discuss statistical power, which is intimately tied to this idea.

7.4 The Central Limit Theorem

The Central Limit Theorem tells us that as sample sizes get larger, the sampling distribution of the mean will become normally distributed, even if the data within each sample are not normally distributed.

First, let's say a little bit about the normal distribution. It's also known as the Gaussian distribution, after Carl Friedrich Gauss, a mathematician who didn't invent it but played a role in its development. The normal distribution is described in terms of two parameters: the mean (which you can think of as the location of the peak), and the standard deviation (which specifies the width of the distribution). The bell-like shape of the distribution never changes, only its location and width. The normal distribution is commonly observed in data collected in the real world, as we have already seen in Chapter 3 - and the central limit theorem gives us some insight into why that occurs.

To see the central limit theorem in action, let's work with the variable AlcoholYear from the NHANES dataset, which is highly skewed, as shown in the left panel of Figure 7.2. This distribution is, for lack of a better word, funky - and definitely not normally distributed. Now let's look at the sampling distribution of the mean for this variable. Figure 7.2 shows the sampling distribution for this variable, which is obtained by repeatedly drawing samples of size 50 from the NHANES dataset and taking the mean. Despite the clear non-normality of the original data, the sampling distribution is remarkably close to the normal.

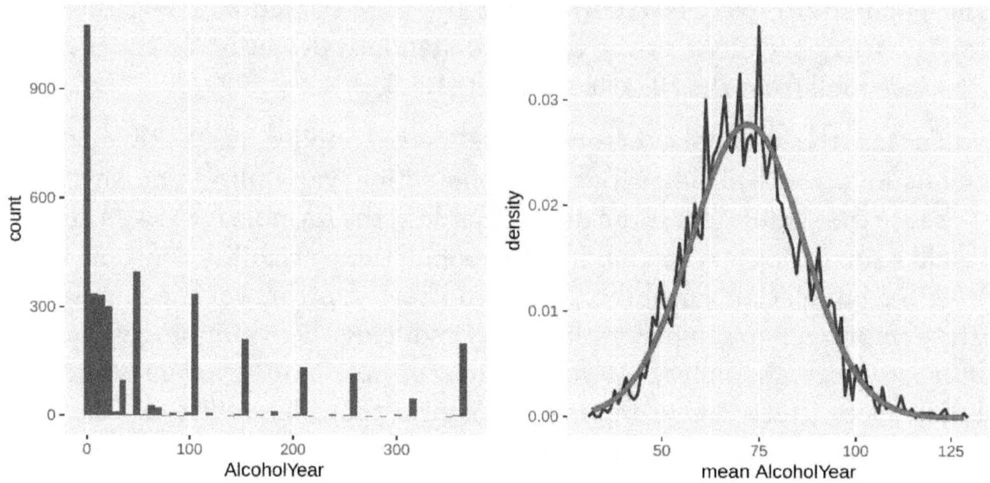

Figure 7.2: Left: Distribution of the variable AlcoholYear in the NHANES dataset, which reflects the number of days that the individual drank in a year. Right: The sampling distribution of the mean for AlcoholYear in the NHANES dataset, obtained by drawing repeated samples of size 50, in blue. The normal distribution with the same mean and standard deviation is shown in red.

The Central Limit Theorem is crucial for statistics as it enables the assumption that the sample distribution of the mean will typically be normal. This indicates that we can utilize statistical methods predicated on the assumption of a normal distribution, as will be demonstrated in the subsequent section. It is significant since it elucidates the prevalence of normal distributions in reality; whenever numerous diverse factors are amalgamated into a singular value, the outcome is likely to conform to a normal distribution. The height of each adult is influenced by a complex interplay of genetics and environmental factors; although these individual contributions may not follow a normal distribution, their aggregation results in a normal distribution.

Chapter-8

Resampling and Computer Simulation

The use of computer simulations has become an essential aspect of modern statistics. For example, one of the most important books in practical computer science, called Numerical Recipes, says the following:

"Offered the choice between mastery of a five-foot shelf of analytical statistics books and middling ability at performing statistical Monte Carlo simulations, we would surely choose to have the latter skill."

In this chapter we will introduce the concept of a Monte Carlo simulation and discuss how it can be used to perform statistical analyses.

8.1 Concept of Monte Carlo simulation

The concept of Monte Carlo simulation was devised by the mathematicians Stan Ulam and Nicholas Metropolis, who were working to develop an atomic weapon for the US as part of the Manhattan Project. They needed to compute the average distance that a neutron would travel in a substance before it collided with an atomic nucleus, but they could not compute this using standard mathematics. Ulam realized that these computations could be simulated using random numbers, just like a casino game. In a casino game such as a roulette wheel, numbers are generated at random; to estimate the probability of a specific outcome, one could play the game hundreds of times.

Ulam's uncle had gambled at the Monte Carlo casino in Monaco, which is apparently where the name came from for this new technique.

There are four steps to performing a Monte Carlo simulation:

1. Define a domain of possible values
2. Generate random numbers within that domain from a probability distribution
3. Perform a computation using the random numbers
4. Combine the results across many repetitions

For instance, I wish to determine the appropriate duration for an in-class quiz. For the time being, we will assume that the distribution of quiz completion times follows a normal distribution, characterized by a mean of 5 minutes and a standard deviation of 1 minute. Considering this, what duration should the test period be to ensure that we anticipate all students will complete the exam 99% of the time? Two methods exist to resolve this issue. The initial step is to determine the solution utilizing a mathematical framework referred to as the statistics of extreme values. This entails intricate mathematics. Alternatively, we might employ Monte Carlo simulation. We must produce random samples from a normal distribution to accomplish this.

8.2 Randomness in statistics

The term "random" is frequently employed informally to describe phenomena that are unusual or unforeseen; nevertheless, in statistics, it possesses a precise definition: a process is deemed random if it is unpredictable. For instance, when I flip a fair coin 10 times, the result of one flip does not furnish any information that enables me to anticipate the outcome of the subsequent flip. It is essential to recognize that unpredictability does not inherently imply a lack of determinism. For instance, when a coin is flipped, the result is governed by the principles of physics; if we have comprehensive knowledge of all conditions, we could accurately forecast the outcome of the flip. Nevertheless, numerous circumstances converge to render the result of the coin flip unpredictable in practice.

Psychologists have demonstrated that humans possess a rather poor understanding of randomness. Initially, we often perceive patterns that are nonexistent. This culminates in the occurrence of pareidolia, when individuals perceive recognize recognizable items inside arbitrary patterns (for instance, identifying a cloud as a human face or seeing the Virgin Mary in a slice of toast). Secondly, individuals often perceive random processes as self-correcting, resulting in the expectation of being "due for a win" following a series of losses in a game of chance, a phenomenon referred to as the "gambler's fallacy."".

8.3 Generating random numbers

Conducting a Monte Carlo simulation necessitates the generation of random numbers. True random number generation, characterized by complete unpredictability, is achievable solely through physical processes like atomic decay or dice rolling, which are often challenging to access and/or too slow for practical computer simulations (although they can be sourced from the NIST Randomness Beacon).

Typically, we utilize pseudo-random numbers produced by a computer algorithm rather than genuinely random numbers; these numbers appear random and are challenging to anticipate, however the sequence will ultimately repeat. The random number generator employed in R will cycle after 2^19937-1 iterations. This exceeds the total number of seconds in the universe's history, and it is typically considered sufficient for most statistical analyses.

Most statistical software encompasses functions that generate random numbers for the principal probability distributions, including the uniform distribution (where all values between 0 and 1 are equally likely), normal distribution, and binomial distribution (e.g., dice rolls, coin tosses). Figure 8.1 illustrates instances of numbers produced by uniform and normal distribution functions.

Random numbers for any distribution can also be generated using the quantile function of that distribution. The quantile function is the inverse of the cumulative distribution function; rather than determining cumulative probabilities for a given set of values, it determines the values corresponding to a specified set of cumulative probabilities. By employing the quantile function, one can produce random numbers from a uniform distribution and subsequently transform them into the desired distribution through its quantile function.

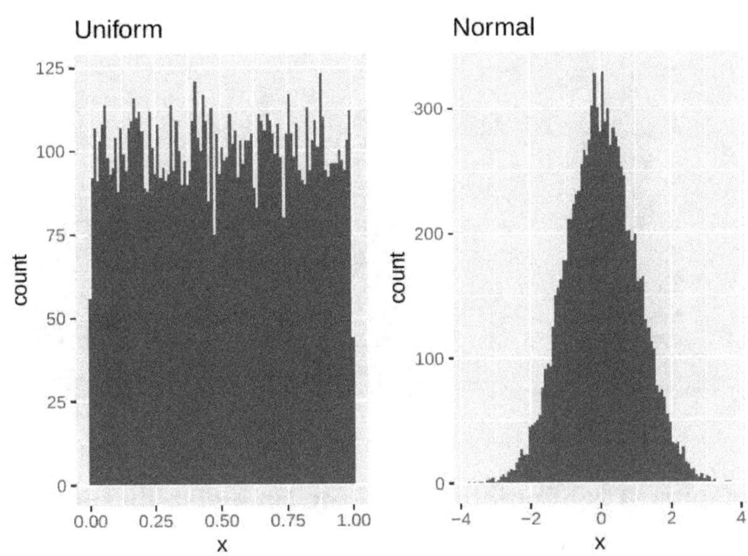

Figure 8.1: Examples of random numbers generated from a uniform (left) or normal (right) distribution.

By default, the random number generators in statistical software will generate a different set of random numbers every time they are run. However, it is also possible to generate exactly the same set of random numbers, by setting what is called the random seed to a specific value. If you were to look at the code that generated these figures, We will do this in many of the examples in this book, in order to make sure that the examples are reproducible.

8.4 Using Monte Carlo simulation

Let's go back to our example of exam finishing times. Say that I administer three quizzes and record the finishing times for each student for each exam, which might look like the distributions presented in Figure 8.2.

What we really want to know to answer our question is not what the distribution of finishing times looks like, but rather what the distribution of the longest finishing time for each quiz looks like. To do this, we can simulate the finishing time for a quiz, using the assumption that the finishing times are distributed normally, as stated above; for each of these simulated quizzes, we then record the longest finishing time. We repeat this simulation a large number of times (5000 should be enough) and record the distribution of finishing times, which is shown in Figure 8.3.

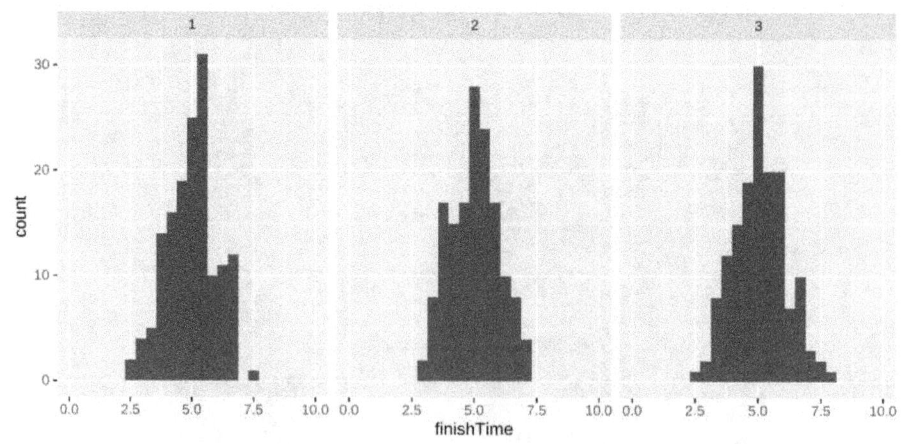

Figure 8.2: Simulated finishing time distributions.

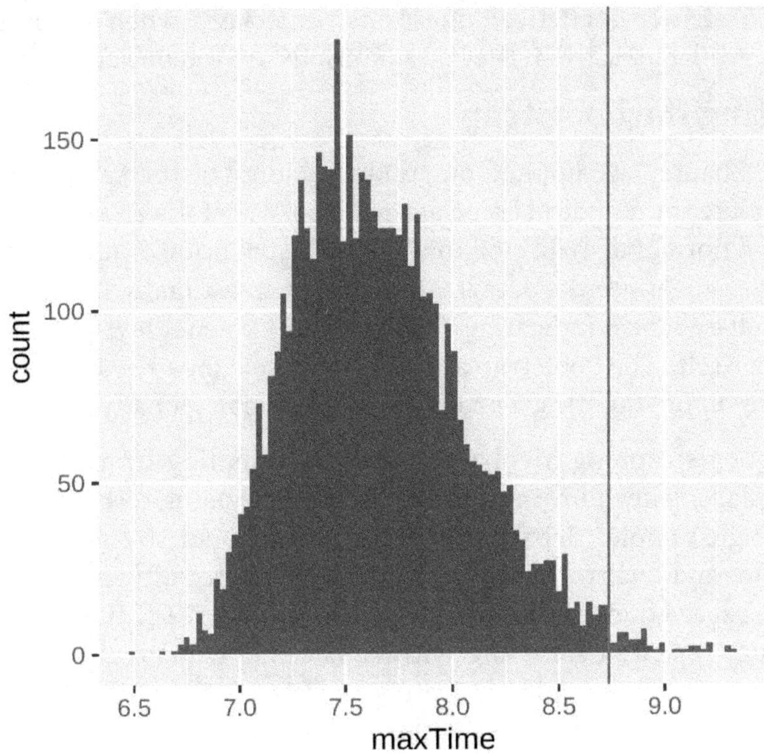

Figure 8.3: Distribution of maximum finishing times across simulations.

This shows that the 99th percentile of the finishing time distribution falls at 8.74 , meaning that if we were to give that much time for the quiz, then everyone should finish 99% of the time. It's always important to remember that our assumptions matter - if they are wrong, then the results of the simulation are useless. In this case, we assumed that the finishing time distribution was normally distributed with a particular mean and standard deviation; if these assumptions are incorrect (and they almost certainly are, since it's rare for elapsed times to be normally distributed), then the true answer could be very different.

8.5 Employing simulation for statistical analysis: The bootstrap method

So far we have used simulation to demonstrate statistical principles, but we can also use simulation to answer real statistical questions. In this section we will introduce a concept known as the bootstrap that lets us use simulation to quantify our uncertainty about statistical estimates. Later in the course, we will see other examples of how simulation can often be used to answer statistical questions, especially when theoretical statistical methods are not available or when their assumptions are too difficult to meet.

8.5.1 Computing the bootstrap

In the preceding chapter, we applied our understanding of the sampling distribution of the mean to calculate the standard error of the mean. What if we cannot presume that the estimates follow a normal distribution, or if their distribution is unknown? The concept of bootstrapping involves use the data itself to derive an estimate. The name derives from the concept of self-reliance, indicating that without external leverage, we must depend solely on the data itself. The bootstrap approach was developed by Bradley Efron from the Stanford Department of Statistics, a prominent statistician globally.

The concept of bootstrapping involves repeatedly sampling from the original dataset, notably with replacement, allowing for the same data point to be represented several times within a single sample. Subsequently, we calculate our statistic of interest for each bootstrap sample and utilize the distribution of these estimates as our sampling distribution. We regard our specific sample as representative of the total population and thereafter conduct repeated sampling with replacement for analytical purposes. This presumes that our specific sample accurately represents the population, which is likely valid for bigger samples but may falter with smaller ones.

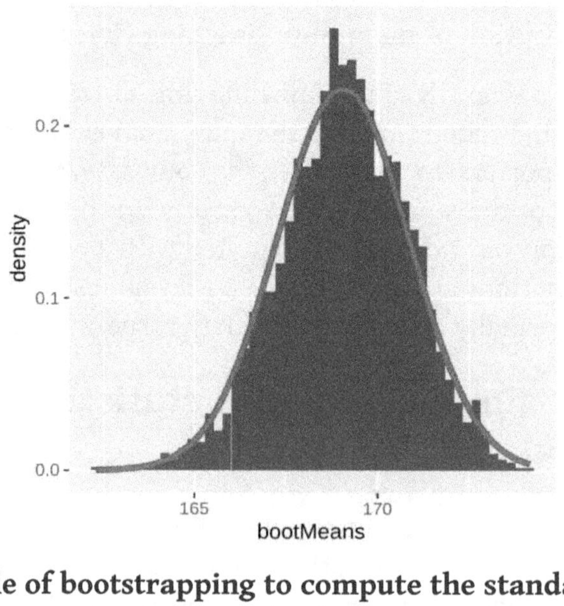

Figure 8.4: An example of bootstrapping to compute the standard error of the mean adult height in the NHANES dataset. The histogram shows the distribution of means across bootstrap samples, while the red line shows the normal distribution based on the sample mean and standard deviation.

We will initiate the process by employing bootstrap methods to estimate the sampling distribution of the mean adult height in the NHANES dataset, enabling us to compare this outcome with the previously described standard error of the mean (SEM).

Figure 8.4 shows that the distribution of means across bootstrap samples is fairly close to the theoretical estimate based on the assumption of normality. We would not usually employ the bootstrap to compute confidence intervals for the mean (since we can generally assume that the normal distribution is appropriate for the sampling distribution of the mean, as long as our sample is large enough), but this example shows how the method gives us roughly the same result as the standard method based on the normal distribution. The bootstrap would more often be used to generate standard errors for estimates of other statistics where we know or suspect that the normal distribution is not appropriate. In addition, in a later chapter you will see how we can also use the bootstrap samples to generate estimates of the uncertainty in our sample statistic as well.

Chapter-9

Hypothesis testing

Hypothesis testing is a fundamental statistical method used to make decisions or draw conclusions about populations based on sample data. It provides a structured framework for evaluating assumptions, known as hypotheses, through objective and quantitative evidence. In this process, researchers begin by formulating two opposing statements: the null hypothesis, which represents the default or existing belief, and the alternative hypothesis, which reflects the claim or effect being investigated. By analyzing sample data, hypothesis testing helps determine whether there is enough statistical support to reject the null hypothesis in favor of the alternative. This approach is widely used in scientific research, business analytics, social sciences, and various fields where uncertainties and variations naturally occur. The strength of hypothesis testing lies in its ability to control errors and provide clear decision-making guidelines. It involves calculating test statistics, assessing significance levels, and interpreting p-values to measure evidence against the null hypothesis. Through these steps, researchers can make informed judgments rather than relying on assumptions or intuition. Hypothesis testing also promotes consistency in research, ensuring that conclusions are based on standardized procedures. Whether comparing group means, testing relationships, or validating experimental effects, hypothesis testing remains a crucial tool for understanding data-driven insights. Its systematic nature makes it essential for verifying claims, supporting theories, and guiding future investigations with confidence. In this chapter we will introduce the ideas behind the use of statistics to make decisions - in particular, decisions about whether a particular hypothesis is supported by the data.

9.1 Null Hypothesis Statistical Testing (NHST)

Null Hypothesis Statistical Testing (NHST) is a widely used framework in statistics for evaluating scientific claims and making data-driven decisions. It begins with the formulation of a **null hypothesis (H_0)**, which typically states that there is no effect, no difference, or no association within the population. Alongside it, an **alternative hypothesis (H_1)** is proposed, representing the presence of an effect or relationship. NHST uses sample data to determine whether the observed results provide enough evidence to reject the null hypothesis in favor of the alternative. This decision is guided by a **significance level (α)**, often set at 0.05, which defines the threshold for acceptable risk of making a Type I error. The process involves calculating a test statistic and comparing it to a theoretical distribution, or converting it into a **p-value** that quantifies the probability of obtaining results as extreme as those observed if the null hypothesis were true. If the p-value falls below the significance level, the null hypothesis is rejected. NHST provides a structured, objective method for interpreting uncertainty in empirical data. Despite its popularity, it has been widely debated due to misunderstandings about p-values and the risk of overreliance on arbitrary thresholds. Nevertheless, NHST continues to serve as a foundational tool in scientific research, psychology, medicine, economics, and many other fields. Its systematic approach helps researchers distinguish between random variation and meaningful effects, supporting reliable and replicable conclusions.

The specific type of hypothesis testing that we will discuss is known (for reasons that will become clear) as null hypothesis statistical testing (NHST). If you pick up almost any scientific or biomedical research publication, you will see NHST being used to test hypotheses, and in their introductory psychology textbook, Gerrig & Zimbardo (2002) referred to NHST as the "backbone of psychological research". Thus, learning how to use and interpret the results from hypothesis testing is essential to understand the results from many fields of research.

It is also important for you to know, however, that NHST is deeply flawed, and that many statisticians and researchers (including myself) think that it has been the cause of serious problems in science, which we will discuss in Chapter 18. For more than 50 years, there have been calls to abandon NHST in favor of other approaches (like those that we will discuss in the following chapters):

- "The test of statistical significance in psychological research may be taken as an instance of a kind of essential mindlessness in the conduct of research" (Bakan, 1966)
- Hypothesis testing is "a wrongheaded view about what constitutes scientific progress" (Luce, 1988)

NHST is also widely misunderstood, largely because it violates our intuitions about how statistical hypothesis testing should work. Let's look at an example to see this.

9.2 Statistical testing of the null hypothesis: An illustration

There is great interest in the use of body-worn cameras by police officers, which are thought to reduce the use of force and improve officer behavior. However, in order to establish this we need experimental evidence, and it has become increasingly common for governments to use randomized controlled trials to test such ideas. A randomized controlled trial of the effectiveness of body-worn cameras was performed by the Washington, DC government and DC Metropolitan Police Department in 2015/2016. Officers were randomly assigned to wear a body-worn camera or not, and their behavior was then tracked over time to determine whether the cameras resulted in less use of force and fewer civilian complaints about officer behavior.

Before we get to the results, let's ask how you would think the statistical analysis might work. Let's say we want to specifically test the hypothesis of whether the use of force is decreased by the wearing of cameras. The randomized controlled trial provides us with the data to test the hypothesis namely, the rates of use of force by officers assigned to either the camera or control groups. The next obvious step is to look at the data and determine whether they provide convincing evidence for or against this hypothesis. That is: What is the likelihood that body-worn cameras reduce the use of force, given the data and everything else we know?

It turns out that this is not how null hypothesis testing works. Instead, we first take our hypothesis of interest (i.e. that body-worn cameras reduce use of force), and flip it on its head, creating a null hypothesis - in this case, the null hypothesis would be that cameras do not reduce use of force. Importantly, we then assume that the null hypothesis is true. We then look at the data, and determine how likely the data would be if the null hypothesis were true. If the the data are sufficiently unlikely under the null hypothesis that we can reject the null in favor of the alternative hypothesis which is our hypothesis of interest. If there is not sufficient evidence to reject the null, then we say that we retain (or "fail to reject") the null, sticking with our initial assumption that the null is true.

Understanding some of the concepts of NHST, particularly the notorious "p-value", is invariably challenging the first time one encounters them, because they are so counter-intuitive. As we will see later, there are other approaches that provide a much more intuitive way to address hypothesis testing (but have their own complexities). However, before we get to those, it's important for you to have a deep understanding of how hypothesis testing works, because it's clearly not going to go away any time soon.

9.3 The process of null hypothesis testing

We can break the process of null hypothesis testing down into a number of steps:

1. Formulate a hypothesis that embodies our prediction (before seeing the data)
2. Specify null and alternative hypotheses
3. Collect some data relevant to the hypothesis

4. Fit a model to the data that represents the alternative hypothesis and compute a test statistic
5. Compute the probability of the observed value of that statistic assuming that the null hypothesis is true
6. Assess the "statistical significance" of the result

For a hands-on example, let's use the NHANES data to ask the following question: Is physical activity related to body mass index? In the NHANES dataset, participants were asked whether they engage regularly in moderate or vigorous-intensity sports, fitness or recreational activities (stored in the variable PhysActive). The researchers also measured height and weight and used them to compute the Body Mass Index (BMI):

$$BMI = \frac{\text{weight } (kg)}{\text{height } (m)^2}$$

9.3.1 Step 1: Formulate a hypothesis of interest

We hypothesize that BMI is greater for people who do not engage in physical activity, compared to those who do.

9.3.2 Step 2: Specify the null and alternative hypotheses

For step 2, we need to specify our null hypothesis (which we call H_0) and our alternative hypothesis (which we call H_A). H_0 is the baseline against which we test our hypothesis of interest: that is, what would we expect the data to look like if there was no effect? The null hypothesis always involves some kind of equality ($=, \leq$, or $\geq$). H_A describes what we expect if there actually is an effect. The alternative hypothesis always involves some kind of inequality ($\neq$, >, or <). Importantly, null hypothesis testing operates under the assumption that the null hypothesis is true unless the evidence shows otherwise.

We also have to decide whether we want to test a directional or non-directional hypotheses. A non-directional hypothesis simply predicts that there will be a difference, without predicting which direction it will go. For the BMI/activity example, a non-directional null hypothesis would be:

$H0: BMI_{\text{active}} = BMI_{\text{inactive}}$ and the corresponding non-directional alternative hypothesis would be:

$$HA: BMI_{\text{active}} \neq BMI_{\text{inactive}}$$

A directional hypothesis, on the other hand, predicts which direction the difference would go. For example, we have strong prior knowledge to predict that people who engage in physical activity should weigh less than those who do not, so we would propose the following directional null hypothesis:

Table 9.1: Summary of BMI data for active versus inactive individuals

PhysActive	N	mean	sd
No	131	30	9.0
Yes	119	27	5.2

$$H0: BMI_{\text{active}} \geq BMI_{\text{inactive}}$$

and directional alternative:

$$HA: BMI_{\text{active}} < BMI_{\text{inactive}}$$

As we will see later, testing a non-directional hypothesis is more conservative, so this is generally to be preferred unless there is a strong a priori reason to hypothesize an effect in a particular direction. Hypotheses, including whether they are directional or not, should always be specified prior to looking at the data!

9.3.3 Step 3: Collect some data

In this case, we will sample 250 individuals from the NHANES dataset. Figure 9.1 shows an example of such a sample, with BMI shown separately for active and inactive individuals, and Table 9.1 shows summary statistics for each group.

9.3.4 Step 4: Fit a model to the data and compute a test statistic

We next want to use the data to compute a statistic that will ultimately let us decide whether the null hypothesis is rejected or not. To do this, the model needs to quantify the amount of evidence in favor of the alternative hypothesis, relative to the variability in the data. Thus we can think of the test statistic as providing a measure of the size of the effect compared to the variability in the data. In general, this test statistic will have a probability distribution associated with it, because that allows us to determine how likely our observed value of the statistic is under the null hypothesis.

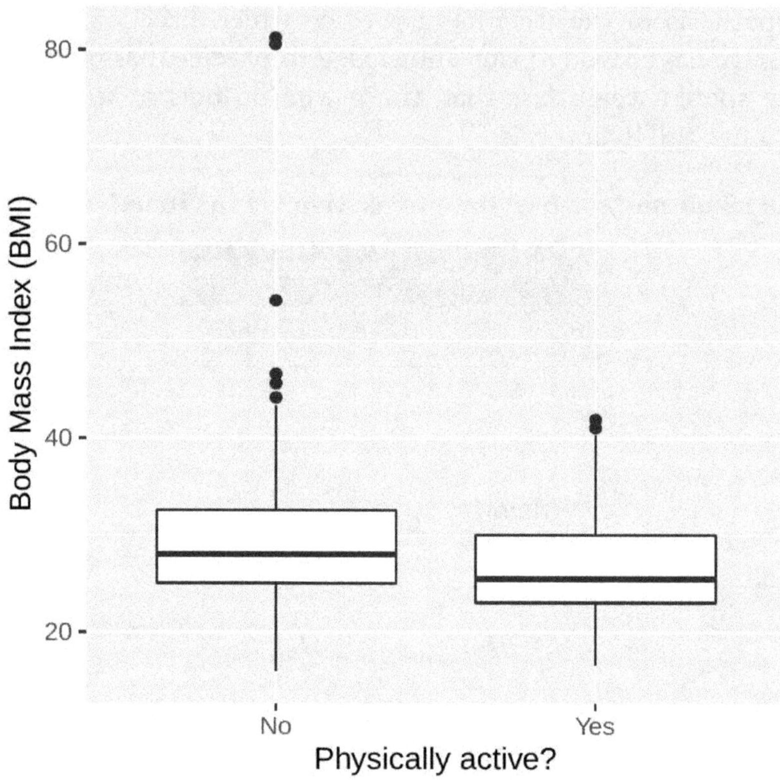

Figure 9.1: Box plot of BMI data from a sample of adults from the NHANES dataset, split by whether they reported engaging in regular physical activity.

For the BMI example, we need a test statistic that allows us to test for a difference between two means, since the hypotheses are stated in terms of mean BMI for each group. One statistic that is often used to compare two means is the *t* statistic, first developed by the statistician William Sealy Gossett, who worked for the Guiness Brewery in Dublin and wrote under the pen name "Student" - hence, it is often called "Student's *t* statistic". The *t* statistic is appropriate for comparing the means of two groups when the sample sizes are relatively small and the population standard deviation is unknown. The *t* statistic for comparison of two independent groups is computed as:

$$t = \frac{\bar{X}_1 - \bar{X}_2}{\sqrt{\frac{S_1^2}{n_1} + \frac{S_2^2}{n_2}}}$$

where $\bar{X}_1$ and $\bar{X}_2$ are the means of the two groups, S_1^2 and S_2^2 are the estimated variances of the groups, and n_1 and n_2 are the sizes of the two groups. Because the variance of a difference between two independent variables is the sum of the variances of each individual variable ($\text{var}(A - B) = \text{var}(A) + \text{var}(B)$), we add the variances for each group divided by their sample sizes in order to compute the standard error of the difference. Thus, one can view the the t statistic as a way of quantifying how large the difference between groups is in relation to the sampling variability of the difference between means.

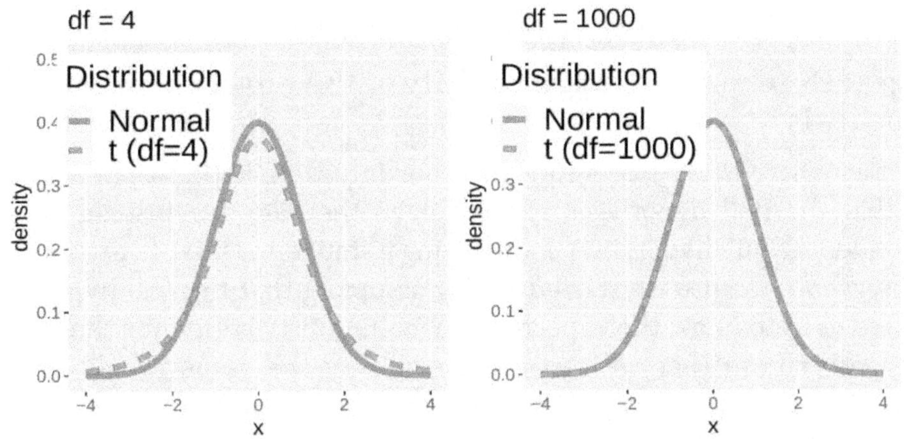

Figure 9.2: Each panel shows the t distribution (in blue dashed line) overlaid on the normal distribution (in solid red line). The left panel shows a *t* distribution with 4 degrees of freedom, in which case the distribution is similar but has slightly wider tails. The right panel shows a *t* distribution with 1000 degrees of freedom, in which case it is virtually identical to the normal.

The t statistic is distributed according to a probability distribution known as a t distribution. The t distribution looks quite similar to a normal distribution, but it differs depending on the number of degrees of freedom. When the degrees of freedom are large (say 1000), then the t distribution looks essentially like the normal distribution, but when they are small then the t distribution has longer tails than the normal (see Figure 9.2). In the simplest case, where the groups are the same size and have equal variance, the degrees of freedom for the t test is the number of observations minus 2 , since we have computed two means and thus given up two degrees of freedom. In this case it's pretty clear from the box plot that the inactive group is more variable than then active group, and the numbers in each group differ, so we need to use a slightly more complex formula for the degrees of freedom, which is often referred to as a "Welch t-test". The formula is:

$$\text{d.f.} = \frac{\left(\frac{S_1^2}{n_1} + \frac{S_2^2}{n_2}\right)^2}{\frac{(S_1^2/n_1)^2}{n_1 - 1} + \frac{(S_2^2/n_2)^2}{n_2 - 1}}$$

This will be equal to $n_1 + n_2 - 2$ when the variances and sample sizes are equal, and otherwise will be smaller, in effect imposing a penalty on the test for differences in sample size or variance. For this example, that comes out to 241.12 which is slightly below the value of 248 that one would get by subtracting 2 from the sample size.

9.3.5 Step 5: Determine the probability of the observed result under the null hypothesis

This is the step where NHST starts to violate our intuition. Rather than determining the likelihood that the null hypothesis is true given the data, we instead determine the likelihood under the null hypothesis of observing a statistic at least as extreme as one that we have observed - because we started out by assuming that the null hypothesis is true! To do this, we need to know the expected probability distribution for the statistic under the null hypothesis, so that we can ask how likely the result would be under that distribution. Note that when I say "how likely the result would be", what I really mean is "how likely the observed result or one more extreme would be". There are (at least) two reasons that we need to add this caveat. The first is that when we are talking about continuous values, the probability of any particular value is zero (as you might remember if you've taken a calculus class). More importantly, we are trying to determine how weird our result would be if the null hypothesis were true, and any result that is more extreme will be even more weird, so we want to count all of those weirder possibilities when we compute the probability of our result under the null hypothesis.

We can obtain this "null distribution" either using a theoretical distribution (like the t distribution), or using randomization. Before we move to our BMI example, let's start with some simpler examples.

9.3.5.1 P -values: A very simple example

Let's say that we wish to determine whether a particular coin is biased towards landing heads. To collect data, we flip the coin 100 times, and let's say we count 70 heads. In this example, $H_0: P(\text{ heads }) \leq 0.5$ and $H_A: P(\text{ heads }) > 0.5$, and our test statistic is simply the number of heads that we counted. The question that we then want to ask is: How likely is it that we would observe 70 or more heads in 100 coin flips if the true probability of heads is 0.5 ? We can imagine that this might happen very occasionally just by chance, but doesn't seem very likely. To quantify this probability, we can use the binomial distribution:

$$P(X \leq k) = \sum_{i=0}^{k} \binom{N}{k} p^i (1-p)^{(n-i)}$$

This equation will tell us the probability of a certain number of heads (k) or fewer, given a particular probability of heads (p) and number of events (N). However, what we really want to know is the probability of a certain number or more, which we can obtain by subtracting from one, based on the rules of probability:

$$P(X \geq k) = 1 - P(X < k)$$

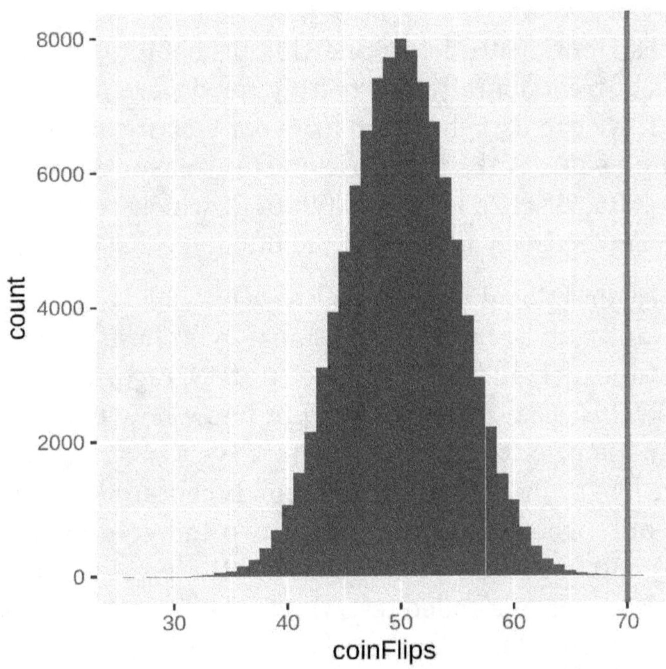

Figure 9.3: Distribution of numbers of heads (out of 100 flips) across 100,000 simulated runs with the observed value of 70 flips represented by the vertical line.

Using the binomial distribution, the probability of 69 or fewer heads given P (heads) = 0.5 is 0.999961 , so the probability of 70 or more heads is simply one minus that value (0.000039). This computation shows us that the likelihood of getting 70 or more heads if the coin is indeed fair is very small.

Now, what if we didn't have a standard function to tell us the probability of that number of heads? We could instead determine it by simulation - we repeatedly flip a coin 100 times using a true probability of 0.5 , and then compute the distribution of the number of heads across those simulation runs. Figure 9.3 shows the result from this simulation. Here we can see that the probability computed via simulation (0.000030) is very close to the theoretical probability (0.000039).

9.3.5.2 Computing p-values using the *t* distribution

Now let's compute a p-value for our BMI example using the *t* distribution. First we compute the *t* statistic using the values from our sample that we calculated above, where we find that $t = 3.86$. The question that we then want to ask is: What is the likelihood that we would find a *t* statistic of this size, if the true difference between groups is zero or less (i.e. the directional null hypothesis)?

We can use the *t* distribution to determine this probability. Above we noted that the appropriate degrees of freedom (after correcting for differences in variance and sample size) was $t = 241.12$. We can use a function from our statistical software to determine the probability of finding a value of the *t* statistic greater than or equal to our observed value. We find that $p(t > 3.86, df = 241.12) = 0.000072$, which tells us that our observed *t* statistic value of 3.86 is relatively unlikely if the null hypothesis really is true.

In this case, we used a directional hypothesis, so we only had to look at one end of the null distribution. If we wanted to test a non-directional hypothesis, then we would need to be able to identify how unexpected the size of the effect is, regardless of its direction. In the context of the t-test, this means that we need to know how likely it is that the statistic would be as extreme in either the positive or negative direction. To do this, we multiply the observed *t* value by -1 , since the *t* distribution is centered around zero, and then add together the two tail probabilities to get a two-tailed p-value: $p(t > 3.86 \text{ or } t < -3.86, df = 241.12) = 0.000145$. Here we see that the p value for the two-tailed test is twice as large as that for the one-tailed test, which reflects the fact that an extreme value is less surprising since it could have occurred in either direction.

How do you choose whether to use a one-tailed versus a two-tailed test? The two-tailed test is always going to be more conservative, so it's always a good bet to use that one, unless you had a very strong prior reason for using a one-tailed test. In that case, you should have written down the hypothesis before you ever looked at the data. In Chapter 18 we will discuss the idea of pre-registration of hypotheses, which formalizes the idea of writing down your hypotheses before you ever see the actual data. You should never make a decision about how to perform a hypothesis test once you have looked at the data, as this can introduce serious bias into the results.

Table 9.2: Squatting data for the two groups

group	squat	shuffledSquat
E	265	125
FB	310	230
FB	335	125
FB	230	315
FB	315	115
XC	155	335
XC	125	155
XC	125	125
XC	125	265
XC	115	310

9.3.5.3 Computing p-values using randomization

So far we have seen how we can use the t -distribution to compute the probability of the data under the null hypothesis, but we can also do this using simulation. The basic idea is that we generate simulated data like those that we would expect under the null hypothesis, and then ask how extreme the observed data are in comparison to those simulated data. The key question is: How can we generate data for which the null hypothesis is true? The general answer is that we can randomly rearrange the data in a particular way that makes the data look like they would if the null was really true. This is similar to the idea of bootstrapping, in the sense that it uses our own data to come up with an answer, but it does it in a different way.

9.3.5.4 Randomization: a simple example

Let's start with a simple example. Let's say that we want to compare the mean squatting ability of football players with cross-country runners, with $H_0: \mu_{FB} \leq \mu_{XC}$ and $H_A: \mu_{FB} > \mu_{XC}$. We measure the maximum squatting ability of 5 football players and 5 cross-country runners (which we will generate randomly, assuming that $\mu_{FB} = 300, \mu_{XC} = 140$, and $\sigma = 30$). The data are shown in Table 9.2.

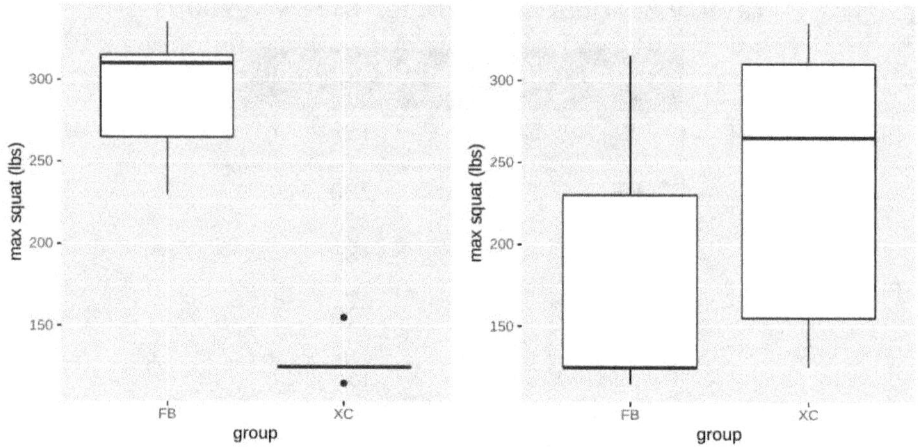

Figure 9.4: Left: Box plots of simulated squatting ability for football players and cross-country runners.Right: Box plots for subjects assigned to each group after scrambling group labels.

From the plot on the left side of Figure 9.4 it's clear that there is a large difference between the two groups. We can do a standard t-test to test our hypothesis; for this example we will use the t.test() command in *R*, which gives the following result:

```
##

## Welch Two Sample t-test

##

## data: squat by group

## t = 8, df = 5, p-value = 2e-04

## alternative hypothesis: true difference in means between group FB and
group XC is

## 95 percent confidence interval:

## 121 Inf

## sample estimates:

## mean in group FB mean in group XC

## 291 129
```

If we look at the p -value reported here, we see that the likelihood of such a difference under the null hypothesis is very small, using the *t* distribution to define the null.

Now let's see how we could answer the same question using randomization. The basic idea is that if the null hypothesis of no difference between groups is true, then it shouldn't matter which group one comes from (football players versus cross-country runners) - thus, to create data that are like our actual data but also conform to the null hypothesis, we can randomly reorder the data for the individuals in the dataset, and then recompute the difference between the groups. The results of such a shuffle are shown in the column labeled "shuffleSquat" in Table 9.2, and the boxplots of the resulting data are in the right panel of Figure 9.4.

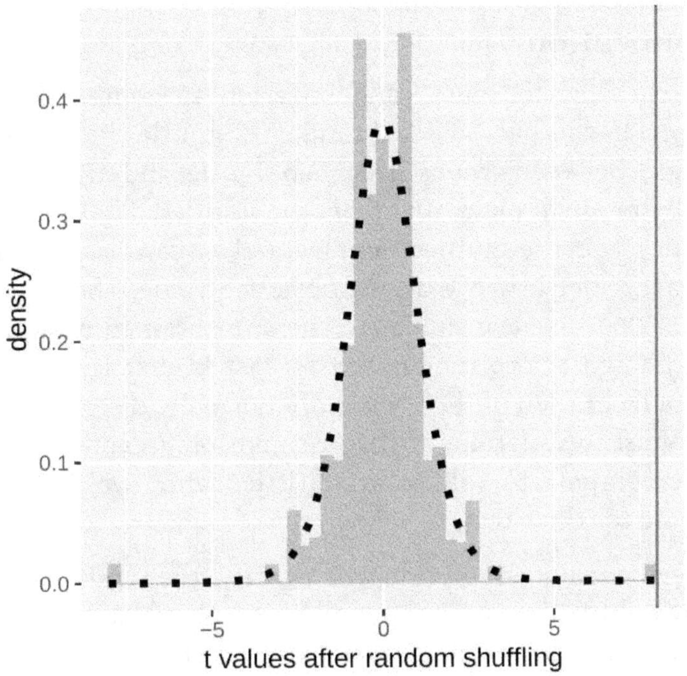

Figure 9.5: Histogram of t -values for the difference in means between the football and cross-country groups after randomly shuffling group membership. The vertical line denotes the actual difference observed between the two groups, and the dotted line shows the theoretical t distribution for this analysis.

After scrambling the data, we see that the two groups are now much more similar, and in fact the cross-country group now has a slightly higher mean.

Now let's do that 10000 times and store the *t* statistic for each iteration; if you are doing this on your own computer, it will take a moment to complete. Figure 9.5 shows the histogram of the t values across all of the random shuffles. As expected under the null hypothesis, this distribution is centered at zero (the mean of the distribution is 0.007). From the figure we can also see that the distribution of t values after shuffling roughly follows the theoretical t distribution under the null hypothesis (with mean $= 0$), showing that randomization worked to generate null data. We can compute the p-value from the randomized data by measuring how many of the shuffled values are at least as extreme as the observed value: $\mathrm{p}(\mathrm{t} > 8.01, \mathrm{df} = 8)$ using randomization $= 0.00410$. This p-value is very similar to the p-value that we obtained using the t distribution, and both are quite extreme, suggesting that the observed data are very unlikely to have arisen if the null hypothesis is true - and in this case we know that it's not true, because we generated the data.

9.3.5.4.1 Randomization

BMI/activity example Now let's use randomization to compute the p-value for the BMI/activity example. In this case, we will randomly shuffle the PhysActive variable and compute the difference between groups after each shuffle, and then compare our observed t statistic to the distribution of t statistics from the shuffled datasets. Figure 9.6 shows the distribution of t values from the shuffled samples, and we can also compute the probability of finding a value as large or larger than the observed value. The p -value obtained from randomization (0.000000) is very similar to the one obtained using the t distribution (0.000075). The advantage of the randomization test is that it doesn't require that we assume that the data from each of the groups are normally distributed, though the t-test is generally quite robust to violations of that assumption. In addition, the randomization test can allow us to compute p -values for statistics when we don't have a theoretical distribution like we do for the t-test.

We do have to make one main assumption when we use the randomization test, which we refer to as exchangeability. This means that all of the observations are distributed in the same way, such that we can interchange them without changing the overall distribution. The main place where this can break down is when there are related observations in the data; for example, if we had data from individuals in 4 different families, then we couldn't assume that individuals were exchangeable, because siblings would be closer to each other than they are to individuals from other families. In general, if the data were obtained by random sampling, then the assumption of exchangeability should hold.

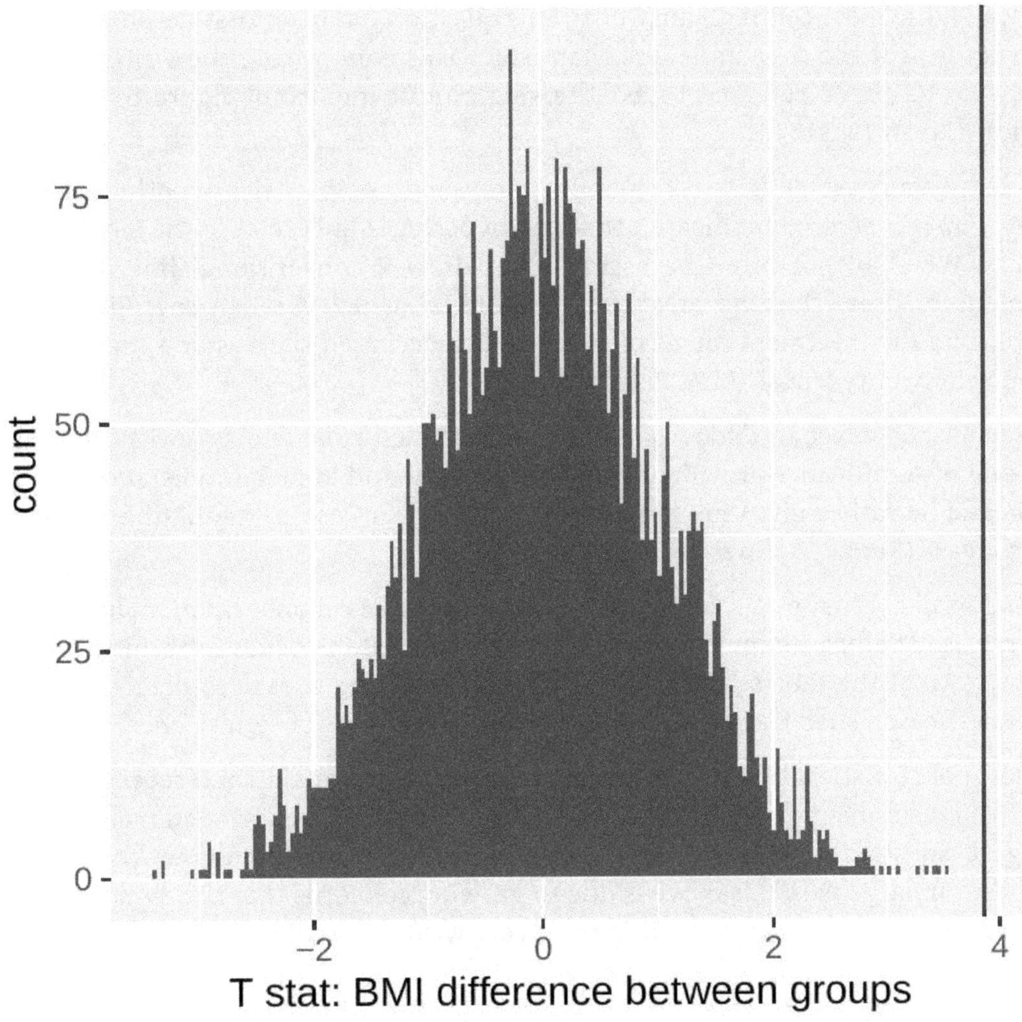

Figure 9.6: Histogram of t statistics after shuffling of group labels, with the observed value of the *t* statistic shown in the vertical line, and values at least as extreme as the observed value shown in lighter gray

9.3.6 Step 6: Assess the "statistical significance" of the result

The next step is to determine whether the p -value that results from the previous step is small enough that we are willing to reject the null hypothesis and conclude instead that the alternative is true. How much evidence do we require? This is one of the most controversial questions in statistics, in part because it requires a subjective judgment - there is no "correct" answer.

Historically, the most common answer to this question has been that we should reject the null hypothesis if the p-value is less than 0.05 . This comes from the writings of Ronald Fisher, who has been referred to as "the single most important figure in 20th century statistics" (Efron 1998):

"If P is between .1 and .9 there is certainly no reason to suspect the hypothesis tested. If it is below . 02 it is strongly indicated that the hypothesis fails to account for the whole of the facts. We shall not often be astray if we draw a conventional line at . 05 ... it is convenient to draw the line at about the level at which we can say: Either there is something in the treatment, or a coincidence has occurred such as does not occur more than once in twenty trials" (R. A. Fisher 1925).

However, Fisher never intended $p < 0.05$ to be a fixed rule: "no scientific worker has a fixed level of significance at which from year to year, and in all circumstances, he rejects hypotheses; he rather gives his mind to each particular case in the light of his evidence and his ideas" (Ronald Aylmer Fisher 1956).

Instead, it is likely that p < .05 became a ritual due to the reliance upon tables of p -values that were used before computing made it easy to compute p values for arbitrary values of a statistic. All of the tables had an entry for 0.05 , making it easy to determine whether one's statistic exceeded the value needed to reach that level of significance.

The choice of statistical thresholds remains deeply controversial, and recently (Benjamin et al., 2018) it has been proposed that the default threshold be changed from .05 to .005 , making it substantially more stringent and thus more difficult to reject the null hypothesis. In large part this move is due to growing concerns that the evidence obtained from a significant result at $p < .05$ is relatively weak; we will return to this in our later discussion of reproducibility in Chapter 18.

9.3.6.1 Hypothesis testing as decision-making: The NeymanPearson approach

Whereas Fisher thought that the p-value could provide evidence regarding a specific hypothesis, the statisticians Jerzy Neyman and Egon Pearson disagreed vehemently. Instead, they proposed that we think of hypothesis testing in terms of its error rate in the long run:

"no test based upon a theory of probability can by itself provide any valuable evidence of the truth or falsehood of a hypothesis. But we may look at the purpose of tests from another viewpoint. Without hoping to know whether each separate hypothesis is true or false, we may search for rules to govern our behaviour with regard to them, in following which we insure that, in the long run of experience, we shall not often be wrong" (J. Neyman and Pearson 1933).

That is: We can't know which specific decisions are right or wrong, but if we follow the rules, we can at least know how often our decisions will be wrong in the long run.

To understand the decision making framework that Neyman and Pearson developed, we first need to discuss statistical decision making in terms of the kinds of outcomes that can occur. There are two possible states of reality (H_0 is true, or H_0 is false), and two possible decisions (reject H_0, or retain H_0). There are two ways in which we can make a correct decision:

- We can reject H_0 when it is false (in the language of signal detection theory, we call this a hit)
- We can retain H_0 when it is true (somewhat confusingly in this context, this is called a correct rejection)

There are also two kinds of errors we can make:

- We can reject H_0 when it is actually true (we call this a false alarm, or Type I error)
- We can retain H_0 when it is actually false (we call this a miss, or Type II error)

Neyman and Pearson coined two terms to describe the probability of these two types of errors in the long run:

- P(Type I error) $= \alpha$
- P(Type II error) $= \beta$

That is, if we set α to .05 , then in the long run we should make a Type I error 5% of the time. Whereas it's common to set α as .05 , the standard value for an acceptable level of β is .2 - that is, we are willing to accept that 20% of the time we will fail to detect a true effect when it truly exists. We will return to this later when we discuss statistical power in Section 10.3, which is the complement of Type II error.

9.3.7 What is the implication of a significant result?

There is a great deal of confusion about what p -values actually mean (Gigerenzer, 2004). Let's say that we do an experiment comparing the means between conditions, and we find a difference with a p -value of .01 . There are a number of possible interpretations that one might entertain.

9.3.7.1 Does it mean that the probability of the null hypothesis being true is .01 ?

No. Remember that in null hypothesis testing, the p -value is the probability of the data given the null hypothesis $\left(P(data \mid H_0)\right)$. It does not warrant conclusions about the probability of the null hypothesis given the data ($P(H_0 \mid$ data)). We will return to this question when we discuss Bayesian inference in a later chapter, as Bayes theorem lets us invert the conditional probability in a way that allows us to determine the probability of the hypothesis given the data.

9.3.7.2 Does it mean that the probability that you are making the wrong decision is .01 ?

No. This would be $P(H_0 \mid$ data), but remember as above that p -values are probabilities of data under H_0, not probabilities of hypotheses.

9.3.7.3 Does it mean that if you ran the study again, you would obtain the same result 99% of the time?

No. The p -value is a statement about the likelihood of a particular dataset under the null; it does not allow us to make inferences about the likelihood of future events such as replication.

9.3.7.4 Does it mean that you have found a practically important effect?

No. There is an essential distinction between statistical significance and practical significance. As an example, let's say that we performed a randomized controlled trial to examine the effect of a particular diet on body weight, and we find a statistically significant effect at $p < .05$. What this doesn't tell us is how much weight was actually lost, which we refer to as the effect size (to be discussed in more detail in Chapter 10). If we think about a study of weight loss, then we probably don't think that the loss of one ounce (i.e. the weight of a few potato chips) is practically significant. Let's look at our ability to detect a significant difference of 1 ounce as the sample size increases.

Figure 9.7 shows how the proportion of significant results increases as the sample size increases, such that with a very large sample size (about 262,000 total subjects), we will find a significant result in more than 90% of studies when there is a 1 ounce difference in weight loss between the diets. While these are statistically significant, most physicians would not consider a weight loss of one ounce to be practically or clinically significant. We will explore this relationship in more detail when we return to the concept of statistical power in Section 10.3, but it should already be clear from this example that statistical significance is not necessarily indicative of practical significance.

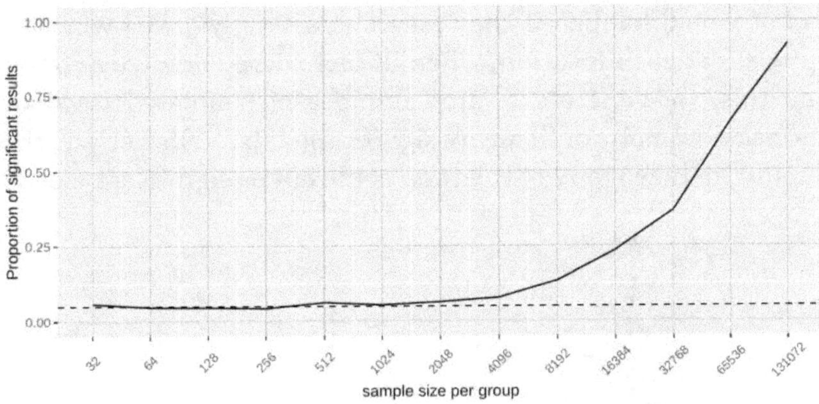

Figure 9.7: The proportion of signifcant results for a very small change (1 ounce, which is about .001 standard deviations) as a function of sample size.

9.4 NHST in contemporary settings: Multiple tests

So far we have discussed examples where we are interested in testing a single statistical hypothesis, and this is consistent with traditional science which often measured only a few variables at a time. However, in modern science we can often measure millions of variables per individual. For example, in genetic studies that quantify the entire genome, there may be many millions of measures per individual, and in the brain imaging research that my group does, we often collect data from more than 100,000 locations in the brain at once. When standard hypothesis testing is applied in these contexts, bad things can happen unless we take appropriate care.

Let's look at an example to see how this might work. There is great interest in understanding the genetic factors that can predispose individuals to major mental illnesses such as schizophrenia, because we know that about 80% of the variation between individuals in the presence of schizophrenia is due to genetic differences. The Human Genome Project and the ensuing revolution in genome science has provided tools to examine the many ways in which humans differ from one another in their genomes. One approach that has been used in recent years is known as a genome-wide association study (GWAS), in which the genome of each individual is characterized at one million or more places to determine which letters of the genetic code they have at each location, focusing on locations where humans tend to differ frequently. After these have been determined, the researchers perform a statistical test at each location in the genome to determine whether people diagnosed with schizoprenia are more or less likely to have one specific version of the genetic sequence at that location.

Let's imagine what would happen if the researchers simply asked whether the test was significant at $p < .05$ at each location, when in fact there is no true effect at any of the locations. To do this, we generate a large number of simulated t values from a null distribution, and ask how many of them are significant at $p < .05$. Let's do this many times, and each time count up how many of the tests come out as significant (see Figure 9.8).

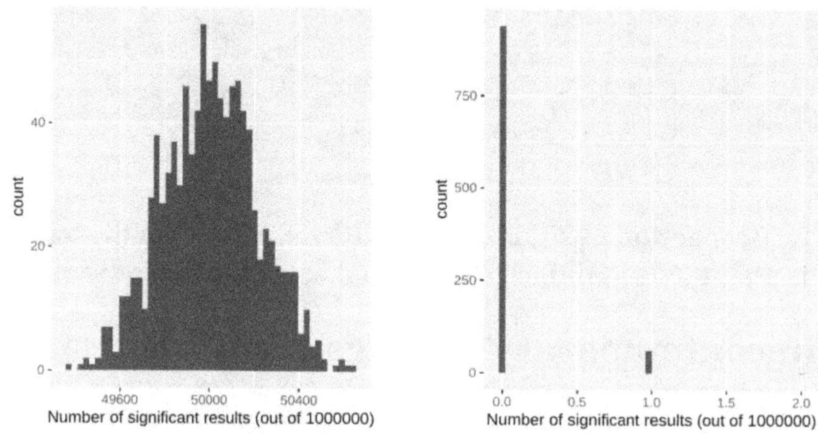

Figure 9.8: Left: A histogram of the number of significant results in each set of one million statistical tests, when there is in fact no true effect. Right: A histogram of the number of significant results across all simulation runs after applying the Bonferroni correction for multiple tests.

This shows that about 5% of all of the tests were significant in each run, meaning that if we were to use $p < .05$ as our threshold for statistical significance, then even if there were no truly significant relationships present, we would still "find" about 500 genes that were seemingly significant in each study (the expected number of significant results is simply $n * \alpha$). That is because while we controlled for the error per test, we didn't control the error rate across our entire family of tests (known as the familywise error), which is what we really want to control if we are going to be looking at the results from a large number of tests. Using $p < .05$, our familywise error rate in the above example is one - that is, we are pretty much guaranteed to make at least one error in any particular study. A straightforward method to adjust for the familywise error is to divide the alpha level by the number of tests; this approach is referred to as the Bonferroni correction, named after the Italian statistician Carlo Bonferroni. According to the statistics shown in our previous example, Figure 9.8 illustrates that merely 5 percent of studies yield significant results when employing the adjusted alpha level of 0.000005, as opposed to the nominal level of 0.05. We have successfully managed the familywise error, ensuring that the probability of mistakes in our study is maintained at approximately 0.05.

Chapter-10

Measuring Impacts and Developing Research Designs

Measuring impacts and developing effective research designs are central to understanding the outcomes and effectiveness of programs, interventions, or policies. Impact measurement allows researchers and practitioners to systematically evaluate the changes attributable to a specific action, distinguishing them from broader trends or external influences. At the same time, a well-structured research design ensures that data collection, analysis, and interpretation are rigorous, reliable, and valid. By combining thoughtful measurement strategies with robust research designs, stakeholders can generate actionable insights, inform evidence-based decision-making, and contribute to the advancement of knowledge across disciplines. The NHANES dataset, so we take a sample from the dataset and estimate the mean. In this sample, the mean weight was 79.92 kilograms. We refer to this as a point estimate since it provides us with a single number to describe our estimate of the population parameter. However, we know from our earlier discussion of sampling error that there is some uncertainty about this estimate, which is described by the standard error. You should also remember that the standard error is determined by two components: the population standard deviation (which is the numerator), and the square root of the sample size (which is in the denominator). The population standard deviation is a generally unknown but fixed parameter that is not under our control, whereas the sample size is under our control. Thus, we can decrease our uncertainty about the estimate by increasing our sample size - up to the limit of the entire population size, at which point there is no uncertainty at all because we can just calculate the population parameter directly from the data of the entire population.

We would often like to have a way to more directly describe our uncertainty about a statistical estimate, which we can accomplish using a confidence interval. Most people are familiar with confidence intervals through the idea of a "margin of error" for political polls. These polls usually try to provide an answer that is accurate within +/- 3 percent. For example, when a candidate is estimated to win an election by 9 percentage points with a margin of error of 3, the percentage by which they will win is estimated to fall within 6-12 percentage points. In statistics we refer to this kind of range of values as a confidence interval, which provides a range of values for our parameter estimate that are consistent with our sample data, rather than just giving us a single estimate based on the data. The wider the confidence interval, the more uncertain we are about our parameter estimate.

10.1 Confidence intervals

Confidence intervals are notoriously confusing, primarily because they don't mean what we might intuitively think they mean. If I tell you that I have computed a "95% confidence interval" for my statistic, then it would seem natural to think that we can have 95% confidence that the true parameter value falls within this interval. However, as we will see throughout the course, concepts in statistics often don't mean what we think they should mean. In the case of confidence intervals, we can't interpret them in this way because the population parameter has a fixed value - it either is or isn't in the interval, so it doesn't make sense to talk about the probability of that occurring. Jerzy Neyman, the inventor of the confidence interval, said:

> *"The parameter is an unknown constant and no probability statement concerning its value may be made." (J. Neyman 1937)*

Instead, we have to view the confidence interval procedure from the same standpoint that we viewed hypothesis testing: As a procedure that in the long run will allow us to make correct statements with a particular probability. Thus, the proper interpretation of the 95% confidence interval is that it is an interval that will contain the true population mean 95% of the time, and in fact we can confirm that using simulation, as you will see below.

The confidence interval for the mean is computed as:

$$CI = \text{point estimate} \pm \text{critical value} * \text{standard error}$$

where the critical value is determined by the sampling distribution of the estimate. The important question, then, is how we obtain our estimate for that sampling distribution.

10.1.1 Confidence intervals utilizing the normal distribution

When the population standard deviation is known, the normal distribution can be employed to calculate a confidence range. Typically, we do not, but in the case of the NHANES dataset, we do, as we are considering the entire dataset as the population (the mean weight is 21.3).Let's say that we want to compute a 95% confidence interval for the mean. The critical value would then be the values of the standard normal distribution that capture 95% of the distribution; these are simply the 2.5th percentile and the 97.5th percentile of the distribution, which we can compute using our statistical software, and come out to ± 1.96. Thus, the confidence interval for the mean ($\bar{X}$) is:

$$CI = \bar{X} \pm 1.96 * SE$$

Using the estimated mean from our sample (79.92) and the known population standard deviation, we can compute the confidence interval of [77.28,82.56].

10.1.2 Confidence intervals using the t distribution

As stated above, if we knew the population standard deviation, then we could use the normal distribution to compute our confidence intervals. However, in general we don't - in which case the *t* distribution is more appropriate as a sampling distribution. Remember that the t distribution is slightly broader than the normal distribution, especially for smaller samples, which means that the confidence intervals will be slightly wider than they would if we were using the normal distribution. This incorporates the extra uncertainty that arises when we estimate parameters based on small samples.

We can compute the 95% confidence interval in a way similar to the normal distribution example above, but the critical value is determined by the 2.5 th percentile and the 97.5 th percentile of the *t* distribution with the appropriate degrees of freedom. Thus, the confidence interval for the mean ($\bar{X}$) is:

$$CI = \bar{X} \pm t_{crit} * SE$$

where t_{crit} is the critical t value. For the NHANES weight example (with sample size of 250), the confidence interval would be $79.92 +/- 1.97 * 1.41$ [77.15-82.69].

Remember that this doesn't tell us anything about the probability of the true population value falling within this interval, since it is a fixed parameter (which we know is 81.77 because we have the entire population in this case) and it either does or does not fall within this specific interval (in this case, it does). Instead, it tells us that in the long run, if we compute the confidence interval using this procedure, 95% of the time that confidence interval will capture the true population parameter.

We can see this using the NHANES data as our population; in this case, we know the true value of the population parameter, so we can see how often the confidence interval ends up capturing that value across many different samples. Figure 10.1.2 shows the confidence intervals for estimated mean weight computed for 100 samples from the NHANES dataset. Of these, 95 captured the true population mean weight, showing that the confidence interval procedure performs as it should.

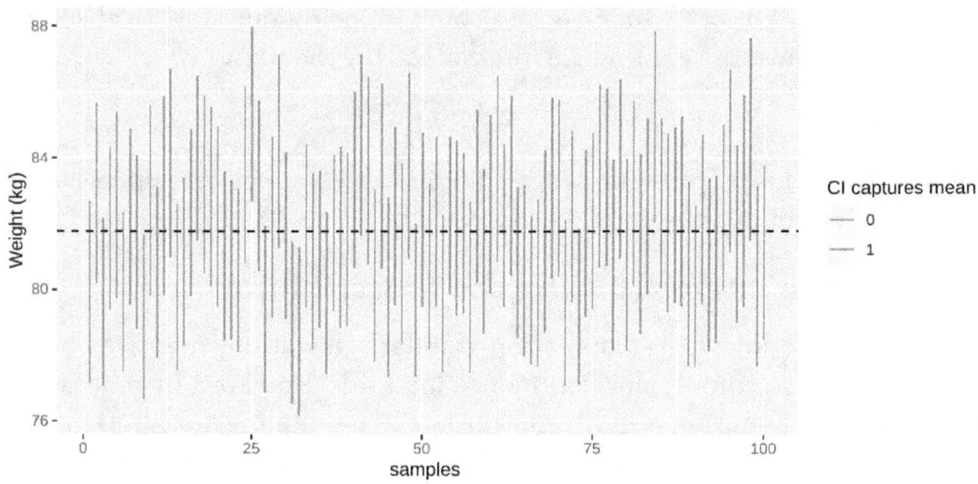

\begin{figure} }

\caption{Samples were repeatedly taken from the NHANES dataset, and the 95% confidence interval of the mean was computed for each sample. Intervals shown in red did not capture the true population mean (shown as the dotted line). } \ end { figure }

10.1.3 Confidence intervals and sample size

Because the standard error decreases with sample size, the confidence interval should get narrower as the sample size increases, providing progressively tighter bounds on our estimate. Figure 10.1 shows an example of how the confidence interval would change as a function of sample size for the weight example. From the figure it's evident that the confidence interval becomes increasingly tighter as the sample size increases, but increasing samples provide diminishing returns, consistent with the fact that the denominator of the confidence interval term is proportional to the square root of the sample size.

10.1.4 Computing confidence intervals using the bootstrap

In some cases we can't assume normality, or we don't know the sampling distribution of the statistic. In these cases, we can use the bootstrap (which we introduced in Chapter 8). As a reminder, the bootstrap involves repeatedly resampling the data with replacement, and then using the distribution of the statistic computed on those samples as a surrogate for the sampling distribution of the statistic.These are the results when we use the built-in bootstrapping function in R to compute the confidence interval for weight in our NHANES sample:

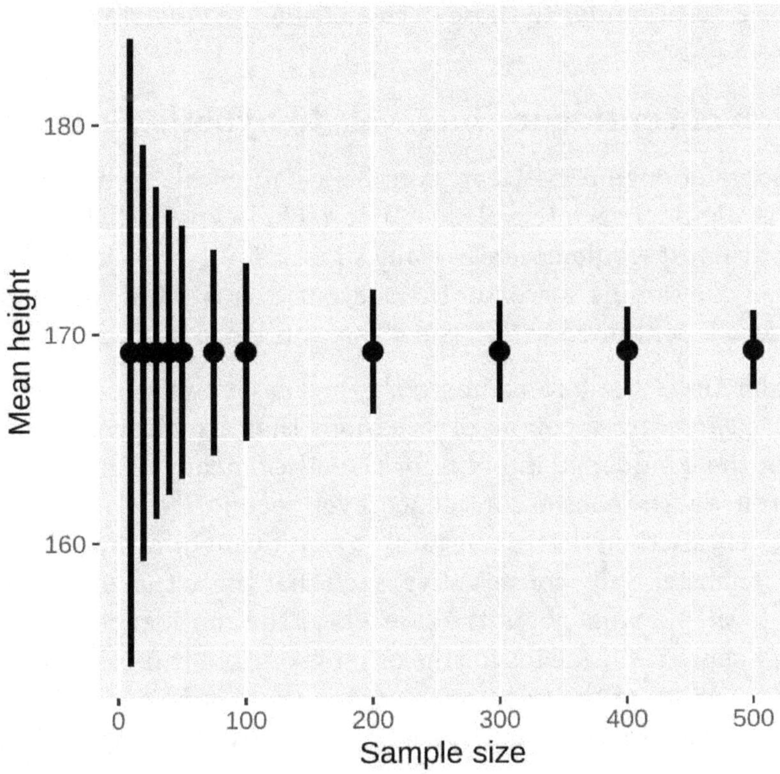

Figure 10.1: An example of the effect of sample size on the width of the confidence interval for the mean.

```
## BOOTSTRAP CONFIDENCE INTERVAL CALCULATIONS

## Based on 1000 bootstrap replicates

##

## CALL :

## boot.ci(boot.out = bs, type = "perc")

##

## Intervals :

## Level Percentile

## 95% (78, 84 )

## Calculations and Intervals on Original Scale
```

These numbers are quite similar to those derived from the t distribution above, albeit not identical.

10.1.5 Relation of confidence intervals to hypothesis tests

There is a close relationship between confidence intervals and hypothesis tests. In particular, if the confidence interval does not include the null hypothesis, then the associated statistical test would be statistically significant. For example, if you are testing whether the mean of a sample is greater than zero with $\alpha = 0.05$, you could simply check to see whether zero is contained within the 95% confidence interval for the mean.

Things get trickier if we want to compare the means of two conditions (Schenker and Gentleman 2001). There are a couple of situations that are clear. First, if each mean is contained within the confidence interval for the other mean, then there is definitely no significant difference at the chosen confidence level. Second, if there is no overlap between the confidence intervals, then there is certainly a significant difference at the chosen level; in fact, this test is substantially conservative, such that the actual error rate will be lower than the chosen level. But what about the case where the confidence intervals overlap one another but don't contain the means for the other group? In this case the answer depends on the relative variability of the two variables, and there is no general answer. However, one should in general avoid using the "eyeball test" for overlapping confidence intervals.

10.2 Effect sizes

"Statistical significance is the least interesting thing about the results. You should describe the results in terms of measures of magnitude - not just, does a treatment affect people, but how much does it affect them." Gene Glass, quoted in (Sullivan and Feinn 2012).

In the previous chapter, we discussed the idea that statistical significance may not necessarily reflect practical significance. In order to discuss practical significance, we need a standard way to describe the size of an effect in terms of the actual data, which we refer to as an effect size. In this section we will introduce the concept and discuss various ways that effect sizes can be calculated.

An effect size is a standardized measurement that compares the size of some statistical effect to a reference quantity, such as the variability of the statistic. In some fields of science and engineering, this idea is referred to as a "signal to noise ratio". There are many different ways that the effect size can be quantified, which depend on the nature of the data.

10.2.1 Cohen's D

One of the most common measures of effect size is known as Cohen's d, named after the statistician Jacob Cohen (who is most famous for his 1994 paper titled "The Earth Is Round ($p < .05$)"). It is used to quantify the difference between two means, in terms of their standard deviation:

$$d = \frac{\bar{X}_1 - \bar{X}_2}{s}$$

where $\bar{X}_1$ and $\bar{X}_2$ are the means of the two groups, and s is the pooled standard deviation (which is a combination of the standard deviations for the two samples, weighted by their sample sizes):

Table 10.1: Interpetation of Cohen's D

D	Interpretation
$0.0 - 0.2$	neglibible
$0.2 - 0.5$	small
$0.5 - 0.8$	medium
$0.8 -$	large

$$s = \sqrt{\frac{(n_1 - 1)s_1^2 + (n_2 - 1)s_2^2}{n_1 + n_2 - 2}}$$

where n_1 and n_2 are the sample sizes and s_1^2 and s_2^2 are the standard deviations for the two groups respectively. Note that this is very similar in spirit to the t statistic - the main difference is that the denominator in the t statistic is based on the standard error of the mean, whereas the denominator in Cohen's D is based on the standard deviation of the data. This means that while the t statistic will grow as the sample size gets larger, the value of Cohen's D will remain the same.

There is a commonly used scale for interpreting the size of an effect in terms of Cohen's d, shown in Table 10.1. It can be useful to look at some commonly understood effects to help understand these interpretations. For example, the effect size for gender differences in adult height (d = 2.05) is very large by reference to our table above. We can also see this by looking at the distributions of male and female heights in a sample from the NHANES dataset. Figure 10.2 shows that the two distributions are quite well separated, though still overlapping, highlighting the fact that even when there is a very large effect size for the difference between two groups, there will be individuals from each group that are more like the other group.

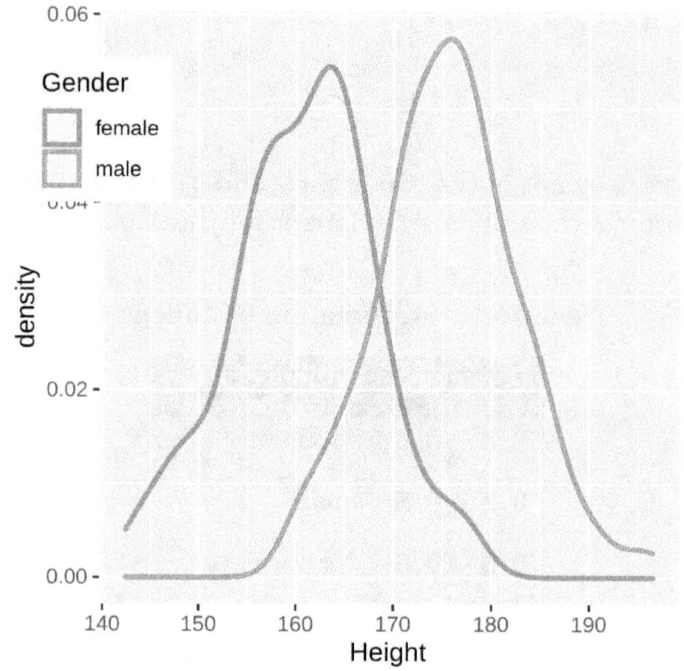

Figure 10.2: Smoothed histogram plots for male and female heights in the NHANES dataset, showing clearly distinct but also clearly overlapping distributions.

It is noteworthy that we never observe impacts of this scale in science, partly because they are so evident that scientific inquiry is unnecessary to identify them. Chapter 18 on reproducibility will demonstrate that substantial reported effects in scientific research frequently indicate the employment of dubious research procedures rather than genuinely significant impacts in nature. It is noteworthy that despite the significant effect, the two distributions still intersect; some girls exceed the average male height, and conversely. In the case of intriguing scientific phenomena, the extent of overlap is typically far bigger; hence, we should refrain from hastily drawing robust generalizations about individuals from disparate populations, even in the presence of a substantial effect size.

10.2.2 Pearson's r

Pearson's r, also known as the correlation coefficient, is a measure of the strength of the linear relationship between two continuous variables. We will discuss correlation in much more detail in Chapter 13, so we will save the details for that chapter; here, we simply introduce r as a way to quantify the relation between two variables.

r is a measure that varies from - 1 to 1 , where a value of 1 represents a perfect positive relationship between the variables, 0 represents no relationship, and -1 represents a perfect negative relationship. Figure 10.3 shows examples of various levels of correlation using randomly generated data.

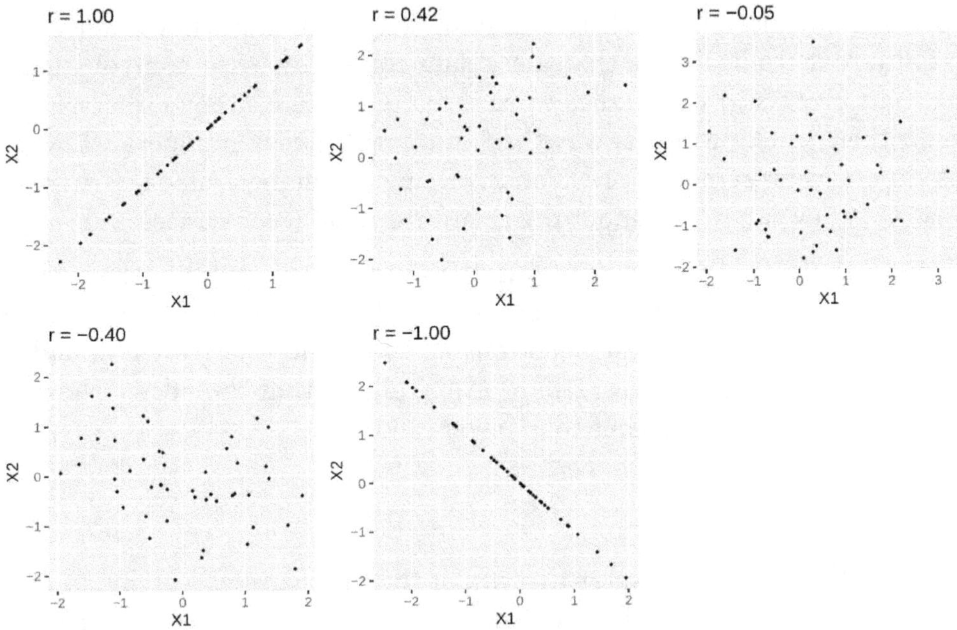

Figure 10.3: Examples of various levels of Pearson's r.

Table 10.2: Lung cancer occurrence separately for current smokers and those who have never smoked

Status	NeverSmoked	CurrentSmoker
No Cancer	2883	3829
Cancer	220	6784

10.2.3 Odds ratio

In our earlier discussion of probability we discussed the concept of odds that is, the relative likelihood of some event happening versus not happening:

$$\text{odds of } A = \frac{P(A)}{P(\neg A)}$$

We also discussed the odds ratio, which is simply the ratio of two odds. The odds ratio is a useful way to describe effect sizes for binary variables.

For example, let's take the case of smoking and lung cancer. A study published in the International Journal of Cancer in 2012 (Pesch et al. 2012) combined data regarding the occurrence of lung cancer in smokers and individuals who have never smoked across a number of different studies. Note that these data come from case-control studies, which means that participants in the studies were recruited because they either did or did not have cancer; their smoking status was then examined. These numbers (shown in Table 10.2) thus do not represent the prevalence of cancer amongst smokers in the general population - but they can tell us about the relationship between cancer and smoking.

We can convert these numbers to odds ratios for each of the groups. The odds of a non-smoker having lung cancer are 0.08 whereas the odds of a current smoker having lung cancer are 1.77 . The ratio of these odds tells us about the relative likelihood of cancer between the two groups: The odds ratio of 23.22 tells us that the odds of lung cancer in smokers are roughly 23 times higher than never-smokers.

10.3 Statistical power

Remember from the previous chapter that under the Neyman-Pearson hypothesis testing approach, we have to specify our level of tolerance for two kinds of errors: False positives (which they called Type I error) and false negatives (which they called Type II error). People often focus heavily on Type I error, because making a false positive claim is generally viewed as a very bad thing; for example, the now discredited claims by Wakefield (1999) that autism was associated with vaccination led to anti-vaccine sentiment that has resulted in substantial increases in childhood diseases such as measles. Similarly, we don't want to claim that a drug cures a disease if it really doesn't. That's why the tolerance for Type I errors is generally set fairly low, usually at $\alpha = 0.05$. But what about Type II errors?

The concept of statistical power is the complement of Type II error - that is, it is the likelihood of finding a positive result given that it exists:

$$\text{power } = 1 - \beta$$

Another important aspect of the Neyman-Pearson model that we didn't discuss earlier is the fact that in addition to specifying the acceptable levels of Type I and Type II errors, we also have to describe a specific alternative hypothesis - that is, what is the size of the effect that we wish to detect? Otherwise, we can't interpret β - the likelihood of finding a large effect is always going to be higher than finding a small effect, so β will differ depending on the size of effect we are trying to detect.

There are three factors that can affect statistical power:

- Sample size: Larger samples provide greater statistical power
- Effect size: A given design will always have greater power to find a large effect than a small effect (because finding large effects is easier)
- Type I error rate: There is a relationship between Type I error and power such that (all else being equal) decreasing Type I error will also decrease power.

We can see this through simulation. First let's simulate a single experiment, in which we compare the means of two groups using a standard t-test. We will vary the size of the effect (specified in terms of Cohen's d), the Type I error rate, and the sample size, and for each of these we will examine how the proportion of significant results (i.e. power) is affected. Figure 10.4 shows an example of how power changes as a function of these factors.

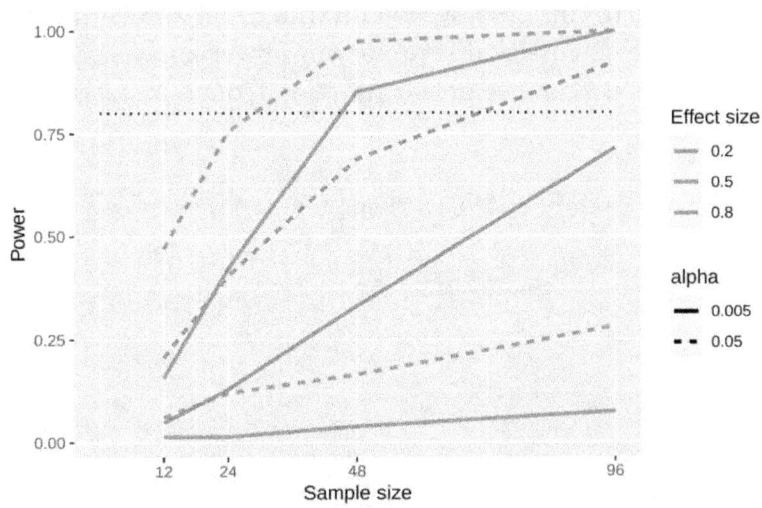

Figure 10.4: Results from power simulation, showing power as a function of sample size, with effect sizes shown as different colors, and alpha shown as line type. The standard criterion of 80 percent power is shown by the dotted black line.

This simulation shows us that even with a sample size of 96 , we will have relatively little power to find a small effect ($d = 0.2$) with $\alpha = 0.005$. This means that a study designed to do this would be futile - that is, it is almost guaranteed to find nothing even if a true effect of that size exists.

There are at least two significant reasons to regard statistical power. Initially, as a researcher, you likely prefer to avoid engaging in unproductive studies. Conducting an underpowered study is fundamentally ineffective, as it significantly reduces the probability of detecting an impact, even if it is present. Secondly, it has been determined that any favorable results derived from an underpowered study are more prone to being erroneous in comparison to those from a well-powered study, a topic we elaborate on further in Chapter 18.

10.3.1 Statistical Power analysis

Fortunately, techniques exist that enable us to ascertain the statistical power of an experiment. The primary application of these techniques is in experimental planning, where we aim to ascertain the requisite sample size to ensure adequate power for detecting our effect of interest. We aim to conduct a study examining the variance of a specific personality trait between iOS and Android device users. Our plan is collect two groups of individuals and measure them on the personality trait, and then compare the two groups using a t -test. In this case, we would think that a medium effect ($d = 0.5$) is of scientific interest, so we will use that level for our power analysis. In order to determine the necessary sample size, we can use power function from our statistical software:

```
##

## Two-sample t test power calculation

##

## n = 64

## delta = 0.5

## sd = 1

## sig.level = 0.05

## power = 0.8

## alternative = two.sided

##

## NOTE: n is number in *each* group
```

This tells us that we would need at least 64 subjects in each group in order to have sufficient power to find a medium-sized effect. It's always important to run a power analysis before one starts a new study, to make sure that the study won't be futile due to a sample that is too small.

It might have occurred to you that if the effect size is large enough, then the necessary sample will be very small. For example, if we run the same power analysis with an effect size of d = 2, then we will see that we only need about 5 subjects in each group to have sufficient power to find the difference.

```
##
## Two-sample t test power calculation
##
## n = 5.1
## d = 2
## sig.level = 0.05
## power = 0.8
## alternative = two.sided
##
## NOTE: n is number in *each* group
```

However, it's rare in science to be doing an experiment where we expect to find such a large effect - just as we don't need statistics to tell us that 16 -year-olds are taller than than 6 -year-olds. When we run a power analysis, we need to specify an effect size that is plausible and/or scientifically interesting for our study, which would usually come from previous research. However, in Chapter 18 we will discuss a phenomenon known as the "winner's curse" that likely results in published effect sizes being larger than the true effect size, so this should also be kept in mind.

Chapter-11

Bayesian Statistics

Bayesian statistics is a powerful framework for statistical inference that combines prior knowledge with observed data to update beliefs about uncertain parameters. Unlike classical (frequentist) approaches, which rely solely on sample data, Bayesian methods treat parameters as random variables and quantify uncertainty through probability distributions. Central to this approach is Bayes' theorem, which provides a formal mechanism to revise prior beliefs in light of new evidence, producing a posterior distribution that reflects both prior information and observed data. This flexibility allows Bayesian statistics to handle complex models, incorporate expert knowledge, and provide intuitive probabilistic interpretations, making it widely applicable in fields ranging from medicine and engineering to machine learning and finance. In this chapter we will take up the approach to statistical modeling and inference that stands in contrast to the null hypothesis testing framework that you encountered in Chapter 9. This is known as "Bayesian statistics" after the Reverend Thomas Bayes, whose theorem you have already encountered in Chapter 6. In this chapter you will learn how Bayes' theorem provides a way of understanding data that solves many of the conceptual problems that we discussed regarding null hypothesis testing, while also introducing some new challenges.

11.1 Generative models

Generative models are a class of machine learning models designed to learn the underlying distribution of data and generate new, realistic samples from that distribution. Unlike discriminative models, which focus solely on predicting labels or outcomes, generative models aim to capture the full structure and patterns of the data itself. By learning how data is generated, these models can create new instances that resemble the original data, making them useful in applications such as image synthesis, text generation, speech modeling, and drug discovery. Popular generative modeling approaches include Variational Autoencoders (VAEs), Generative Adversarial Networks (GANs), and diffusion models, each offering different techniques for modeling complex, high-dimensional data. Say you are walking down the street and a friend of yours walks right by but doesn't say hello. You would probably try to decide why this happened - Did they not see you? Are they mad at you? Are you suddenly cloaked in a magic invisibility shield? One of the basic ideas behind Bayesian statistics is that we want to infer the details of how the data are being generated, based on the data themselves. In this case, you want to use the data (i.e. the fact that your friend did not say hello) to infer the process that generated the data (e.g. whether or not they actually saw you, how they feel about you, etc).

The idea behind a generative model is that a latent (unseen) process generates the data we observe, usually with some amount of randomness in the process. When we take a sample of data from a population and estimate a parameter from the sample, what we are doing in essence is trying to learn the value of a latent variable (the population mean) that gives rise through sampling to the observed data (the sample mean). Figure 11.1 shows a schematic of this idea.

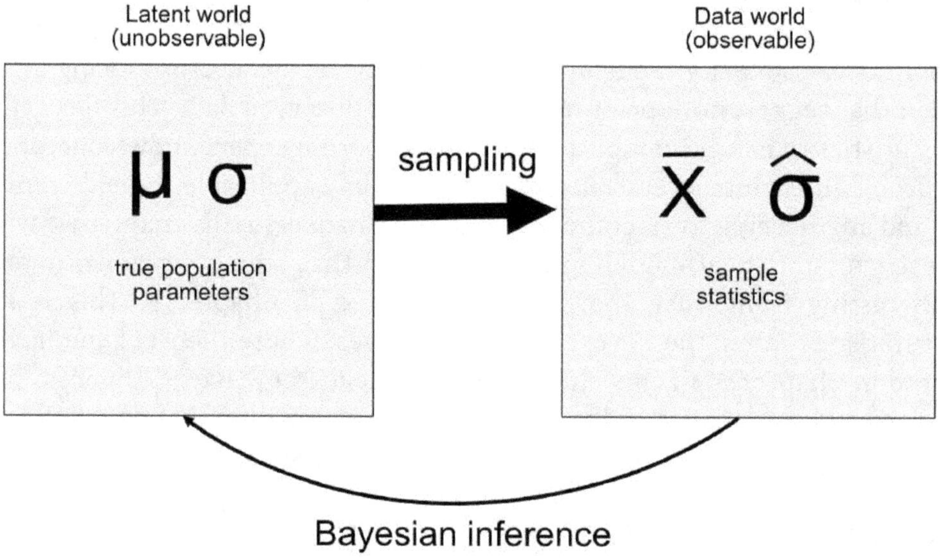

Figure 11.1: A schematic of the idea of a generative model.

If we know the value of the latent variable, then it's easy to reconstruct what the observed data should look like. For example, let's say that we are flipping a coin that we know to be fair, such that we would expect it to land on heads 50% of the time. We can describe the coin by a binomial distribution with a value of $P_{\text{heads}} = 0.5$, and then we could generate random samples from such a distribution in order to see what the observed data should look like. However, in general we are in the opposite situation: We don't know the value of the latent variable of interest, but we have some data that we would like to use to estimate it.

11.2 Bayes' theorem and inverse inference

Bayesian statistics derives its name from the utilization of Bayes' theorem to infer information about the underlying process that produced the data. We seek to determine if a coin is unbiased. To test this, we flip the coin 10 times and come up with 7 heads. Before this test we were pretty sure that the $P_{\text{heads}} = 0.5$, but finding 7 heads out of 10 flips would certainly give us pause if we believed that $P_{\text{heads}} = 0.5$.

We already know how to compute the conditional probability that we would flip 7 or more heads out of 10 if the coin is really fair ($P(n \geq 7 \mid p_{\text{heads}} = 0.5)$), using the binomial distribution.

The resulting probability is 0.055 . That is a fairly small number, but this number doesn't really answer the question that we are asking - it is telling us about the likelihood of 7 or more heads given some particular probability of heads, whereas what we really want to know is the true probability of heads for this particular coin. This should sound familiar, as it's exactly the situation that we were in with null hypothesis testing, which told us about the likelihood of data rather than the likelihood of hypotheses.

Remember that Bayes' theorem provides us with the tool that we need to invert a conditional probability:

$$P(H \mid D) = \frac{P(D \mid H) * P(H)}{P(D)}$$

We can think of this theorem as having four parts:

- prior ($P($ Hypothesis $)$) : Our degree of belief about hypothesis H before seeing the data D
- likelihood (P (Data | Hypothesis)): How likely are the observed data D under hypothesis H ?
- marginal likelihood ($P($ Data $)$): How likely are the observed data, combining over all possible hypotheses?
- posterior (P (Hypothesis | Data)): Our updated belief about hypothesis H , given the data D

In the case of our coin-flipping example:

- prior (P_{heads}) : Our degree of belief about the likelhood of flipping heads, which was $P_{heads} = 0.5$
- likelihood (P(7 or more heads out of 10 flips | $P_{heads} = 0.5$)): How likely are 7 or more heads out of 10 flips if $P_{heads} = 0.5$)?
- marginal likelihood (P (7 or more heads out of 10 flips)): How likely are we to observe 7 heads out of 10 coin flips, in general?
- posterior (P_{heads} | 7 or more heads out of 10 coin flips)): Our updated belief about P_{heads} given the observed coin flips

Here we see one of the primary differences between frequentist and Bayesian statistics. Frequentists do not believe in the idea of a probability of a hypothesis (i.e. our degree of belief about a hypothesis) - for them, a hypothesis is either true or it isn't. Another way to say this is that for the frequentist, the hypothesis is fixed and the data are random, which is why frequentist inference focuses on describing the probability of data given a hypothesis (i.e. the p-value). Bayesians, on the other hand, are comfortable making probability statements about both data and hypotheses.

11.3 Doing Bayesian estimation

We ultimately want to use Bayesian statistics to make decisions about hypotheses, but before we do that we need to estimate the parameters that are necessary to make the decision. Here we will walk through the process of Bayesian estimation. Let's use another screening example: Airport security screening. If you fly a lot, it's just a matter of time until one of the random explosive screenings comes back positive; I had the particularly unfortunate experience of this happening soon after September 11, 2001, when airport security staff were especially on edge.

What the security staff want to know is what is the likelihood that a person is carrying an explosive, given that the machine has given a positive test. Let's walk through how to calculate this value using Bayesian analysis.

11.3.1 Specifying the prior

To use Bayes' theorem, we first need to specify the prior probability for the hypothesis. In this case, we don't know the real number but we can assume that it's quite small. According to the FAA, there were 971,595,898 air passengers in the U.S. in 2017. Let's say that one of those travelers was carrying an explosive in their bag - that would give a prior probability of 1 out of 971 million, which is very small! The security personnel may have reasonably held a stronger prior in the months after the 9/11 attack, so let's say that their subjective belief was that one out of every million flyers was carrying an explosive.

11.3.2 Collect some data

The data are composed of the results of the explosive screening test. Let's say that the security staff runs the bag through their testing apparatus 3 times, and it gives a positive reading on 3 of the 3 tests.

11.3.3 Computing the likelihood

We want to compute the likelihood of the data under the hypothesis that there is an explosive in the bag. Let's say that we know (from the machine's manufacturer) that the sensitivity of the test is 0.99 - that is, when a device is present, it will detect it 99% of the time. To determine the likelihood of our data under the hypothesis that a device is present, we can treat each test as a Bernoulli trial (that is, a trial with an outcome of true or false) with a probability of success of 0.99 , which we can model using a binomial distribution.

11.3.4 Computing the marginal likelihood

We also need to know the overall likelihood of the data - that is, finding 3 positives out of 3 tests. Computing the marginal likelihood is often one of the most difficult aspects of Bayesian analysis, but for our example it's simple because we can take advantage of the specific form of Bayes' theorem for a binary outcome that we introduced in Section 6.7:

$$P(E \mid T) = \frac{P(T \mid E) * P(E)}{P(T \mid E) * P(E) + P(T \mid \neg E) * P(\neg E)}$$

where E refers to the presence of explosives, and T refers to a postive test result.

The marginal likelihood in this case is a weighted average of the likelihood of the data under either presence or absence of the explosive, multiplied by the probability of the explosive being present (i.e. the prior). In this case, let's say that we know (from the manufacturer) that the specificity of the test is 0.99 , such that the likelihood of a positive result when there is no explosive ($P(T \mid \neg E)$) is 0.01 .

11.3.5 Computing the posterior

We now have all of the parts that we need to compute the posterior probability of an explosive being present, given the observed 3 positive outcomes out of 3 tests.

This result shows us that the posterior probability of an explosive in the bag given these positive tests (0.492) is just under 50%, again highlighting the fact that testing for rare events is almost always liable to produce high numbers of false positives, even when the specificity and sensitivity are very high.

An important aspect of Bayesian analysis is that it can be sequential. Once we have the posterior from one analysis, it can become the prior for the next analysis!

11.4 Estimating posterior distributions

In the previous example there were only two possible outcomes - the explosive is either there or it's not - and we wanted to know which outcome was most likely given the data. However, in other cases we want to use Bayesian estimation to estimate the numeric value of a parameter. Let's say that we want to know about the effectiveness of a new drug for pain; to test this, we can administer the drug to a group of patients and then ask them whether their pain was improved or not after taking the drug. We can use Bayesian analysis to estimate the proportion of people for whom the drug will be effective using these data.

11.4.1 Specifying the prior

In this case, we don't have any prior information about the effectiveness of the drug, so we will use a uniform distribution as our prior, since all values are equally likely under a uniform distribution. In order to simplify the example, we will only look at a subset of 99 possible values of effectiveness (from .01 to .99 , in steps of .01). Therefore, each possible value has a prior probability of 1/99.

11.4.2 Collect some data

We need some data in order to estimate the effect of the drug. Let's say that we administer the drug to 100 individuals, we find that 64 respond positively to the drug.

11.4.3 Computing the likelihood

We can compute the likelihood of the observed data under any particular value of the effectiveness parameter using the binomial density function. In Figure 11.2 you can see the likelihood curves over numbers of responders for several different values of P_{respond}. Looking at this, it seems that our observed data are relatively more likely under the hypothesis of $P_{\text{respond}} = 0.7$, somewhat less likely under the hypothesis of $P_{\text{respond}} = 0.5$, and quite unlikely under the hypothesis of $P_{\text{respond}} = 0.3$. One of the fundamental ideas of Bayesian inference is that we should upweight our belief in values of our parameter of interest in proportion to how likely the data are under those values, balanced against what we believed about the parameter values before having seen the data (our prior knowledge).

11.4.4 Computing the marginal likelihood

In addition to the likelihood of the data under different hypotheses, we need to know the overall likelihood of the data, combining across all hypotheses (i.e., the marginal likelihood). This marginal likelihood is primarily important because it helps to ensure that the posterior values are true probabilities. In this case, our use of a set of discrete possible parameter values makes it easy to compute the marginal likelihood, because we can just compute the likelihood of each parameter value under each hypothesis and add them up.

11.4.5 Computing the posterior

We now have all of the parts that we need to compute the posterior probability distribution across all possible values of $p_{respond}$, as shown in Figure 11.3.

11.4.6 Maximum a posteriori (MAP) estimation

Given our data we would like to obtain an estimate of $p_{respond}$ for our sample. One way to do this is to find the value of $p_{respond}$ for which the posterior probability is the highest, which we refer to as the maximum a posteriori (MAP) estimate. We can find this from the data in 11.3 - it's the value shown with a marker at the top of the distribution. Note that the result (0.64) is simply the proportion of responders from our sample - this occurs because the prior was uniform and thus didn't influence our estimate.

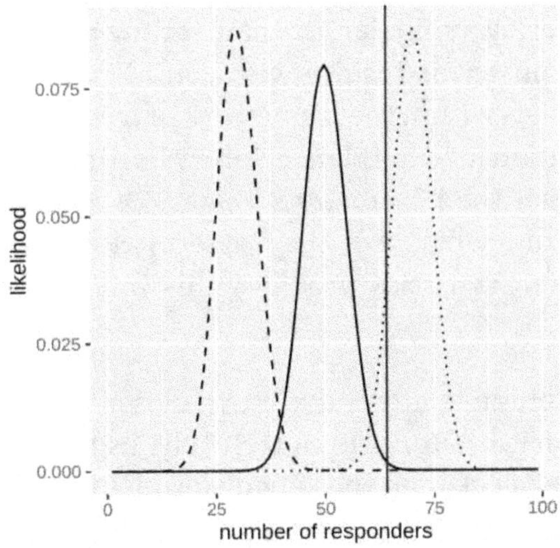

Figure 11.2: Likelihood of each possible number of responders under several different hypotheses (p(respond) = 0. 5 (solid), 0.7 (dotted), 0.3 (dashed). Observed value shown in the vertical line

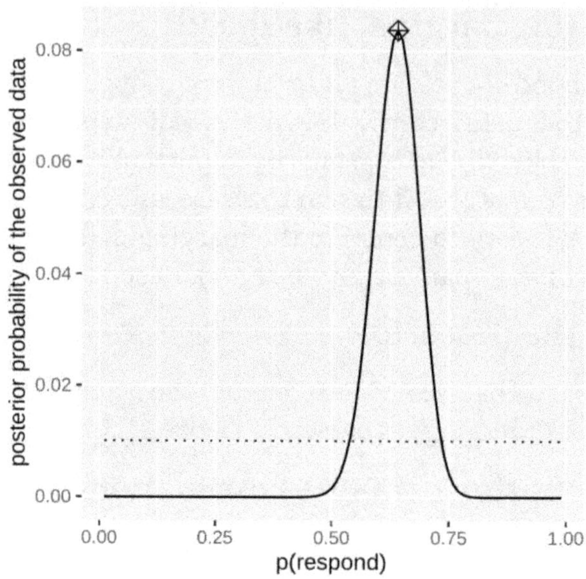

Figure 11.3: Posterior probability distribution for the observed data plotted in solid line against uniform prior distribution (dotted line). The maximum a posteriori (MAP) value is signified by the diamond symbol.

11.4.7 Credible intervals

Frequently, we seek not merely a singular estimate for the posterior, but an interval within which we may assert the posterior resides with confidence. We recently examined the notion of confidence intervals within the framework of frequentist inference, and you may recall that the interpretation of confidence intervals was rather complex: It was an interval that will encompass the parameter's value 95% of the time. Our objective is to establish an interval within which we may assert with confidence that the correct parameter resides; Bayesian statistics provides this interval, referred to as a credible interval.

The interpretation of this credible interval is much closer to what we had hoped we could get from a confidence interval (but could not): It tells us that there is a 95% probability that the value of p_{respond} falls between these two values. Importantly, in this case it shows that we have high confidence that $p_{\text{respond}} > 0.0$, meaning that the drug seems to have a positive effect.

In some cases the credible interval can be computed numerically based on a known distribution, but it's more common to generate a credible interval by sampling from the posterior distribution and then to compute quantiles of the samples. This is particularly useful when we don't have an easy way to express the posterior distribution numerically, which is often the case in real Bayesian data analysis. One such method (rejection sampling) is explained in more detail in the Appendix at the end of this chapter.

11.4.8 Effects of different priors

In the previous example we used a flat prior, meaning that we didn't have any reason to believe that any particular value of $p_{respond}$ was more or less likely. However, let's say that we had instead started with some previous data: In a previous study, researchers had tested 20 people and found that 10 of them had responded positively. This would have lead us to start with a prior belief that the treatment has an effect in 50% of people. We can do the same computation as above, but using the information from our previous study to inform our prior (see panel A in Figure 11.4).

Note that the likelihood and marginal likelihood did not change - only the prior changed. The effect of the change in prior to was to pull the posterior closer to the mass of the new prior, which is centered at 0.5 .

Now let's see what happens if we come to the analysis with an even stronger prior belief. Let's say that instead of having previously observed 10 responders out of 20 people, the prior study had instead tested 500 people and found 250 responders. This should in principle give us a much stronger prior, and as we see in panel B of Figure 11.4 , that's what happens: The prior is much more concentrated around 0.5 , and the posterior is also much closer to the prior. The general idea is that Bayesian inference combines the information from the prior and the likelihood, weighting the relative strength of each.

This example also highlights the sequential nature of Bayesian analysis - the posterior from one analysis can become the prior for the next analysis.

Finally, it is important to realize that if the priors are strong enough, they can completely overwhelm the data. Let's say that you have an absolute prior that $p_{respond}$ is 0.8 or greater, such that you set the prior likelihood of all other values to zero. What happens if we then compute the posterior?

In panel C of Figure 11.4 we see that there is zero density in the posterior for any of the values where the prior was set to zero - the data are overwhelmed by the absolute prior.

11.5 Choosing a prior

The influence of priors on the resultant inferences is the most contentious element of Bayesian statistics. What is the appropriate prior to utilize? If the selection of the prior influences the outcomes (i.e., the posterior), how can you ascertain the reliability of your results? These inquiries are challenging; nonetheless, we must not retreat only because to their complexity. As previously discussed, Bayesian analyses provide interpretable outcomes (credible intervals, etc.). This alone should motivate us to critically consider these problems to achieve results that are rational and comprehensible.

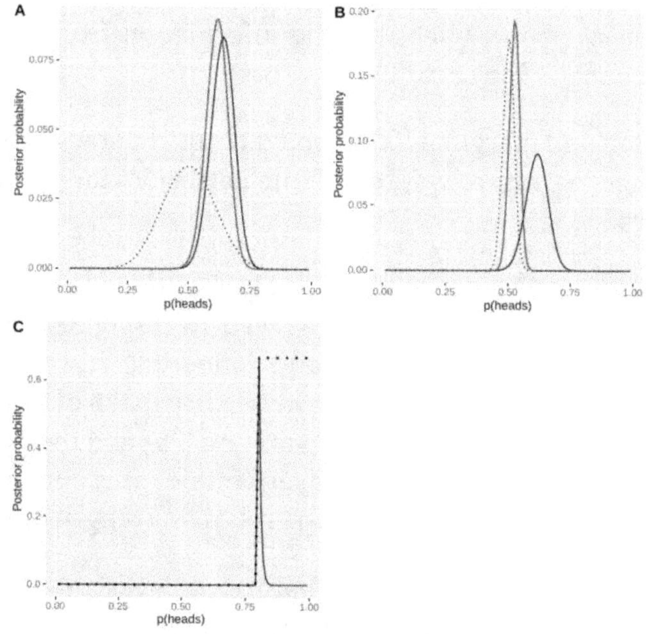

Figure 11.4: A: Effects of priors on the posterior distribution. The original posterior distribution based on a flat prior is plotted in blue. The prior based on the observation of 10 responders out of 20 people is plotted in the dotted black line, and the posterior using this prior is plotted in red. B: Effects of the strength of the prior on the posterior distribution. The blue line shows the posterior obtained using the prior based on 50 heads out of 100 people. The dotted black line shows the prior based on 250 heads out of 500 flips, and the red line shows the posterior based on that prior. C: Effects of the strength of the prior on the posterior distribution. The blue line shows the posterior obtained using an absolute prior which states that p (respond) is 0.8 or greater. The prior is shown in the dotted black line.

There are various ways to choose one's priors, which (as we saw above) can impact the resulting inferences.

Sometimes we have a very specific prior, as in the case where we expected our coin to lands heads 50% of the time, but in many cases we don't have such strong a starting point. Uninformative priors attempt to influence the resulting posterior as little as possible, as we saw in the example of the uniform prior above. It's also common to use weakly informative priors (or default priors), which influence the result only very slightly. For example, if we had used a binomial distribution based on one heads out of two coin flips, the prior would have been centered around 0.5 but fairly flat, influencing the posterior only slightly. It is also possible to use priors based on the scientific literature or pre-existing data, which we would call empirical priors. In general, however, we will stick to the use of uninformative/weakly informative priors, since they raise the least concern about influencing our results.

11.6 Bayesian hypothesis testing

Having acquired proficiency in Bayesian estimation, we now shift our focus to the application of Bayesian methods in hypothesis testing. Consider two politicians who hold divergent views of popular support for an additional tax to fund national parks. Senator Smith believes that only 40% of individuals support the tax, whereas Senator Jones asserts that 60% are in favor. They organize a poll to assess this, querying 1,000 randomly selected individuals over their support for the tax. Of the individuals surveyed, 490 expressed support for the tax. Based on this data, we want to ascertain if it substantiates the assertions of one senator over the other, and to what extent. The Bayes factor can be employed to evaluate whether hypothesis is superior by assessing the predictive accuracy of each in relation to the observed data.

11.6.1 Bayes factors

Bayes factors are a fundamental tool in Bayesian statistics for comparing the relative evidence provided by data in favor of two competing hypotheses. They quantify how much more likely the observed data are under one hypothesis compared to another, providing a continuous measure of support rather than a simple "reject" or "fail to reject" decision as in classical hypothesis testing. A Bayes factor greater than one indicates evidence in favor of the first hypothesis, while a value less than one favors the second. This approach allows researchers to incorporate prior beliefs and assess evidence in a probabilistic and interpretable manner, making it widely used in fields such as psychology, medicine, and social sciences.

The Bayes factor characterizes the relative likelihood of the data under two different hypotheses. It is defined as:

$$BF = \frac{p(\text{data} \mid H_1)}{p(\text{data} \mid H_2)}$$

for two hypotheses H_1 and H_2. In the case of our two senators, we know how to compute the likelihood of the data under each hypothesis using the binomial distribution; let's assume for the moment that our prior probability for each senator being correct is the same ($P_{H_1} = P_{H_2} = 0.5$). We will put Senator Smith in the numerator and Senator Jones in the denominator, so that a value greater than one will reflect greater evidence for Senator Smith, and a value less than one will reflect greater evidence for Senator Jones. The resulting Bayes Factor (3325.26) provides a measure of the evidence that the data provides regarding the two hypotheses - in this case, it tells us the data support Senator Smith more than 3000 times more strongly than they support Senator Jones.

11.6.2 Bayesian factors for statistical hypotheses

Bayes factors provide a Bayesian framework for evaluating statistical hypotheses by quantifying the strength of evidence in the data for one hypothesis relative to another. Given two competing hypotheses—typically a null hypothesis (H_0) and an alternative hypothesis (H_1)—the Bayes factor is calculated as the ratio of the likelihood of the observed data under H_1 to that under H_0. Values greater than one indicate evidence in favor of the alternative, while values less than one support the null hypothesis. Unlike traditional p-values, Bayes factors allow for a graded measure of evidence, incorporate prior information, and enable researchers to directly compare hypotheses in a probabilistic and interpretable manner.

In the previous example we had specific predictions from each senator, whose likelihood we could quantify using the binomial distribution. In addition, our prior probability for the two hypotheses was equal. However, in real data analysis we generally must deal with uncertainty about our parameters, which complicates the Bayes factor, because we need to compute the marginal likelihood (that is, an integrated average of the likelihoods over all possible model parameters, weighted by their prior probabilities). However, in exchange we gain the ability to quantify the relative amount of evidence in favor of the null versus alternative hypotheses.

Let's say that we are a medical researcher performing a clinical trial for the treatment of diabetes, and we wish to know whether a particular drug reduces blood glucose compared to placebo. We recruit a set of volunteers and randomly assign them to either drug or placebo group, and we measure the change in hemoglobin A1C (a marker for blood glucose levels) in each group over the period in which the drug or placebo was administered. What we want to know is: Is there a difference between the drug and placebo?

First, let's generate some data and analyze them using null hypothesis testing (see Figure 11.5). Then let's perform an independent-samples t-test, which shows that there is a significant difference between the groups:

```
##
## Welch Two Sample t-test
##
```

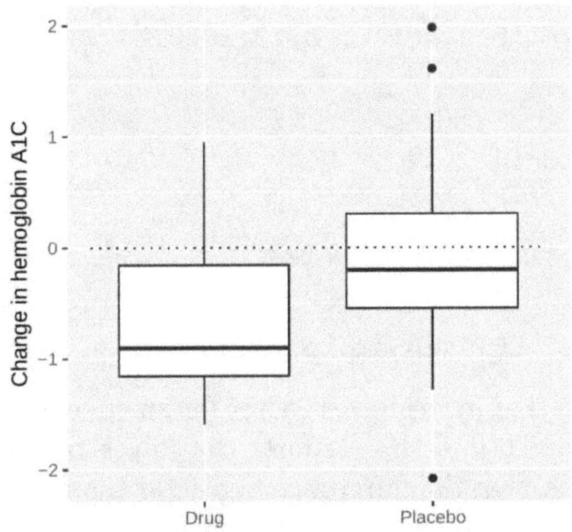

Figure 11.5: Box plots showing data for drug and placebo groups.

```
## data: hbchange by group
## t = 2, df = 32, p-value = 0.02
## alternative hypothesis: true difference in means between group 0 and
group
## 95 percent confidence interval:
## 0.11 Inf
## sample estimates:
```

```
## mean in group 0 mean in group 1

## -0.082 -0.650
```

This test tells us that there is a significant difference between the groups, but it doesn't quantify how strongly the evidence supports the null versus alternative hypotheses. To measure that, we can compute a Bayes factor using ttestBF function from the BayesFactor package in R:

```
## Bayes factor analysis

## --------------

## [1] Alt., r=0.707 0<d<Inf: :3.4 ±0%

## [2] Alt., r=0.707 !(0<d<Inf) : 0.12 ±0.01%

##

## Against denominator:

## Null, mu1-mu2 = 0

## ---

## Bayes factor type: BFindepSample, JZS
```

We are particularly interested in the Bayes Factor for an effect greater than zero, which is listed in the line marked "[1]" in the report. The Bayes factor here tells us that the alternative hypothesis (i.e. that the difference is greater than zero) is about 3 times more likely than the point null hypothesis (i.e. a mean difference of exactly zero) given the data. Thus, while the effect is significant, the amount of evidence it provides us in favor of the alternative hypothesis is rather weak.

11.6.2.1 One-sided tests

We generally are less interested in testing against the null hypothesis of a specific point value (e.g. mean difference $= 0$) than we are in testing against a directional null hypothesis (e.g. that the difference is less than or equal to zero). We can also perform a directional (or one-sided) test using the results from ttestBF analysis, since it provides two Bayes factors: one for the alternative hypothesis that the mean difference is greater than zero, and one for the alternative hypothesis that the mean difference is less than zero. If we want to assess the relative evidence for a positive effect, we can compute a Bayes factor comparing the relative evidence for a positive versus a negative effect by simply dividing the two Bayes factors returned by the function:

```
## Bayes factor analysis
## --------------
## [1] Alt., r=0.707 0<d<Inf : 29 ±0.01%
##
## Against denominator:
## Alternative, r = 0.707106781186548, mu =/= 0 !(0<d<Inf)
## ---
## Bayes factor type: BFindepSample, JZS
```

Now we see that the Bayes factor for a positive effect versus a negative effect is substantially larger (almost 30).

11.6.2.2 Interpreting Bayes Factors

How do we know whether a Bayes factor of 2 or 20 is good or bad? There is a general guideline for interpretation of Bayes factors suggested by Kass & Rafferty (1995):

BF	Strength of evidence
1 to 3	not worth more than a bare mention
3 to 20	positive
20 to 150	strong
> 150	very strong

Based on this, even though the statisical result is significant, the amount of evidence in favor of the alternative vs. the point null hypothesis is weak enough that it's hardly worth even mentioning, whereas the evidence for the directional hypothesis is relatively strong.

11.6.3 Assessing evidence for the null hypothesis

The Bayes factor evaluates evidence for two hypotheses, enabling the assessment of support for the null hypothesis, a capability not afforded by conventional null hypothesis testing, which presumes the null is true from the outset. This can be useful in assessing whether a non-significant finding genuinely indicates a lack of effect or rather signifies weak evidence overall.

11.7 Appendix:

11.7.1 Rejection sampling

We will generate samples from our posterior distribution using a simple algorithm known as rejection sampling. The idea is that we choose a random value of x (in this case p_{respond}) and a random value of y (in this case, the posterior probability of p_{respond}) each from a uniform distribution. We then only accept the sample if $y < f(x)$ - in this case, if the randomly selected value of y is less than the actual posterior probability of y . Figure 11.6 shows an example of a histogram of samples using rejection sampling, along with the 95% credible intervals obtained using this method (with the values presented in Table ??).

	x
2.5%	0.54
97.5%	0.73

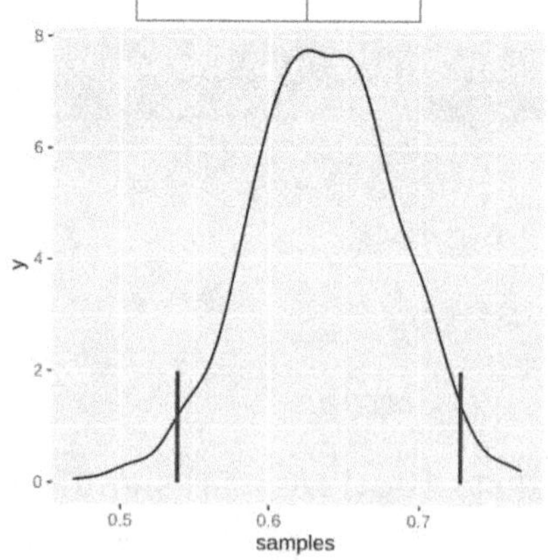

Figure 11.6: Rejection sampling example. The black line shows the density of all possible values of p (respond); the blue lines show the 2.5th and 97.5th percentiles of the distribution, which represent the 95 percent credible interval for the estimate of p (respond).

Chapter-12

Modeling Categorical Associations

Modeling categorical associations is a fundamental aspect of statistical analysis that focuses on understanding relationships between categorical variables. Categorical variables represent data that can be divided into distinct groups or categories, such as gender, marital status, or education level. Unlike continuous variables, categorical data do not have a natural ordering or distance, which requires specialized statistical techniques for analysis. One of the primary goals in modeling categorical associations is to determine whether variables are independent or whether a relationship exists between them. Contingency tables are commonly used to summarize the joint distribution of categorical variables, providing a basis for assessing associations. Chi-square tests are widely applied to evaluate the significance of observed associations, comparing expected frequencies under independence with actual data. For more complex relationships, log-linear models can be employed, allowing the examination of interactions among multiple categorical variables. Logistic regression is another key approach, especially when modeling a binary outcome variable based on one or more categorical predictors. These models provide estimates of odds ratios, which quantify the strength and direction of associations. Modeling categorical associations is crucial in social sciences, epidemiology, marketing, and many other fields where data are naturally categorical. Proper modeling helps uncover patterns, guide decision-making, and support hypothesis testing. Advanced methods, such as multinomial logistic regression or hierarchical models, enable the analysis of more complex structures and multiple categories. Bayesian approaches can also be incorporated, allowing the use of prior knowledge in assessing associations. Visualization tools, like mosaic plots or association plots, enhance the interpretability of relationships among categories. Understanding these associations provides insights into underlying processes, risk factors, and dependencies. Statistical software packages offer robust implementations of these techniques, facilitating practical application. Accurate modeling requires careful attention to sample size, sparsity, and the coding of categorical variables. Interactions between categories can reveal nuanced relationships that simple pairwise comparisons may miss. Ultimately, modeling categorical associations is about translating discrete data into meaningful insights, supporting both scientific understanding and practical decision-making. So far we have discussed the general concepts of statistical modeling and hypothesis testing, and applied them to some simple analyses; now we will turn to the question of how to model particular kinds of relationships in our data. In this chapter we will focus on the modeling of categorical relationships, by which we mean relationships between variables that are measured qualitatively. These data are usually expressed in terms of counts; that is, for each value of the variable (or combination of values of multiple variables), how many observations take that value? For example, when we count how many people from each major are in our class, we are fitting a categorical model to the data.

12.1 Example: Candy colors

Let's say that I have purchased a bag of 100 candies, which are labeled as having 1/3 chocolates, 1/3 licorices, and 1/3 gumballs. When I count the candies in the bag, we get the following numbers: 30 chocolates, 33 licorices, and 37 gumballs. Because I like chocolate much more than licorice or gumballs, I feel slightly ripped off and I'd like to know if this was just a random accident. To answer that question, I need to know: What is the likelihood that the count would come out this way if the true probability of each candy type is the averaged proportion of 1/3 each?

Table 12.1: Observed counts, expectations under the null hypothesis, and squared differences in the candy data

Candy Type	count	nullExpectation	squared difference
chocolate	30	33	11.11
licorice	33	33	0.11
gumball	37	33	13.44

12.2 Pearson's chi-squared test

The Pearson chi-squared test provides us with a way to test whether a set of observed counts differs from some specific expected values that define the null hypothesis:

$$\chi^2 = \sum_i \frac{(\text{observed}_i - \text{expected}_i)^2}{\text{expected}_i}$$

In the case of our candy example, the null hypothesis is that the proportion of each type of candy is equal. To compute the chi-squared statistic, we first need to come up with our expected counts under the null hypothesis: since the null is that they are all the same, then this is just the total count split across the three categories (as shown in Table 12.1). We then take the difference between each count and its expectation under the null hypothesis, square them, divide them by the null expectation, and add them up to obtain the chi-squared statistic.

The chi-squared statistic for this analysis comes out to 0.74 , which on its own is not interpretable, since it depends on the number of different values that were added together. However, we can take advantage of the fact that the chi-squared statistic is distributed according to a specific distribution under the null hypothesis, which is known as the chi-squared distribution. This distribution is defined as the sum of squares of a set of standard normal random variables; it has a number of degrees of freedom that is equal to the number of variables being added together. The shape of the distribution depends on the number of degrees of freedom. The left panel of Figure 12.1 shows examples of the distribution for several different degrees of freedom.

Let's verify that the chi-squared distribution accurately describes the sum of squares of a set of standard normal random variables, using simulation.

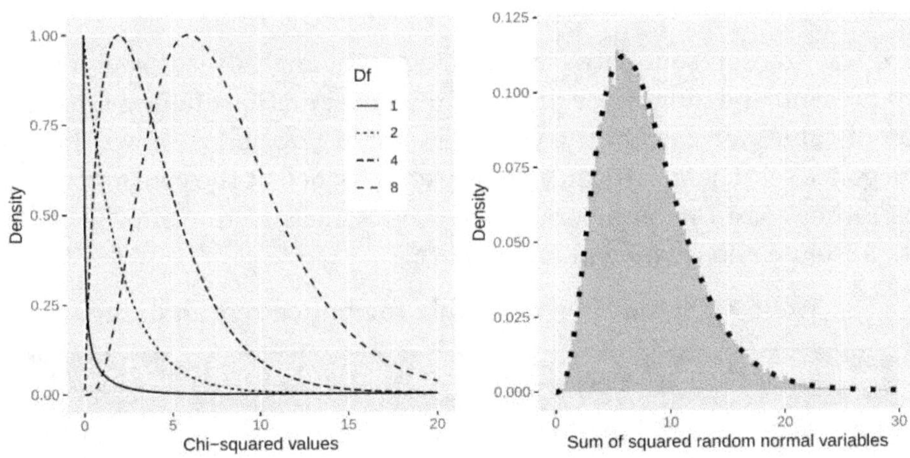

Figure 12.1: Left: Examples of the chi-squared distribution for various degrees of freedom. Right: Simulation of sum of squared random normal variables. The histogram is based on the sum of squares of 50,000 sets of 8 random normal variables; the dotted line shows the values of the theoretical chi-squared distribution with 8 degrees of freedom.

To do this, we repeatedly draw sets of 8 random numbers, and add up each set after squaring each value. The right panel of Figure 12.1 shows that the theoretical distribution matches closely with the results of a simulation that repeatedly added together the squares of a set of random normal variables.

For the candy example, we can compute the likelihood of our observed chisquared value of 0.74 under the null hypothesis of equal frequency across all candies. We use a chi-squared distribution with degrees of freedom equal to k - 1 (where k = the number of categories) since we lost one degree of freedom when we computed the mean in order to generate the expected values. The resulting p-value (P(Chi-squared) > 0.74 = 0.691) shows that the observed counts of candies are not particularly surprising based on the proportions printed on the bag of candy, and we would not reject the null hypothesis of equal proportions.

12.3 Contingency tables and the two-way test

Another application of the chi-squared test is to determine the relationship between two categorical variables. For a more realistic illustration, consider the inquiry regarding whether a Black driver is more prone to being searched when stopped by a police officer in comparison to a white driver. The Stanford Open Policing Project has conducted a study and offers data for analyzing the issue. We will utilize data from the State of Connecticut due to its relatively modest size, facilitating analysis.

The standard way to represent data from a categorical analysis is through a contingency table, which presents the number or proportion of observations falling into each possible combination of values for each of the variables. Table 12.2 below shows the contingency table for the police search data. It can also be useful to look at the contingency table using proportions rather than raw numbers, since they are easier to compare visually, so we include both absolute and relative numbers here.

Table 12.2: Contingency table for police search data

searched	Black	White	Black (relative)	White (relative)
FALSE	36244	239241	0.13	0.86
TRUE	1219	3108	0.00	0.01

The Pearson chi-squared test allows us to test whether observed frequencies are different from expected frequencies, so we need to determine what frequencies we would expect in each cell if searches and race were unrelated - which we can define as being independent. Remember from the chapter on probability that if X and Y are independent, then:

$$P(X \cap Y) = P(X) * P(Y)$$

That is, the joint probability under the null hypothesis of independence is simply the product of the marginal probabilities of each individual variable. The marginal probabilities are simply the probabilities of each event occuring regardless of other events. We can compute those marginal probabilities, and then multiply them together to get the expected proportions under independence.

	Black	White	
Not searched	P(NS) *P(B)	P(NS) *P(W)	P(NS)
Searched	P(S) *P(B)	P(S) *P(W)	P(S)
	P(B)	P(W)	

We then compute the chi-squared statistic, which comes out to 828.3. To compute a p-value, we need to compare it to the null chi-squared distribution in order to determine how extreme our chi-squared value is compared to our expectation under the null hypothesis. The degrees of freedom for this distribution are $df = ($ nRows -1) $* ($ nColumns -1) - thus, for a 2X2 table like the one here, $df = (2-1)*(2-1) = 1$. The intuition here is that computing the expected frequencies requires us to use three values: the total number of observations and the marginal probability for each of the two variables. Thus, once those values are computed, there is only one number that is free to vary, and thus there is one degree of freedom. Given this, we can compute the p -value for the chi-squared statistic, which is about as close to zero as one can get: 3.79×10^{-182}. This shows that the observed data would be highly unlikely if there was truly no relationship between race and police searches, and thus we should reject the null hypothesis of independence.

We can also perform this test easily using our statistical software:

```
##
## Pearson's Chi-squared test
##
```

Table 12.4: Summary of standardized residuals for police stop data

searched	driver_race	Standardized residuals
FALSE	Black	-3.3
TRUE	Black	26.6
FALSE	White	1.3
TRUE	White	-10.4

data: summaryDf2wayTable and 1

X-squared = 828, df = 1, p-value <2e-16

12.4 Standardized residuals

When we find a significant effect with the chi-squared test, this tells us that the data are unlikely under the null hypothesis, but it doesn't tell us how the data differ. To get a deeper insight into how the data differ from what we would expect under the null hypothesis, we can examine the residuals from the model, which reflects the deviation of the data (i.e., the observed frequencies) from the model (i.e., the expected frequencies) in each cell. Rather than looking at the raw residuals (which will vary simply depending on the number of observations in the data), it's more common to look at the standardized residuals (sometimes called Pearson residuals), which are computed as:

$$\text{standardized residual}_{ij} = \frac{\text{observed}_{ij} - \text{expected}_{ij}}{\sqrt{\text{expected}_{ij}}}$$

where i and j are the indices for the rows and columns respectively.

Table 12.4 shows these for the police stop data. These standardized residuals can be interpreted as Z scores - in this case, we see that the number of searches for Black individuals are substantially higher than expected based on independence, and the number of searches for white individuals are substantially lower than expected. This provides us with the context that we need to interpret the signficant chi-squared result.

12.5 Odds ratios

We can also represent the relative likelihood of different outcomes in the contingency table using the odds ratio that we introduced earlier, in order to better understand the magnitude of the effect. First, we represent the odds of being stopped for each race, then we compute their ratio:

$$\text{odds } s_{\text{searched} \mid \text{black}} = \frac{N_{\text{searched} \cap \text{black}}}{N_{\text{not searched} \cap \text{black}}} = \frac{1219}{36244} = 0.034$$

odds

$$\text{odds ratio} = \frac{N_{\text{searched} \mid \text{white}} = \frac{\text{odds}}{N_{\text{searched searched} \cap \text{white}}} = \frac{3108}{239241} = 0.013}{\text{odds}} = 2.59$$

odarched | white

The odds ratio shows that the odds of being searched are 2.59 times higher for Black versus white drivers, based on this dataset.

12.6 Bayes factor

We discussed Bayes factors in the earlier chapter on Bayesian statistics - you may remember that it represents the ratio of the likelihood of the data under each of the two hypotheses:

$$K = \frac{P(\text{ data } \mid H_A)}{P(\text{ data } \mid H_0)} = \frac{P(H_A \mid \text{ data }) * P(H_A)}{P(H_0 \mid \text{ data }) * P(H_0)}$$

We can compute the Bayes factor for the police search data using our statistical software:

```
## Bayes factor analysis

## --------------

## [1] Non-indep. (a=1) : 1.8e+142 ±0%

##

## Against denominator:

## Null, independence, a = 1

## ---
```

```
## Bayes factor type: BFcontingencyTable, independent multinomial
```

Table 12.5: Relationship between depression and sleep problems in the NHANES dataset

Depressed	NoSleepTrouble	YesSleepTrouble
None	2614	676
Several	418	249
Most	138	145

This shows that the evidence in favor of a relationship between driver race and police searches in this dataset is exceedingly strong $-1.8 * 10^{142}$ is about as close to infinity as we can imagine getting in statistics.

12.7 Categorical analysis beyond the 2 X 2 table

Categorical analysis can also be applied to contingency tables where there are more than two categories for each variable.

For example, let's look at the NHANES data and compare the variable *De* pressed which denotes the "self-reported number of days where the participant felt down, depressed or hopeless". This variable is coded as None, Several, or Most. Let's test whether this variable is related to the SleepTrouble variable which denotes whether the individual has reported sleeping problems to a doctor.

Simply by looking at these data, we can tell that it is likely that there is a relationship between the two variables; notably, while the total number of people with sleep trouble is much less than those without, for people who report being depresssed most days the number with sleep problems is greater than those without. We can quantify this directly using the chi-squared test:

```
##

## Pearson's Chi-squared test

##

## data: depressedSleepTroubleTable

## X-squared = 191, df = 2, p-value <2e-16
```

This test shows that there is a strong relationship between depression and sleep trouble. We can also compute the Bayes factor to quantify the strength of the evidence in favor of the alternative hypothesis:

```
## Bayes factor analysis
## --------------
## [1] Non-indep.(a=1) : 1.8e+35 ±0%
##
## Against denominator:
## Null, independence, a = 1
## ---
## Bayes factor type: BFcontingencyTable, joint multinomial
```

Here we see that the Bayes factor is very large ($1.8 * 10^{35}$), showing that the evidence in favor of a relation between depression and sleep problems is very strong.

12.8 Beware of Simpson's paradox

The contingency tables presented above represent summaries of large numbers of observations, but summaries can sometimes be misleading. Let's take an example from baseball. The table below shows the batting data (hits/at bats and batting average) for Derek Jeter and David Justice over the years 1995-1997:

Player	1995		1996		1997		Combined	
Derek Jeter	12/48	.250	183/582	.314	190/654	.291	385/1284	**.300**
David Justice	104/411	**.253**	45/140	**.321**	163/495	**.329**	312/1046	.298

Upon closer examination, one will observe that something unusual is occurring: In each individual year, Justice maintained a superior batting average compared to Jeter; but, when aggregating the data throughout the three years, Jeter's average ultimately surpasses that of Justice. This exemplifies a phenomena termed Simpson's paradox, when a trend observable in a consolidated dataset may be absent in its individual subsets. This transpires when an additional variable fluctuates among the various subsets; in this instance, the number of at-bats differs among years, with Justice having significantly more at-bats in 1995, a year characterized by low batting averages. This is referred to as a lurking variable, and it is crucial to remain vigilant for such variables when analyzing categorical data.

Chapter-13

Modeling Continuous Relationships

Modeling continuous relationships is a central task in statistics and data analysis, focusing on understanding how one or more continuous variables relate to another continuous outcome. Continuous variables can take an infinite number of values within a range, such as height, weight, temperature, or income, which allows for precise measurement and modeling. The primary goal in modeling these relationships is to quantify how changes in predictor variables influence the outcome variable, identify trends, and make predictions. Linear regression is one of the most commonly used techniques, providing a simple framework to model the relationship between a dependent variable and one or more independent variables. Beyond linear models, more complex approaches such as polynomial regression, spline regression, and generalized additive models can capture non-linear patterns. Correlation analysis helps to assess the strength and direction of linear associations, while scatterplots and other visualization tools aid in exploring relationships visually. Modeling continuous relationships is crucial in fields like economics, engineering, biology, and social sciences, where understanding how variables interact is key for decision-making and forecasting. Assumptions such as linearity, independence, homoscedasticity, and normality of residuals are important to ensure valid inferences. Multivariate techniques extend the analysis to multiple predictors, allowing for the assessment of combined effects and interactions. Advanced methods, including machine learning models like random forests or neural networks, can capture complex, high-dimensional relationships that traditional models may miss. Proper modeling requires careful consideration of outliers, measurement errors, and collinearity among predictors. Visualization, diagnostics, and model validation play a critical role in confirming the reliability and predictive performance of the models. Overall, modeling continuous relationships transforms numerical data into actionable insights, supporting hypothesis testing, prediction, and informed decision-making.

13.1 An illustration: Hate crimes and economic disparity

In 2017, the website Fivethirtyeight.com published an article titled "Higher Rates of Hate Crimes Are Tied to Income Inequality," which examined the correlation between the incidence of hate crimes and income disparity following the 2016 Presidential election.

The story reported an analysis of hate crime data from the FBI and the Southern Poverty Law Center, on the basis of which they report:

> *"we found that income inequality was the most significant determinant of population-adjusted hate crimes and hate incidents across the United States".*

The data for this research are accessible through the FiveThirtyEight package for the R statistical software, facilitating our access to them. The analysis presented in the narrative examined the correlation between income inequality, as measured by the Gini index (see to the Appendix for further details), and the incidence of hate crimes across each state.

13.2 Is income inequality related to hate crimes?

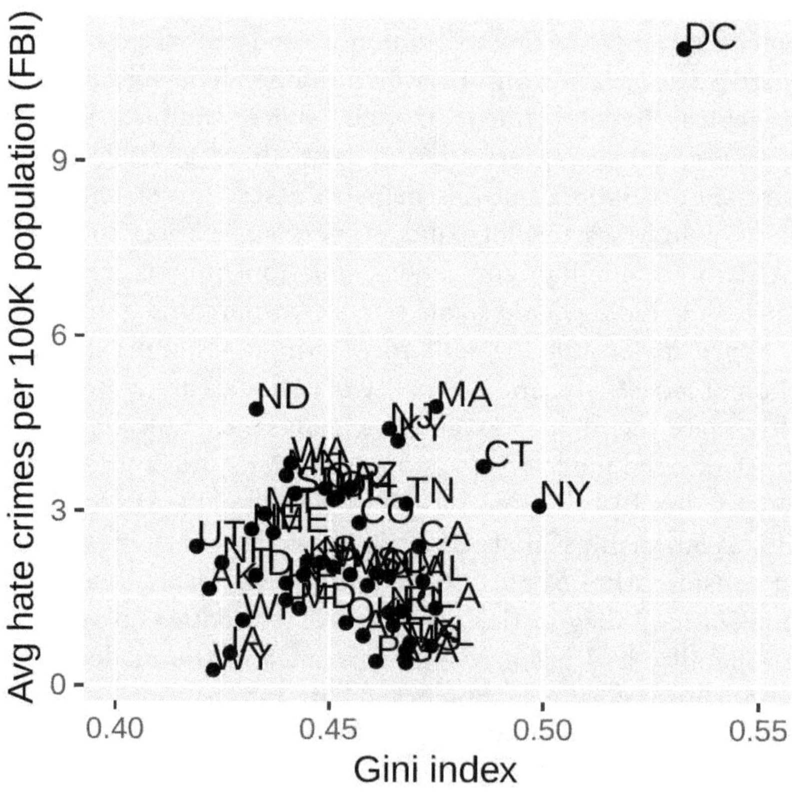

Figure 13.1: Plot of rates of hate crimes vs. Gini index.

The relationship between income inequality and rates of hate crimes is shown in Figure 13.1. Looking at the data, it seems that there may be a positive relationship between the two variables. How can we quantify that relationship?

Table 13.1: Data for toy example of covariance

x	y	y_dev	x_dev	crossproduct
3	5	-3.6	-4.6	16.56
5	4	-4.6	-2.6	11.96
8	7	-1.6	0.4	-0.64
10	10	1.4	2.4	3.36
12	17	8.4	4.4	36.96

13.3 Covariance and correlation

One way to quantify the relationship between two variables is the covariance. Remember that variance for a single variable is computed as the average squared difference between each data point and the mean:

$$s^2 = \frac{\sum_{i=1}^{n} (x_i - \bar{x})^2}{N - 1}$$

This tells us how far each observation is from the mean, on average, in squared units. Covariance tells us whether there is a relation between the deviations of two different variables across observations. It is defined as:

$$\text{covariance} = \frac{\sum_{i=1}^{n} (x_i - \bar{x})(y_i - \bar{y})}{N - 1}$$

This value will be far from zero when individual data points deviate by similar amounts from their respective means; if they are deviant in the same direction then the covariance is positive, whereas if they are deviant in opposite directions the covariance is negative. Let's look at a toy example first. The data are shown in Table 13.1, along with their individual deviations from the mean and their crossproducts.

The covariance is simply the mean of the crossproducts, which in this case is 17.05. We don't usually use the covariance to describe relationships between variables, because it varies with the overall level of variance in the data. Instead, we would usually use the correlation coefficient (often referred to as Pearson's correlation after the statistician Karl

Pearson). The correlation is computed by scaling the covariance by the standard deviations of the two variables:

$$r = \frac{\text{covariance}}{s_x s_y} = \frac{\sum_{i=1}^{n} (x_i - \bar{x})(y_i - \bar{y})}{(N-1)s_x s_y}$$

In this case, the value is 0.89 . The correlation coefficient is useful because it varies between - 1 and 1 regardless of the nature of the data - in fact, we already discussed the correlation coefficient earlier in our discussion of effect sizes. As we saw in that previous chapter, a correlation of 1 indicates a perfect linear relationship, a correlation of -1 indicates a perfect negative relationship, and a correlation of zero indicates no linear relationship.

13.3.1 Hypothesis testing for correlations

The correlation value of 0.42 between hate crimes and income inequality seems to indicate a reasonably strong relationship between the two, but we can also imagine that this could occur by chance even if there is no relationship. We can test the null hypothesis that the correlation is zero, using a simple equation that lets us convert a correlation value into a *t* statistic:

$$t_r = \frac{r\sqrt{N-2}}{\sqrt{1-r^2}}$$

Under the null hypothesis $H_0: r = 0$, this statistic is distributed as a t distribution with $N - 2$ degrees of freedom. We can compute this using our statistical software:

```
##

## Pearson's product-moment correlation

##

## data: hateCrimes$avg_hatecrimes_per_100k_fbi and
hateCrimes$gini_index

## t = 3, df = 48, p-value = 0.002

## alternative hypothesis: true correlation is not equal to 0

## 95 percent confidence interval:

## 0.16 0.63

## sample estimates:
```

```
## cor
## 0.42
```

This test shows that the likelihood of an r value this extreme or more is quite low under the null hypothesis, so we would reject the null hypothesis of $r = 0$. Note that this test assumes that both variables are normally distributed.

We could also test this by randomization, in which we repeatedly shuffle the values of one of the variables and compute the correlation, and then compare our observed correlation value to this null distribution to determine how likely our observed value would be under the null hypothesis. The results are shown in Figure 13.2. The p -value computed using randomization is reasonably similar to the answer given by the t -test.

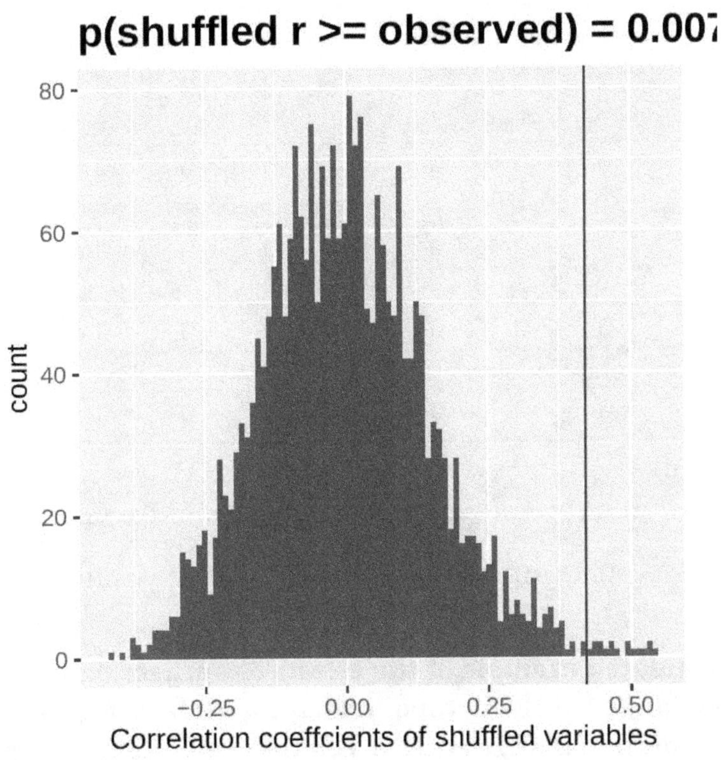

Figure 13.2: Histogram of correlation values under the null hypothesis, obtained by shuffling values. Observed value is denoted by blue line.

We could also use Bayesian inference to estimate the correlation; see the Appendix for more on this.

13.3.2 Robust correlations

You may have noticed something a bit odd in Figure 13.1 - one of the datapoints (the one for the District of Columbia) seemed to be quite separate from the others. We refer to this as an outlier, and the standard correlation coefficient is very sensitive to outliers. For example, in Figure 13.3 we can see how a single outlying data point can cause a very high positive correlation value, even when the actual relationship between the other data points is perfectly negative.

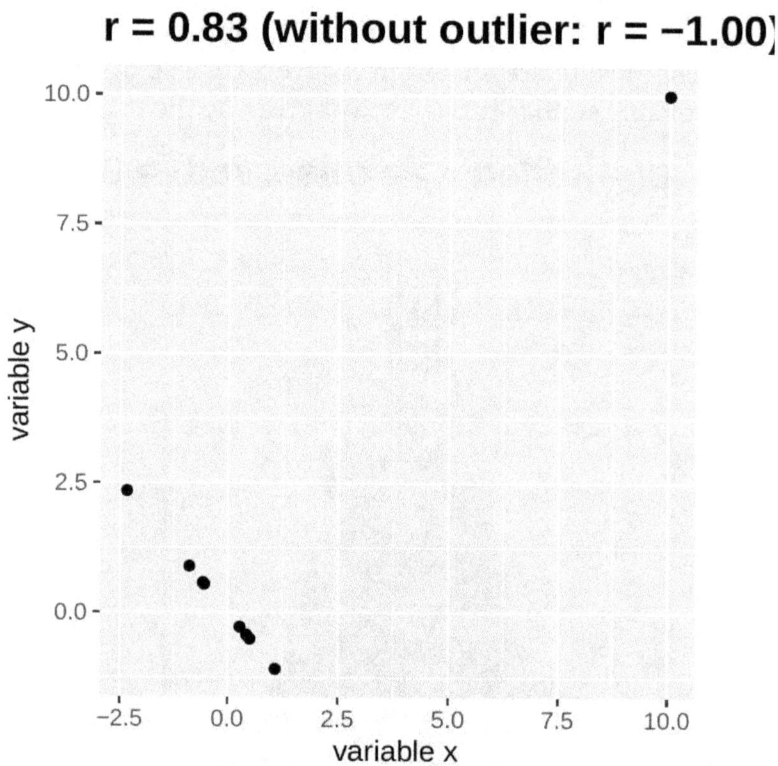

Figure 13.3: An simulated example of the effects of outliers on correlation. Without the outlier the remainder of the datapoints have a perfect negative correlation, but the single outlier changes the correlation value to highly positive.

One way to address outliers is to compute the correlation on the ranks of the data after ordering them, rather than on the data themselves; this is known as the Spearman correlation. Whereas the Pearson correlation for the example in Figure 13.3 was 0.83 , the Spearman correlation is -0.45 , showing that the rank correlation reduces the effect of the outlier and reflects the negative relationship between the majority of the data points.

We can compute the rank correlation on the hate crime data as well:

```
##
## Spearman's rank correlation rho
##
## data: hateCrimes$avg_hatecrimes_per_100k_fbi and
hateCrimes$gini_index
## S = 20146, p-value = 0.8
## alternative hypothesis: true rho is not equal to 0
## sample estimates:
## rho
## 0.033
```

Now we see that the correlation is no longer significant (and in fact is very near zero), suggesting that the claims of the FiveThirtyEight blog post may have been incorrect due to the effect of the outlier.

13.4 Correlation and causation

When we say that one thing causes another, what do we mean? There is a long history in philosophy of discussion about the meaning of causality, but in statistics one way that we commonly think of causation is in terms of experimental control. That is, if we think that factor X causes factor Y , then manipulating the value of X should also change the value of Y .

In medicine, there is a set of ideas known as Koch's postulates which have historically been used to determine whether a particular organism causes a disease. The basic idea is that the organism should be present in people with the disease, and not present in those without it - thus, a treatment that eliminates the organism should also eliminate the disease. Further, infecting someone with the organism should cause them to contract the disease. An example of this was seen in the work of Dr. Barry Marshall, who had a hypothesis that stomach ulcers were caused by a bacterium (Helicobacter pylori). To demonstrate this, he infected himself with the bacterium, and soon thereafter developed severe inflammation in his stomach. He then treated himself with an antibiotic, and his stomach soon recovered. He later won the Nobel Prize in Medicine for this work.

Often we would like to test causal hypotheses but we can't actually do an experiment, either because it's impossible ("What is the relationship between human carbon emissions and the earth's climate?") or unethical ("What are the effects of severe abuse on child brain development?"). However, we can still collect data that might be relevant to those questions. For example, we can potentially collect data from children who have been abused as well as those who have not, and we can then ask whether their brain development differs.

Let's say that we did such an analysis, and we found that abused children had poorer brain development than non-abused children. Would this demonstrate that abuse causes poorer brain development? No. Whenever we observe a statistical association between two variables, it is certainly possible that one of those two variables causes the other. However, it is also possible that both of the variables are being influenced by a third variable; in this example, it could be that child abuse is associated with family stress, which could also cause poorer brain development through less intellectual engagement, food stress, or many other possible avenues. The point is that a correlation between two variables generally tells us that something is probably causing somethign else, but it doesn't tell us what is causing what.

13.4.1 Causal graphs

One useful way to describe causal relations between variables is through a causal graph, which shows variables as circles and causal relations between them as arrows. For example, Figure 13.4 shows the causal relationships between study time and two variables that we think should be affected by it: exam grades and exam finishing times.

However, in reality the effects on finishing time and grades are not due directly to the amount of time spent studying, but rather to the amount of knowledge that the student gains by studying. We would usually say that knowledge is a latent variable - that is, we can't measure it directly but we can see it reflected in variables that we can measure (like grades and finishing times).

Here we would say that knowledge mediates the relationship between study time and grades/finishing times. That means that if we were able to hold knowledge constant (for example, by administering a drug that causes imme- diate forgetting), then the amount of study time should no longer have an effect on grades and finishing times.

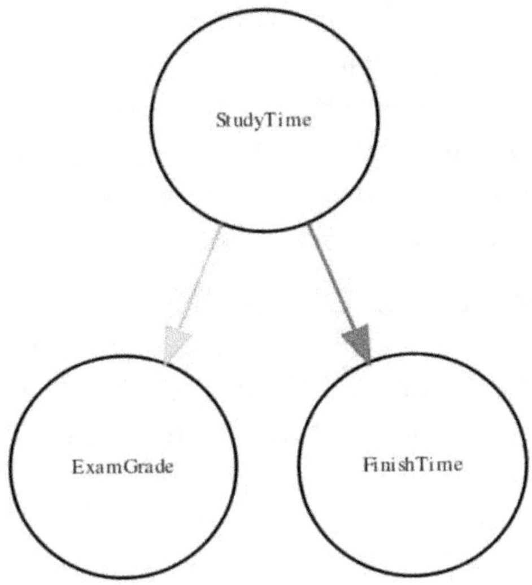

Figure 13.4: A graph showing causal relationships between three variables: study time, exam grades, and exam finishing time. A green arrow represents a positive relationship (i.e. more study time causes exam grades to increase), and a red arrow represents a negative relationship (i.e. more study time causes faster completion of the exam).

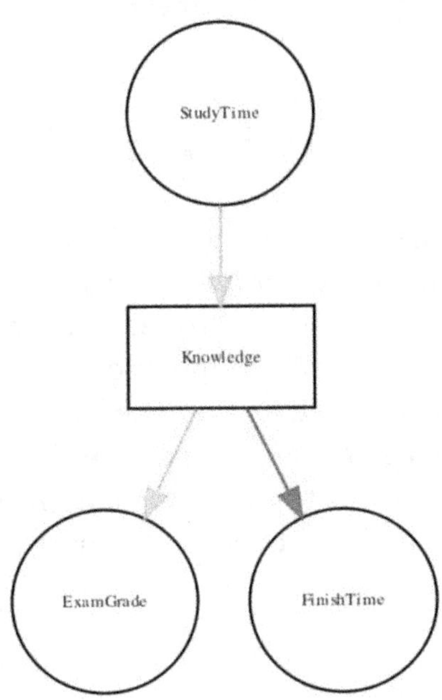

Figure 13.5: A graph showing the same causal relationships as above, but now also showing the latent variable (knowledge) using a square box.

It is important to observe that a mere assessment of exam scores and completion times would often reveal an inverse correlation, since those who complete exams more swiftly tend to achieve higher grades. Nevertheless, if we were to construe this association as a causative relationship, it would imply that to achieve superior grades, one should complete the examination more swiftly. This example illustrates the complexities involved in inferring causality from non-experimental data.

In the fields of statistics and machine learning, a vibrant research community is actively investigating the conditions and methodologies for inferring causal correlations from non-experimental data. Nevertheless, these methods frequently necessitate robust assumptions and should typically be employed with some caution.

13.5 Appendix:

13.5.1 Quantifying inequality: The Gini index

Before we look at the analysis reported in the story, it's first useful to understand how the Gini index is used to quantify inequality. The Gini index is usually defined in terms of a curve that describes the relation between income and the proportion of the population that has income at or less than that level, known as a Lorenz curve. However, another way to think of it is more intuitive: It is the relative mean absolute difference between incomes, divided by two:

$$G = \frac{\sum_{i=1}^{n} \sum_{j=1}^{n} \left| x_i - x_j \right|}{2n \sum_{i=1}^{n} x_i}$$

Figure 13.6 shows the Lorenz curves for several different income distributions. The top left panel (A) shows an example with 10 people where everyone has exactly the same income. The length of the intervals between points are equal, indicating each person earns an identical share of the total income in the population. The top right panel (B) shows an example where income is normally distributed. The bottom left panel shows an example with high inequality; everyone has equal income ($40,000) except for one person, who has income of $40,000,000. According to the US Census, the United States had a Gini index of 0.469 in 2010, falling roughly half way between our normally distributed and maximally inequal examples.

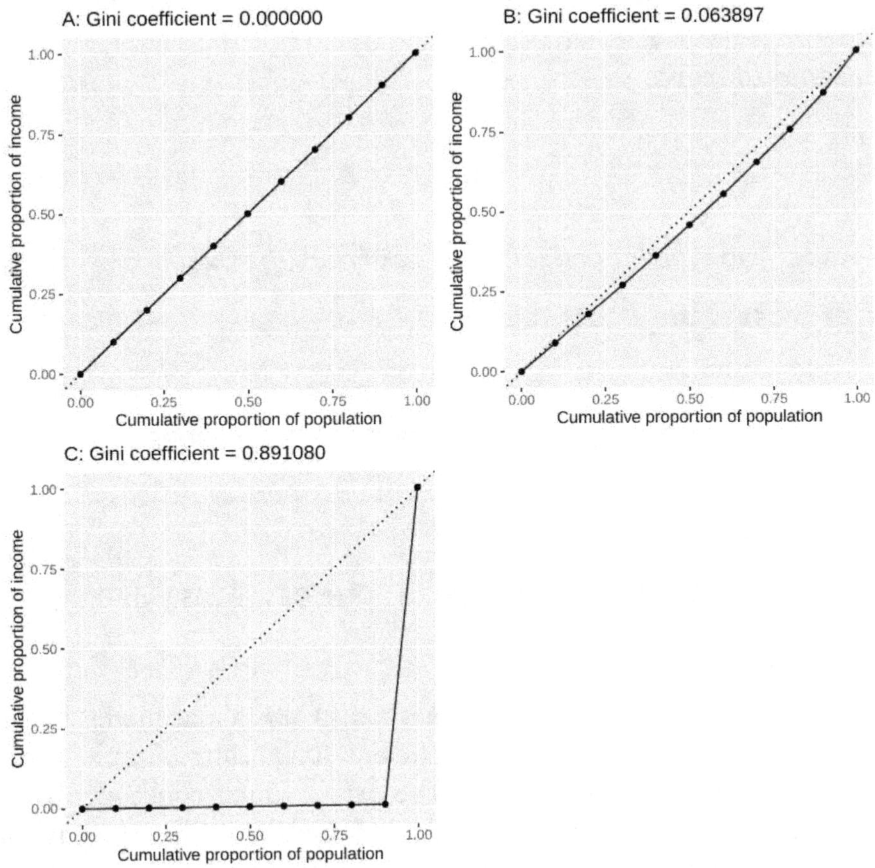

Figure 13.6: Lorenz curves for A) perfect equality, B) normally distributed income, and C) high inequality (equal income except for one very wealthy individual).

13.5.2 Bayesian correlation analysis

We can also analyze the FiveThirtyEight data using Bayesian analysis, which has two advantages. First, it provides us with a posterior probability - in this case, the probability that the correlation value exceeds zero. Second, the Bayesian estimate combines the observed evidence with a prior, which has the effect of regularizing the correlation estimate, effectively pulling it towards zero. Here we can compute it using BayesFactor package in R .

```
## Bayes factor analysis

## --------------

## [1] Alt., r=0.333 : 21 ±0%
```

```
##

## Against denominator:

## Null, rho = 0

## ---

## Bayes factor type: BFcorrelation, Jeffreys-beta*

## Summary of Posterior Distribution

##

## Parameter | Median | 95% CI | pd | ROPE | % in ROPE | BF |

## ----------------------------------------------------------------------
--------------------

## rho | 0.38 | [0.13, 0.58] | 99.88% | [-0.05, 0.05] | 0% | 20.85 | B
```

The correlation derived from the Bayesian method (0.38) is marginally lower than that obtained from the standard correlation coefficient (0.42), attributable to the estimate being influenced by both the evidence and the prior, which consequently reduces the estimate towards zero. Nonetheless, it is important to observe that the Bayesian analysis lacks robustness in the presence of the outlier, yet it still indicates substantial evidence that the correlation exceeds zero (with a Bayes factor exceeding 20).

Chapter-14

The General Linear Model

The General Linear Model (GLM) is a versatile and foundational framework in statistics that unifies many common techniques for analyzing relationships between variables. It models a continuous dependent variable as a linear combination of one or more independent variables, which can be continuous or categorical. The GLM extends simple and multiple linear regression to accommodate complex designs, including analysis of variance (ANOVA), analysis of covariance (ANCOVA), and regression with multiple predictors. At its core, the GLM assumes that the response variable can be expressed as a linear function of predictors plus an error term that is normally distributed with constant variance. This flexibility allows researchers to examine main effects, interactions, and covariate adjustments within a single coherent framework. By providing estimates of effect sizes, confidence intervals, and hypothesis tests, the GLM is widely used across fields such as psychology, medicine, economics, and social sciences. Its strength lies in its ability to model data efficiently, handle multiple predictors simultaneously, and provide interpretable results, making it a cornerstone of statistical modeling.

Remember that early in the book we described the basic model of statistics:

$$\text{data} = \text{model} + \text{error}$$

where our general goal is to find the model that minimizes the error, subject to some other constraints (such as keeping the model relatively simple so that we can generalize beyond our specific dataset). In this chapter we will focus on a particular implementation of this approach, which is known as the general linear model (or GLM). You have already seen the general linear model in the earlier chapter on Fitting Models to Data, where we modeled height in the NHANES dataset as a function of age; here we will provide a more general introduction to the concept of the GLM and its many uses. Nearly every model used in statistics can be framed in terms of the general linear model or an extension of it.

Before we discuss the general linear model, let's first define two terms that will be important for our discussion:

- dependent variable: This is the outcome variable that our model aims to explain (usually referred to as Y)

- independent variable: This is a variable that we wish to use in order to explain the dependent variable (usually referred to as X).

There may be multiple independent variables, but for this course we will focus primarily on situations where there is only one dependent variable in our analysis.

A general linear model is one in which the model for the dependent variable is composed of a linear combination of independent variables that are each multiplied by a weight (which is often referred to as the Greek letter betaβ), which determines the relative contribution of that independent variable to the model prediction.

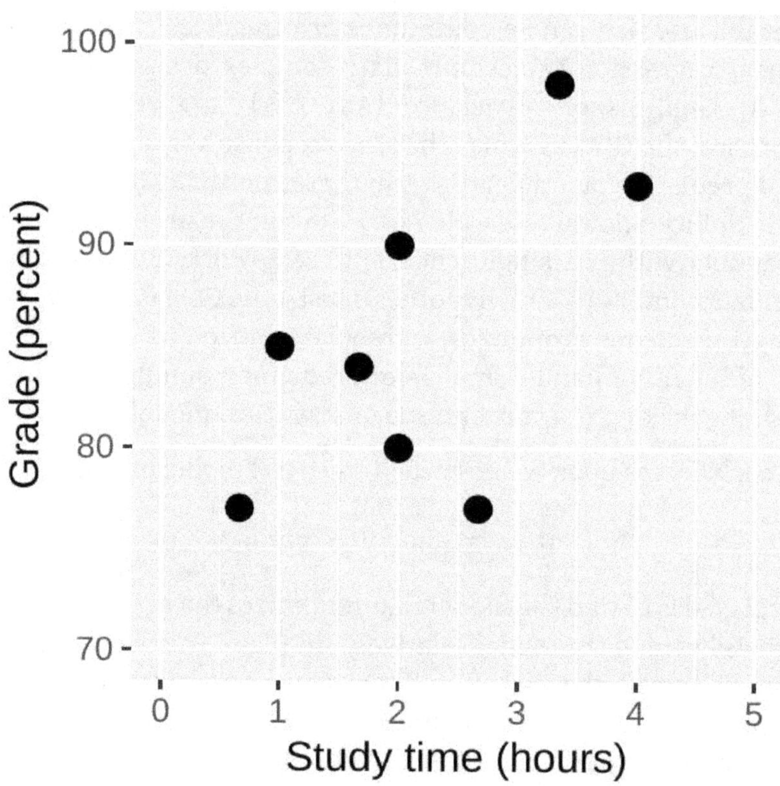

Figure 14.1: Relation between study time and grades

As an example, let's generate some simulated data for the relationship between study time and exam grades (see Figure 14.1). Given these data, we might want to engage in each of the three fundamental activities of statistics:

- Describe: How strong is the relationship between grade and study time?

- Decide: Is there a statistically significant relationship between grade and study time?
- Predict: Given a particular amount of study time, what grade do we expect?

In the previous chapter we learned how to describe the relationship between two variables using the correlation coefficient. Let's use our statistical software to compute that relationship for these data and test whether the correlation is significantly different from zero:

```
##
## Pearson's product-moment correlation
##
## data: df$grade and df$studyTime
## t = 2,df = 6,p-value = 0.09
## alternative hypothesis: true correlation is not equal to 0
## 95 percent confidence interval:
## -0.13 0.93
## sample estimates:
## cor
## 0.63
```

The correlation is quite high, but notice that the confidence interval around the estimate is very wide, spanning nearly the entire range from zero to one, which is due in part to the small sample size.

14.1 Linear regression

We can use the general linear model to describe the relation between two variables and to decide whether that relationship is statistically significant; in addition, the model allows us to predict the value of the dependent variable given some new value(s) of the independent variable(s). Most importantly, the general linear model will allow us to build models that incorporate multiple independent variables, whereas the correlation coefficient can only describe the relationship between two individual variables.

The specific version of the GLM that we use for this is referred to as as linear regression. The term regression was coined by Francis Galton, who had noted that when he compared parents and their children on some feature (such as height), the children of extreme parents (i.e. the very tall or very short parents) generally fell closer to the mean than did their parents. This is an extremely important point that we return to below.

The simplest version of the linear regression model (with a single independent variable) can be expressed as follows:

$$y = x * \beta_x + \beta_0 + \epsilon$$

The β_x value tells us how much we would expect y to change given a one-unit

change in x. The intercept β_0 is an overall offset, which tells us what value we would expect y to have when $x = 0$; you may remember from our early modeling discussion that this is important to model the overall magnitude of the data, even if x never actually attains a value of zero. The error term ϵ refers to whatever is left over once the model has been fit; we often refer to these as the residuals from the model. If we want to know how to predict y (which we call $\hat{y}$) after we estimate the β values, then we can drop the error term:

$$\hat{y} = x * \hat{\beta}_x + \hat{\beta}_0$$

Note that this is simply the equation for a line, where $\hat{\beta}_x$ is our estimate of the slope and $\hat{\beta}_0$ is the intercept. Figure 14.2 shows an example of this model applied to the study time data.

We will refrain from elaborating on the methodology for estimating the optimal slope and intercept from the data; for those interested, further information may be found in the Appendix.

14.1.1 Regression to the mean

The concept of regression to the mean was one of Galton's essential contributions to science, and it remains a critical point to understand when we interpret the results of experimental data analyses. Let's say that we want to study the effects of a reading intervention on the performance of poor readers. To test our hypothesis, we might go into a school and recruit those individuals in the bottom 25% of the distribution on some reading test, administer the intervention, and then examine their performance on the test after the intervention. Let's say that the intervention actually has no effect, such that reading scores for each individual are simply independent samples from a normal distribution. Results from a computer simulation of this hypothetic experiment are presented in Table 14.1.

If we look at the difference between the mean test performance at the first and second test, it appears that the intervention has helped these students substantially, as their scores have gone up by more than ten points on the test! However, we know that in fact the students didn't improve at all, since in both cases the scores were simply selected from a random normal distribution.

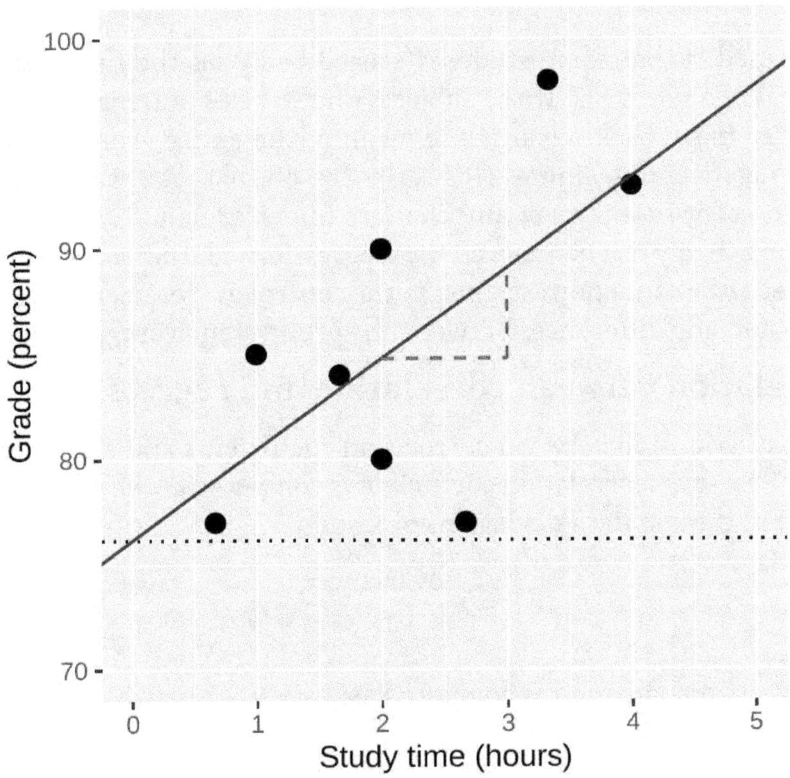

Figure 14.2: The linear regression solution for the study time data is shown in the solid line The value of the intercept is equivalent to the predicted value of the y variable when the x variable is equal to zero; this is shown with a dotted line. The value of beta is equal to the slope of the line - that is, how much *y* changes for a unit change in *x*. This is shown schematically in the dashed lines, which show the degree of increase in grade for a single unit increase in study time.

Table 14.1: Reading scores for Test 1 (which is lower, because it was the basis for selecting the students) and Test 2 (which is higher because it was not related to Test 1).

	Score
Test 1	88
Test 2	101

What has happened is that some students scored badly on the first test simply due to random chance. If we select just those subjects on the basis of their first test scores, they are guaranteed to move back towards the mean of the entire group on the second test, even if there is no effect of training. This is the reason that we always need an untreated control group in order to interpret any changes in performance due to an intervention; otherwise we are likely to be tricked by regression to the mean. In addition, the participants need to be randomly assigned to the control or treatment group, so that there won't be any systematic differences between the groups (on average).

14.1.2 The relation between correlation and regression

There is a close relationship between correlation coefficients and regression coefficients. Remember that Pearson's correlation coefficient is computed as the ratio of the covariance and the product of the standard deviations of x and y :

$$\hat{r} = \frac{\text{covariance}_{xy}}{s_x * s_y}$$

whereas the regression beta for x is computed as:

$$\hat{\beta}_x = \frac{\text{covariance}_{xy}}{s_x * s_x}$$

Based on these two equations, we can derive the relationship between $\hat{r}$ and bêta:

$$\text{covariance}_{xy} = \hat{r} * s_x * s_y$$

$$\hat{\beta}_x = \frac{\hat{r} * s_x * s_y}{s_x * s_x} = r * \frac{s_y}{s_x}$$

That is, the regression slope is equal to the correlation value multiplied by the ratio of standard deviations of y and x . One thing this tells us is that when the standard deviations of x and y are the same (e.g. when the data have been converted to Z scores), then the correlation estimate is equal to the regression slope estimate.

14.1.3 Standard errors for regression models

If we want to make inferences about the regression parameter estimates, then we also need an estimate of their variability. To compute this, we first need to compute the residual variance or error variance for the model - that is, how much variability in the dependent variable is not explained by the model. We can compute the model residuals as follows:

$$\text{residual } = y - \hat{y} = y - (x * \hat{\beta}_x + \hat{\beta}_0)$$

We then compute the sum of squared errors (SSE):

$$SS_{\text{error}} = \sum_{i=1}^{n} (y_i - \hat{y}_i)^2 = \sum_{i=1}^{n} \text{residuals}^2$$

and from this we compute the mean squared error:

$$MS_{\text{error}} = \frac{SS_{\text{error}}}{df} = \frac{\sum_{i=1}^{n} (y_i - \hat{y}_i)^2}{N - p}$$

where the degrees of freedom (df) are determined by subtracting the number of estimated parameters (2 in this case: $\hat{\beta}_x$ and $\hat{\beta}_0$) from the number of observations (N). Once we have the mean squared error, we can compute the standard error for the model as:

$$SE_{\text{model}} = \sqrt{MS_{\text{error}}}$$

In order to get the standard error for a specific regression parameter estimate, SE_{β_x}, we need to rescale the standard error of the model by the square root of the sum of squares of the X variable:

$$SE_{\hat{\beta}_x} = \frac{SE_{\text{model}}}{\sqrt{\sum (x_i - \bar{x})^2}}$$

14.1.4 Statistical tests for regression parameters

Once we have the parameter estimates and their standard errors, we can compute a t statistic to tell us the likelihood of the observed parameter estimates compared to some expected value under the null hypothesis. In this case we will test against the null hypothesis of no effect (i.e. $\beta = 0$):

$$t_{N-p} = \frac{\hat{\beta} - \beta_{\text{expected}}}{SE_{\hat{\beta}}}$$

$$t_{N-p} = \frac{\hat{\beta} - 0}{SE_{\hat{\beta}}}$$

$$t_{N-p} = \frac{\hat{\beta}}{SE_{\hat{\beta}}}$$

In general we would use statistical software to compute these rather than computing them by hand. Here are the results from the linear model function in R :

```
##
## Call:
## lm(formula = grade ~ studyTime, data = df)
##
## Residuals:

\begin{tabular}{lrrrrr}
\#\# & Min & 1Q & Median & 3Q & Max \\
\#\# & -10.656 & -2.719 & 0.125 & 4.703 & 7.469
\end{tabular}
##
## Coefficients:

\begin{tabular}{lrrrl}
```

```
\#\# & Estimate & Std. & Error t value & $\operatorname{Pr}(>|t|)$ & \\

\#\# & (Intercept) & 76.16 & 5.16 & 14.76 & $6.1 e-06$ \\

\#\# studyTime & 4.31 & 2.14 & 2.01 & 0.091 & .

\end{tabular}

## ---

## Signif. codes: 0 '***' 0.001 '**' 0.01 '*' 0.05 '.' 0.1 ' ' 1

##

## Residual standard error: 6.4 on 6 degrees of freedom

## Multiple R-squared: 0.403, Adjusted R-squared: 0.304

## F-statistic: 4.05 on 1 and 6 DF, p-value: 0.0907
```

In this case we see that the intercept is significantly different from zero (which is not very interesting) and that the effect of studyTime on grades is marginally significant ($p = .09$) - the same p -value as the correlation test that we performed earlier.

14.1.5 Assessing the model's goodness of fit

Sometimes it's useful to quantify how well the model fits the data overall, and one way to do this is to ask how much of the variability in the data is accounted for by the model. This is quantified using a value called R^2 (also known as the coefficient of determination). If there is only one x variable, then this is easy to compute by simply squaring the correlation coefficient:

$$R^2 = r^2$$

In the case of our study time example, $R^2 = 0.4$, which means that we have accounted for about 40% of the variance in grades.

More generally we can think of R^2 as a measure of the fraction of variance in the data that is accounted for by the model, which can be computed by breaking the variance into multiple components:

THIS IS CONFUSING, CHANGE TO RESIDUAL RATHER THAN ERROR

$$SS_{\text{total}} = SS_{\text{model}} + SS_{\text{error}}$$

where SS_{total} is the variance of the data (y) and SS_{model} and SS_{error} are computed as shown earlier in this chapter. Using this, we can then compute the coefficient of determination as:

$$R^2 = \frac{SS_{\text{model}}}{SS_{\text{total}}} = 1 - \frac{SS_{\text{error}}}{SS_{\text{total}}}$$

A small value of R^2 tells us that even if the model fit is statistically significant, it may only explain a small amount of information in the data.

14.2 Fitting more complex models

Often we would like to understand the effects of multiple variables on some particular outcome, and how they relate to one another. In the context of our study time example, let's say that we discovered that some of the students had previously taken a course on the topic. If we plot their grades (see Figure 14.3), we can see that those who had a prior course perform much better than those who had not, given the same amount of study time. We would like to build a statistical model that takes this into account, which we can do by extending the model that we built above:

$$\hat{y} = \hat{\beta}_1 * \text{studyTime} + \hat{\beta}_2 * \text{priorClass} + \hat{\beta}_0$$

To model whether each individual has had a previous class or not, we use what we call dummy coding in which we create a new variable that has a value of one to represent having had a class before, and zero otherwise. This means that for people who have had the class before, we will simply add the value of $\hat{\beta}_2$ to our predicted value for them - that is, using dummy coding $\hat{\beta}_2$ simply reflects the difference in means between the two groups. Our estimate of $\hat{\beta}_1$ reflects the regression slope over all of the data points - we are assuming that regression slope is the same regardless of whether someone has had a class before (see Figure 14.3).

```
##
## Call:
## lm(formula = grade ~ studyTime + priorClass, data = df)
##
```

```
## Residuals:

\begin{tabular}{lrrrrrrr}

\#\# & 1 & 2 & 3 & 4 & 5 & 6 & 7 & 8 \\

\#\# & 3.5833 & 0.7500 & -3.5833 & -0.0833 & 0.7500 & -6.4167 & 2.0833 &
2.9167

\end{tabular}

##

## Coefficients:

\begin{tabular}{|l|l|l|l|l|}

\hline \#\# & Estimate Std. & Error & t value & $\operatorname{Pr}(>|t|)$
\\

\hline \#\# (Intercept) & 70.08 & 3.77 & 18.60 & 8.3e-06 *** \\

\hline \#\# studyTime & 5.00 & 1.37 & 3.66 & 0.015 * \\

\hline \#\# priorClass1 & 9.17 & 2.88 & 3.18 & 0.024 * \\

\hline

\end{tabular}

## ---

## Signif. codes: 0 '***' 0.001 '**' 0.01 '*' 0.05 '.' 0.1 ' ' 1

##

## Residual standard error: 4 on 5 degrees of freedom

## Multiple R-squared: 0.803, Adjusted R-squared: 0.724

## F-statistic: 10.2 on 2 and 5 DF, p-value: 0.0173
```

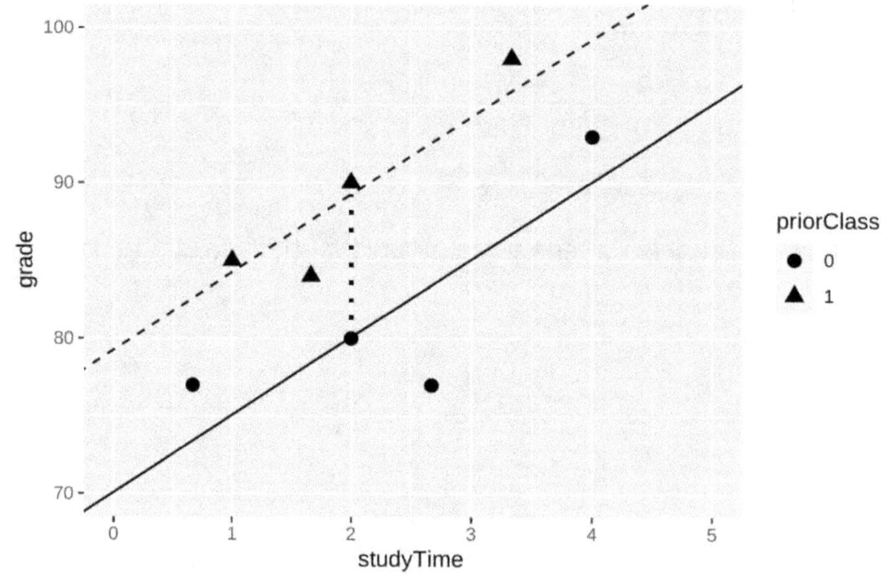

Figure 14.3: The relation between study time and grade including prior experience as an additional component in the model. The solid line relates study time to grades for students who have not had prior experience, and the dashed line relates grades to study time for students with prior experience. The dotted line corresponds to the difference in means between the two groups.

14.3 Interrelations among variables

In the prior model, we posited that the influence of study time on grades (i.e., the regression slope) was identical for both groups. In certain instances, we may conceive that the influence of one variable may vary based on the value of another variable, which we denote as an interaction between variables. Let's use a new example that asks the question: What is the effect of caffeine on public speaking? First let's generate some data and plot them. Looking at panel A of Figure 14.4, there doesn't seem to be a relationship, and we can confirm that by performing linear regression on the data:

```
##
## Call:
## lm(formula = speaking ~ caffeine, data = df)
##
## Residuals:
```

```
\begin{tabular}{lrrrr}
\#\# & Min & 1Q & Median & 3Q & Max \\
\#\# & -33.10 & -16.02 & 5.01 & 16.45 & 26.98
\end{tabular}
##
## Coefficients:

\begin{tabular}{lrrr}
\#\# & Estimate Std. Error t value & $\operatorname{Pr}(>|t|)$ \\
\#\# (Intercept) & -7.413 & 9.165 & -0.81 & 0.43 \\
\#\# caffeine & 0.168 & 0.151 & 1.11 & 0.28
\end{tabular}
##
## Residual standard error: 19 on 18 degrees of freedom
## Multiple R-squared: 0.0642, Adjusted R-squared: 0.0122
## F-statistic: 1.23 on 1 and 18 DF, p-value: 0.281
```

But now let's say that we find research suggesting that anxious and nonanxious people react differently to caffeine. First let's plot the data separately for anxious and non-anxious people.

As we see from panel B in Figure 14.4, it appears that the relationship between speaking and caffeine is different for the two groups, with caffeine improving performance for people without anxiety and degrading performance for those with anxiety. We'd like to create a statistical model that addresses this question. First let's see what happens if we just include anxiety in the model.

```
##
```

```
## Call:

## lm(formula = speaking ~ caffeine + anxiety, data = df)

##

## Residuals:


\begin{tabular}{rrrrrr}

\#\# & Min & 1Q & Median & 3Q & Max \\

\#\# & -32.97 & -9.74 & 1.35 & 10.53 & 25.36

\end{tabular}

##

## Coefficients:


\begin{tabular}{lrrrr}

\#\# & Estimate Std. Error t value & $\operatorname{Pr}(>|t|)$ \\

\#\# (Intercept) & -12.581 & 9.197 & -1.37 & 0.19 \\

\#\# caffeine & 0.131 & 0.145 & 0.91 & 0.38 \\

\#\# anxietynotAnxious & 14.233 & 8.232 & 1.73 & 0.10

\end{tabular}

##

## Residual standard error: 18 on 17 degrees of freedom

## Multiple R-squared: 0.204, Adjusted R-squared: 0.11

## F-statistic: 2.18 on 2 and 17 DF, p-value: 0.144
```

Here we see there are no significant effects of either caffeine or anxiety, which might seem a bit confusing. The problem is that this model is trying to use the same slope relating speaking to caffeine for both groups. If we want to fit them using lines with separate slopes, we need to include an interaction in the model, which is equivalent to fitting different lines for each of the two groups; this is often denoted by using the * symbol in the model.

```
##
## Call:
## lm(formula = speaking ~ caffeine + anxiety + caffeine * anxiety,
## data = df)
##
## Residuals:

\begin{tabular}{lrrrr}
\#\# & Min & 1Q & Median & 3Q \\
\#\# & -11.385 & -7.103 & -0.444 & 6.171 \\
Max
\end{tabular} 13.458
##
## Coefficients:

\begin{tabular}{lrrrr}
\#\# & Estimate Std. Error t value $\operatorname{Pr}(>|t|)$ & \\
\#\# (Intercept) & 17.4308 & 5.4301 & 3.21 & $0.00546 * *$ \\
\#\# caffeine & -0.4742 & 0.0966 & -4.91 & $0.00016 * * *$ \\
\#\# anxietynotAnxious & -43.4487 & 7.7914 & -5.58 & $4.2 \mathrm{e}-05
* * *$
\end{tabular}
```

```
## caffeine:anxietynotAnxious 1.0839 0.1293 8.38 3.0e-07 ***

## ---

## Signif. codes: 0 '***' 0.001 '**' 0.01 '*' 0.05 '.' 0.1 ' ' 1

##

## Residual standard error: 8.1 on 16 degrees of freedom

## Multiple R-squared: 0.852, Adjusted R-squared: 0.825

## F-statistic: 30.8 on 3 and 16 DF, p-value: 7.01e-07
```

From these results we see that there are significant effects of both caffeine and anxiety (which we call main effects) and an interaction between caffeine and anxiety. Panel C in Figure 14.4 shows the separate regression lines for each group.

One important point to note is that we have to be very careful about interpreting a significant main effect if a significant interaction is also present, since the interaction suggests that the main effect differs according to the values of another variable, and thus is not easily interpretable.

Sometimes we want to compare the relative fit of two different models, in order to determine which is a better model; we refer to this as model comparison. For the models above, we can compare the goodness of fit of the model with and without the interaction, using what is called an analysis of variance:

```
## Analysis of Variance Table

##

## Model 1: speaking ~ caffeine + anxiety

## Model 2: speaking ~ caffeine + anxiety + caffeine * anxiety

## Res.Df RSS Df Sum of Sq F Pr(>F)

## 1 17 5639

## 2 16 1046 1 4593 70.3 3e-07 ***

## ---

## Signif. codes: 0 '***' 0.001 '**' 0.01 '*' 0.05 '.' 0.1 ' ' 1
```

This tells us that there is good evidence to prefer the model with the interaction over the one without an interaction. Model comparison is relatively simple in this case because the two models are nested - one of the models is a simplified version of the other model, such that all of the variables in the simpler model are contained in the more complex model. Model comparison with non-nested models can get much more complicated.

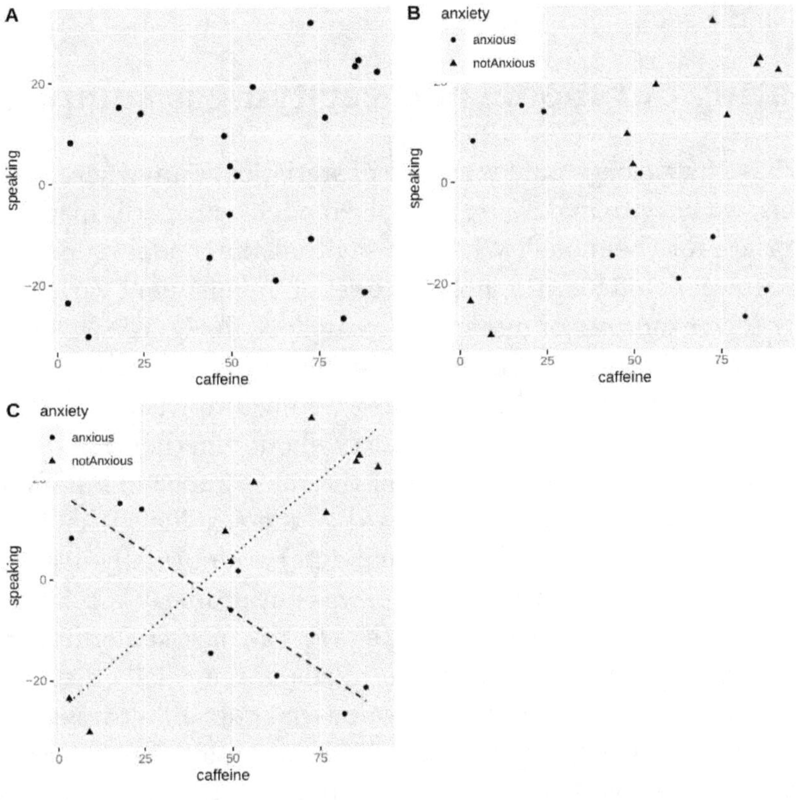

Figure 14.4: A: The relationship between caffeine and public speaking. B: The relationship between caffeine and public speaking, with anxiety represented by the shape of the data points. C: The relationship between public speaking and caffeine, including an interaction with anxiety. This results in two lines that separately model the slope for each group (dashed for anxious, dotted for non-anxious).

14.4 Transcending linear predictors and outcomes

It is essential to recognize that although it is termed the generic linear model, the same framework can be employed to represent effects that do not adhere to a linear trajectory, such as curves. The term "linear" in the general linear model pertains not to the form of the response but to the linearity concerning its parameters; specifically, the predictors in the model are multiplied by the parameters rather than exhibiting a nonlinear relationship, such as being raised to a power of the parameter. It is also prevalent to examine data with binary results instead of continuous ones, as discussed in the chapter on categorical outcomes. There are methods to modify the general linear model, referred to as generalized linear models, that facilitate this type of analysis. These models will be examined later in the book.

14.5 Evaluating our model and verifying assumptions

The saying "garbage in, garbage out" is as true of statistics as anywhere else. In the case of statistical models, we have to make sure that our model is properly specified and that our data are appropriate for the model. When we say that the model is "properly specified", we mean that we have included the appropriate set of independent variables in the model. We have already seen examples of mis specified models, in Figure 5.3. Remember that we saw several cases where the model failed to properly account for the data, such as failing to include an intercept. When building a model, we need to ensure that it includes all of the appropriate variables. We also need to worry about whether our model satisfies the assumptions of our statistical methods. One of the most important assumptions that we make when using the general linear model is that the residuals (that is, the difference between the model's predictions and the actual data) are normally distributed. This can fail for many reasons, either because the model was not properly specified or because the data that we are modeling are inappropriate. We can use something called a $Q - Q$ (quantile-quantile) plot to see whether our residuals are normally distributed. You have already encountered quantiles - they are the value that cuts off a particular proportion of a cumulative distribution. The Q-Q plot presents the quantiles of two distributions against one another; in this case, we will present the quantiles of the actual data against the quantiles of a normal distribution fit to the same data. Figure 14.5 shows examples of two such Q-Q plots. The left panel shows a Q-Q plot for data from a normal distribution, while the right panel shows a Q – Q plot from non-normal data. The data points in the right panel diverge substantially from the line, reflecting the fact that they are not normally distributed.

```
qq_df <- tibble(norm=rnorm(100),
        unif=runif(100))
p1 <- ggplot(qq_df,aes(sample=norm)) +
    geom_qq() +
```

```
    geom_qq_line() +
    ggtitle('Normal data')
p2 <- ggplot(qq_df,aes(sample=unif)) +
    geom_qq() +
    geom_qq_line()+
    ggtitle('Non-normal data')
plot_grid(p1,p2)
```

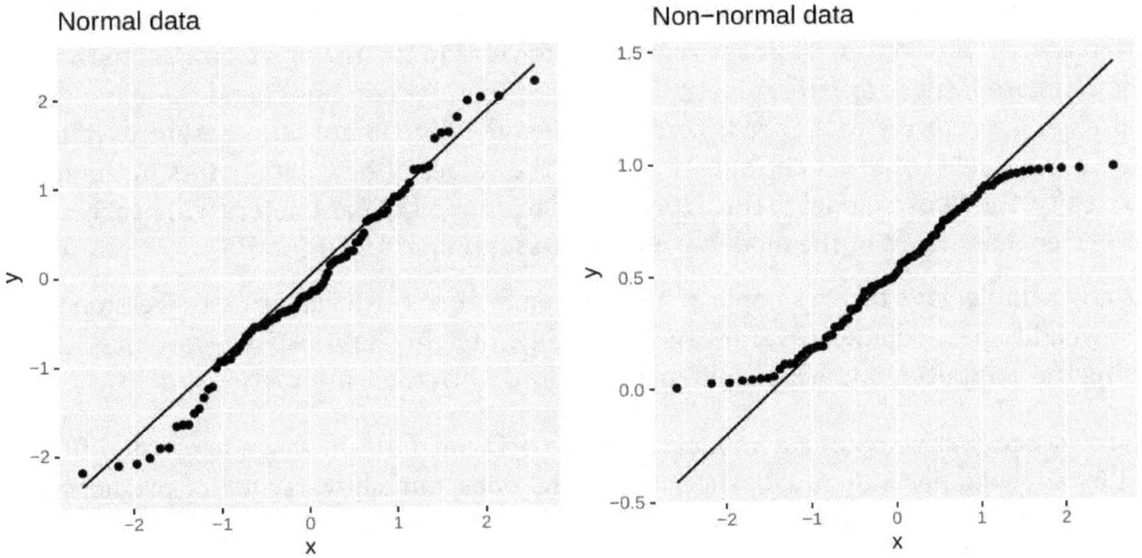

Figure 14.5: Q-Q plotsof normal (left) and non-normal (right) data. The line shows the point at which the x and y axes are equal.

Model diagnostics will be explored in more detail in a later chapter.

Table 14.2: Root mean squared error for model applied to original data and new data, and after shuffling the order of the y variable (in essence making the null hypothesis true)

Data type	RMSE (original data)	RMSE (new data)
True data	3.0	25
Shuffled data	7.8	59

14.6 Precise definition of "predict"

When we talk about "prediction" in daily life, we are generally referring to the ability to estimate the value of some variable in advance of seeing the data. However, the term is often used in the context of linear regression to refer to the fitting of a model to the data; the estimated values ($\hat{y}$) are sometimes referred to as "predictions" and the independent variables are referred to as "predictors". This has an unfortunate connotation, as it implies that our model should also be able to predict the values of new data points in the future. In reality, the fit of a model to the dataset used to obtain the parameters will nearly always be better than the fit of the model to a new dataset (Copas 1983).

As an example, let's take a sample of 48 children from NHANES and fit a regression model for weight that includes several regressors (age, height, hours spent watching TV and using the computer, and household income) along with their interactions.

Here we see that whereas the model fit on the original data showed a very good fit (only off by a few kg per individual), the same model does a much worse job of predicting the weight values for new children sampled from the same population (off by more than 25 kg per individual). This happens because the model that we specified is quite complex, since it includes not just each of the individual variables, but also all possible combinations of them (i.e. their interactions), resulting in a model with 32 parameters. Since this is almost as many coefficients as there are data points (i.e., the heights of 48 children), the model overfits the data, just like the complex polynomial curve in our initial example of overfitting in Section 5.4.

Another way to see the effects of overfitting is to look at what happens if we randomly shuffle the values of the weight variable (shown in the second row of the table). Randomly shuffling the value should make it impossible to predict weight from the other variables, because they should have no systematic relationship. The results in the table show that even when there is no true relationship to be modeled (because shuffling should have obliterated the relationship), the complex model still shows a very low error in its predictions on the fitted data, because it fits the noise in the specific dataset. However, when that model is applied to a new dataset, we see that the error is much larger, as it should be.

14.6.1 Cross-validation

One method that has been developed to help address the problem of overfitting is known as cross-validation. This technique is commonly used within the field of machine learning, which is focused on building models that will generalize well to new data, even when we don't have a new dataset to test the model. The idea behind cross-validation is that we fit our model repeatedly, each time leaving out a subset of the data, and then test the ability of the model to predict the values in each held-out subset.

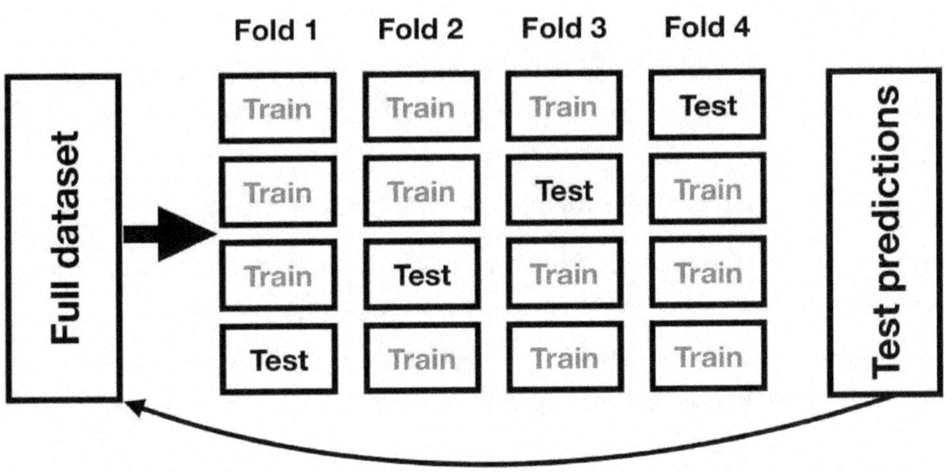

Figure 14.6: A schematic of the cross-validation procedure.

Let's see how that would work for our weight prediction example. In this case we will perform 12 -fold cross-validation, which means that we will break the data into 12 subsets, and then fit the model 12 times, in each case leaving out one of the subsets and then testing the model's ability to accurately predict the value of the dependent variable for those held-out data points. Most statistical software provides tools to apply cross-validation to one's data. Using this function we can run cross-validation on 100 samples from the NHANES dataset, and compute the RMSE for cross-validation, along with the RMSE for the original data and a new dataset, as we computed above.

Table 14.3: R-squared from cross-validation and new data, showing that cross-validation provides a reasonable estimate of the model's performance on new data.

	R-squared
Original data	0.95
New data	0.34
Cross-validation	0.60

Here we see that cross-validation gives us an estimate of predictive accuracy that is much closer to what we see with a completely new dataset than it is to the inflated accuracy that we see with the original dataset - in fact, it's even slightly more pessimistic than the average for a new dataset, probably because only part of the data are being used to train each of the models.

Note that using cross-validation properly is tricky, and it is recommended that you consult with an expert before using it in practice. However, this section has hopefully shown you three things:

- "Prediction" doesn't always mean what you think it means
- Complex models can overfit data very badly, such that one can observe seemingly good prediction even when there is no true signal to predict
- You should view claims about prediction accuracy very skeptically unless they have been done using the appropriate methods.

14.7 Appendix

14.7.1 Estimating linear regression parameters

We generally estimate the parameters of a linear model from data using linear algebra, which is the form of algebra that is applied to vectors and matrices. If you aren't familiar with linear algebra, don't worry - you won't actually need to use it here, as R will do all the work for us. However, a brief excursion in linear algebra can provide some insight into how the model parameters are estimated in practice.

First, let's introduce the idea of vectors and matrices; you've already encountered them in the context of R , but we will review them here. A matrix is a set of numbers that are arranged in a square or rectangle, such that there are one or more dimensions across which the matrix varies. It is customary to place different observation units (such as people) in the rows, and different variables in the columns. Let's take our study time data from above. We could arrange these numbers in a matrix, which would have eight rows (one for each student) and two columns (one for study time, and one for grade). If you are thinking "that sounds like a data frame in R " you are exactly right! In fact, a data frame is a specialized version of a matrix, and we can convert a data frame to a matrix using the as .matrix() function.

```
df <-
    tibble(
        studyTime = c(2, 3, 5, 6, 6, 8, 10, 12) / 3,
        priorClass = c(0, 1, 1, 0, 1, 0, 1, 0)
    ) %>%
    mutate(

        grade =
            studyTime * betas[1] +
            priorClass * betas[2] +
            round(rnorm(8, mean = 70, sd = 5))
    )
df_matrix <-
    df %>%
    dplyr::select(studyTime, grade) %>%
    as.matrix()
```

We can write the general linear model in linear algebra as follows:

$$Y = X * \beta + E$$

This looks very much like the earlier equation that we used, except that the letters are all capitalized, which is meant to express the fact that they are vectors.

We know that the grade data go into the Y matrix, but what goes into the X matrix? Remember from our initial discussion of linear regression that we need to add a constant in addition to our independent variable of interest, so our X matrix (which we call the design matrix) needs to include two columns: one representing the study time variable, and one column with the same value for each individual (which we generally fill with all ones). We can view the resulting design matrix graphically (see Figure 14.7).

The rules of matrix multiplication tell us that the dimensions of the matrices have to match with one another; in this case, the design matrix has dimensions of 8 (rows) X 2 (columns) and the Y variable has dimensions of 8 X 1 . Therefore, the β matrix needs to have dimensions 2 X 1 , since an 8 X 2 matrix multiplied by a 2×1 matrix results in an 8×1 matrix (as the matching middle dimensions drop out). The interpretation of the two values in the β matrix is that they are the values to be multipled by study time and 1 respectively to obtain the estimated grade for each individual. We can also view the linear model as a set of individual equations for each individual:

$\hat{y}_1 = \text{studyTime}_{\ 1} * \beta_1 + 1 * \beta_2$

$\hat{y}_2 = \text{studyTime}_{\ 2} * \beta_1 + 1 * \beta_2$

Independent variable		Design matrix		
0.67		77	1	
1.0		85	1	
1.67		84	1	
2.0	=	80		1
2.0		1		
2.67		77	1	
3.33		98	1	
4.0	93	1		

Figure 14.7: A depiction of the linear model for the study time data in terms of matrix algebra.

...

$\hat{y}_8 = \text{studyTime}_{\ 8} * \beta_1 + 1 * \beta_2$

Remember that our goal is to determine the best fitting values of β given the known values of X and Y. A naive way to do this would be to solve for β using simple algebra - here we drop the error term E because it's out of our control:

$$\hat{\beta} = \frac{Y}{X}$$

The challenge here is that X and β are now matrices, not single numbers but the rules of linear algebra tell us how to divide by a matrix, which is the same as multiplying by the inverse of the matrix (referred to as X^{-1}). We can do this in R :

```
# compute beta estimates using linear algebra

#create Y variable 8 x 1 matrix


Y <- as.matrix(df$grade)

    #create X variable 8 x 2 matrix

X <- matrix(0, nrow = 8, ncol = 2)

#assign studyTime values to first column in X matrix

X[, 1] <- as.matrix(df$studyTime)

#assign constant of 1 to second column in X matrix

X[, 2] <- 1

# compute inverse of X using ginv()

# %*% is the R matrix multiplication operator

beta_hat <- ginv(X) %*% Y #multiple the inverse of X by Y

print(beta_hat)

## [,1]

## [1,] 8.2

## [2,] 68.0
```

Individuals interested in the rigorous application of statistical methods are strongly urged to dedicate time to mastering linear algebra, as it underpins practically all instruments utilized in conventional statistics.

Chapter-15

Comparing Means

Comparing means is a fundamental aspect of statistical analysis that involves examining whether the average values of a variable differ across two or more groups. It is widely used in research to assess the effect of treatments, interventions, or categorical factors on a continuous outcome. For two groups, the independent samples t-test is commonly applied, testing whether the difference between group means is statistically significant. When comparing means across more than two groups, analysis of variance (ANOVA) is typically employed, partitioning the total variation in the data into between-group and within-group components. Post-hoc tests, such as Tukey's HSD or Bonferroni correction, are often used after ANOVA to identify specific group differences. Paired t-tests are used when the data consist of related measurements, such as before-and-after observations on the same subjects. Comparing means is not only important for hypothesis testing but also for estimating effect sizes and understanding the practical significance of differences. Assumptions such as normality of the outcome variable, homogeneity of variances, and independence of observations are critical for valid inferences. Modern extensions include Welch's t-test for unequal variances and robust statistical methods that reduce sensitivity to violations of assumptions. Visualization tools, like boxplots and error bar graphs, complement statistical tests by providing intuitive insights into group differences. Comparing means is widely applied in medicine, psychology, social sciences, education, and business to inform decisions, evaluate interventions, and guide policy.We have already encountered a number of cases where we wanted to ask questions about the mean of a sample. In this chapter, we will delve deeper into the various ways that we can compare means across groups.

15.1 Evaluating the worth of an individual mean

The simplest question we might want to ask of a mean is whether it has a specific value. Let's say that we want to test whether the mean diastolic blood pressure value in adults from the NHANES dataset is above 80 , which is cutoff for hypertension according to the American College of Cardiology. We take a sample of 200 adults in order to ask this question; each adult had their blood pressure measured three times, and we use the average of these for our test.

One simple way to test for this difference is using a test called the sign test, which asks whether the proportion of positive differences between the actual value and the hypothesized value is different than what we would expect by chance. To do this, we take the differences between each data point and the hypothesized mean value and compute their sign. If the data are normally distributed and the actual mean is equal to the hypothesized mean, then the proportion of values above the hypothesized mean (or below it) should be 0.5 , such that the proportion of positive differences should also be 0.5 . In our sample, we see that 19.0 percent of individuals have a diastolic blood pressure above 80 . We can then use a binomial test to ask whether this proportion of positive differences is greater than 0.5 , using the binomial testing function in our statistical software:

```
##

## Exact binomial test

##

## data: npos and nrow(NHANES_sample)

## number of successes = 38, number of trials = 200, p-value = 1

## alternative hypothesis: true probability of success is greater than
0.5

## 95 percent confidence interval:

## 0.15 1.00

## sample estimates:

## probability of success

## 0.19
```

Here we see that the proportion of individuals with positive signs is not very surprising under the null hypothesis of $p \leq 0.5$, which should not surprise us given that the observed value is actually less than 0.5 .

We can also ask this question using Student's t -test, which you have already encountered earlier in the book. We will refer to the mean as $\bar{X}$ and the hypothesized population mean as μ. Then, the t test for a single mean is:

$$t = \frac{\bar{X} - \mu}{SEM}$$

where SEM (as you may remember from the chapter on sampling) is defined as:

$$SEM = \frac{\hat{\sigma}}{\sqrt{n}}$$

In essence, the t statistic asks how large the deviation of the sample mean from the hypothesized quantity is with respect to the sampling variability of the mean.

We can compute this for the NHANES dataset using our statistical software:

```
##
## One Sample t-test


##
## data: NHANES_adult$BPDiaAve
## t = -55, df = 4593, p-value = 1
## alternative hypothesis: true mean is greater than 80
## 95 percent confidence interval:
## 69 Inf
## sample estimates:
## mean of x
## 70
```

This shows us that the mean diastolic blood pressure in the dataset (69.5) is actually much lower than 80 , so our test for whether it is above 80 is very far from significance.

Remember that a large p -value doesn't provide us with evidence in favor of the null hypothesis, since we had already assumed that the null hypothesis is true to start with.

However, as we discussed in the chapter on Bayesian analysis, we can use the Bayes factor to quantify evidence for or against the null hypothesis:

```
ttestBF(NHANES_sample$BPDiaAve, mu=80, nullInterval=c(-Inf, 80))

## Bayes factor analysis

## --------------

## [1] Alt., r=0.707 - Inf<d<80 : 2.7e+16 ±NA%

## [2] Alt., r=0.707 !(-Inf<d<80) : NaNe-Inf ±NA%

##

## Against denominator:

## Null, mu = 80

## ---

## Bayes factor type: BFoneSample, JZS
```

The first Bayes factor listed here ($2.73 * 10^{16}$) denotes the fact that there is exceedingly strong evidence in favor of the null hypothesis over the alternative.

15.2 Comparing two means

A more common question that often arises in statistics is whether there is a difference between the means of two different groups. Let's say that we would like to know whether regular marijuana smokers watch more television, which we can also ask using the NHANES dataset. We take a sample of 200 individuals from the dataset and test whether the number of hours of television watching per day is related to regular marijuana use. The left panel of Figure 15.1 shows these data using a violin plot.

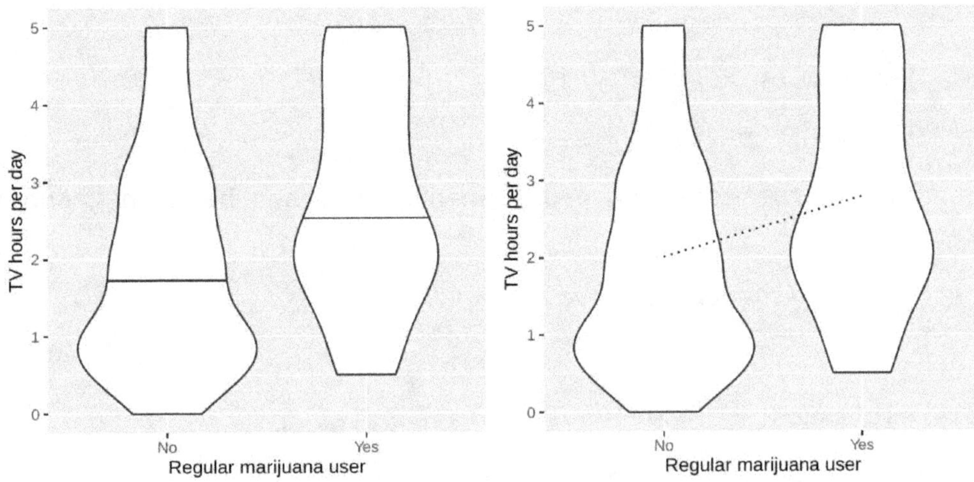

Figure 15.1: Left: Violin plot showing distributions of TV watching separated by regular marijuana use. Right: Violin plots showing data for each group, with a dotted line connecting the predicted values for each group, computed on the basis of the results of the linear model.

We can also use Student's t test to test for differences between two groups of independent observations (as we saw in an earlier chapter); we will turn later in the chapter to cases where the observations are not independent. As a reminder, the t -statistic for comparison of two independent groups is computed as:

$$t = \frac{\bar{X}_1 - \bar{X}_2}{\sqrt{\frac{S_1^2}{n_1} + \frac{S_2^2}{n_2}}}$$

where $\bar{X}_1$ and $\bar{X}_2$ are the means of the two groups, S_1^2 and S_2^2 are the variances for each of the groups, and n_1 and n_2 are the sizes of the two groups. Under the null hypothesis of no difference between means, this statistic is distributed according to a t distribution, with degrees of freedom computed using the Welch test (as discussed previously) since the number of individuals differs between the two groups. In this case, we started with the specific hypothesis that smoking marijuana is associated with greater TV watching, so we will use a one-tailed test. Here are the results from our statistical software:

```
##
## Welch Two Sample t-test
```

```
##
## data: TVHrsNum by RegularMarij
## t = -3, df = 85, p-value = 6e-04
## alternative hypothesis: true difference in means between group No and group Yes is
## 95 percent confidence interval:
## -Inf -0.39
## sample estimates:
## mean in group No mean in group Yes
## 2.0 2.8
```

In this case we see that there is a statistically significant difference between groups, in the expected direction - regular pot smokers watch more TV.

15.3 The t-test as a linear model

The t -test is often presented as a specialized tool for comparing means, but it can also be viewed as an application of the general linear model. In this case, the model would look like this:

$$\hat{TV} = \hat{\beta}_1 * \text{Marijuana} + \hat{\beta}_0$$

Since smoking is a binary variable, we treat it as a dummy variable like we discussed in the previous chapter, setting it to a value of 1 for smokers and zero for nonsmokers. In that case, $\hat{\beta}_1$ is simply the difference in means between the two groups, and $\hat{\beta}_0$ is the mean for the group that was coded as zero. We can fit this model using the general linear model function in our statistical software, and see that it gives the same t statistic as the t -test above, except that it's positive in this case because of the way that our software arranges the groups:

```
##
## Call:
```

```
## lm(formula = TVHrsNum ~ RegularMarij, data = NHANES_sample)
##
## Residuals:

\begin{tabular}{lrrrr}
\#\# & Min & 1Q & Median & 3Q & Max \\
\#\# & -2.2843 & -1.0067 & -0.0067 & 0.9933 & 2.9933
\end{tabular}
##
## Coefficients:

\begin{tabular}{lrrrr}
\#\# & Estimate Std. Error t value & $\operatorname{Pr}(>|t|)$ & \\
\#\# (Intercept) & 2.007 & 0.116 & 17.27 & $<2 e-16$ & $* * *$ \\
\#\# RegularMarijYes & 0.778 & 0.230 & 3.38 & 0.00087 & $* * *$
\end{tabular}
## ---
## Signif. codes: 0 '***' 0.001 '**' 0.01 '*' 0.05 '.' 0.1 ' ' 1
##
## Residual standard error: 1.4 on 198 degrees of freedom
## Multiple R-squared: 0.0546, Adjusted R-squared: 0.0498
## F-statistic: 11.4 on 1 and 198 DF, p-value: 0.000872
```

We can also view the linear model results graphically (see the right panel of Figure 15.1). In this case, the predicted value for nonsmokers is $\hat{\beta}_0(2.0)$ and the predicted value for smokers is $\hat{\beta}_0 + \hat{\beta}_1(2.8)$.

To calculate the standard errors for this study, we can employ the identical equations utilized for linear regression, as this is really another instance of linear regression. Indeed, a comparison of the p-value from the aforementioned t-test with the p-value derived from the linear regression analysis for the marijuana use variable reveals that the latter is precisely double the former, as the linear regression analysis conducts a two-tailed test.

15.3.1 Effect sizes for the comparison of two means

The most commonly used effect size for a comparison between two means is Cohen's d, which (as you may remember from Chapter 10) is an expression of the effect size in terms of standard deviation units. For the t -test estimated using the general linear model outlined above (i.e. with a single dummy-coded variable), this is expressed as:

$$d = \frac{\hat{\beta}_1}{\sigma_{\text{residual}}}$$

We can obtain these values from the analysis output above, giving us a $d = 0.55$, which we would generally interpret as a medium sized effect.

We can also compute R^2 for this analysis, which tells us what proportion of the variance in TV watching is accounted for by marijuana smoking. This value (which is reported at the bottom of the summary of the linear model analysis above) is 0.05 , which tells us that while the effect may be statistically significant, it accounts for relatively little of the variance in TV watching.

15.4 Bayes factor for discrepancies in means

As we discussed in the chapter on Bayesian analysis, Bayes factors provide a way to better quantify evidence in favor of or against the null hypothesis of no difference. We can perform that analysis on the same data:

```
## Bayes factor analysis

## --------------

## [1] Alt., r=0.707 0<d<Inf : 0.041 ±0%

## [2] Alt., r=0.707 !(0<d<Inf) : 61 ±0%
```

```
##
## Against denominator:
## Null, mu1-mu2 = 0
## ---
## Bayes factor type: BFindepSample, JZS
```

Because of the way that the data are organized, the second line shows us the relevant Bayes factor for this analysis, which is 61.4 . This shows us that the evidence against the null hypothesis is quite strong.

15.5 Contrasting paired observations

In experimental research, we often use within-subjects designs, in which we compare the same person on multiple measurements. The measurements that come from this kind of design are often referred to as repeated measures. For example, in the NHANES dataset blood pressure was measured three times. Let's say that we are interested in testing whether there is a difference in mean systolic blood pressure between the first and second measurement across individuals in our sample (Figure 15.2).

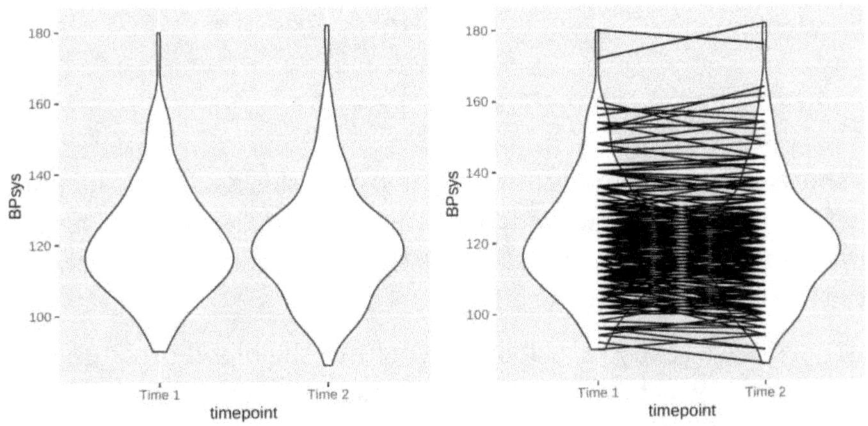

Figure 15.2: Left: Violin plot of systolic blood pressure on first and second recording, from NHANES. Right: Same violin plot with lines connecting the two data points for each individual.

We see that there does not seem to be much of a difference in mean blood pressure (about one point) between the first and second measurement. First let's test for a difference using an independent samples t-test, which ignores the fact that pairs of data points come from the the same individuals.

```
##

## Two Sample t-test

##

## data: BPsys by timepoint

## t = 0.6, df = 398, p-value = 0.5

## alternative hypothesis: true difference in means between group BPSys1 and

## 95 percent confidence interval:

## -2.1 4.1

## sample estimates:

## mean in group BPSys1 mean in group BPSys2


##
```

This analysis shows no significant difference. However, this analysis is inappropriate since it assumes that the two samples are independent, when in fact they are not, since the data come from the same individuals. We can plot the data with a line for each individual to show this (see the right panel in Figure 15.2).

In this analysis, what we really care about is whether the blood pressure for each person changed in a systematic way between the two measurements, so another way to represent the data is to compute the difference between the two timepoints for each individual, and then analyze these difference scores rather than analyzing the individual measurements. In Figure 15.3, we show a histogram of these difference scores, with a blue line denoting the mean difference.

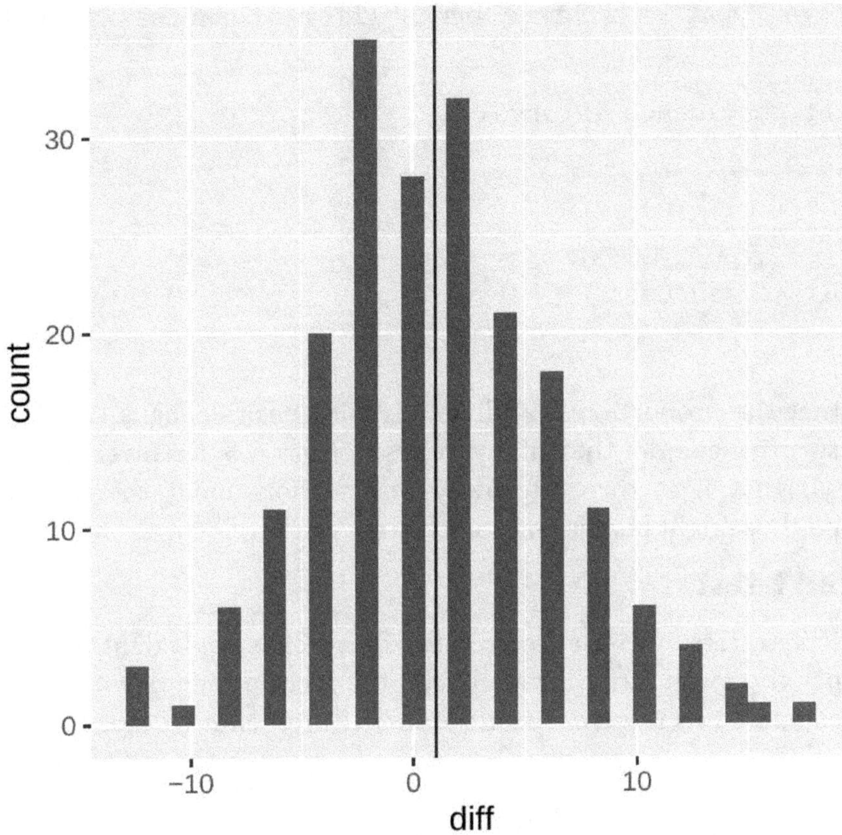

Figure 15.3: Histogram of difference scores between first and second BP measurement. The vertical line represents the mean difference in the sample.

15.5.1 Sign test

One simple way to test for differences is using the sign test. To do this, we take the differences and compute their sign, and then we use a binomial test to ask whether the proportion of positive signs differs from 0.5 .

```
##
## Exact binomial test
##
## data: npos and nrow(NHANES_sample)
## number of successes = 96, number of trials = 200, p-value = 0.6
```

```
## alternative hypothesis: true probability of success is not equal to
0.5

## 95 percent confidence interval:

## 0.41 0.55

## sample estimates:

## probability of success

## 0.48
```

Here we see that the proportion of individuals with positive signs (0.48) is not large enough to be surprising under the null hypothesis of $p = 0.5$. However, one problem with the sign test is that it is throwing away information about the magnitude of the differences, and thus might be missing something.

15.5.2 Paired t-test

A more common strategy is to use a paired t-test, which is equivalent to a one-sample t - test for whether the mean difference between the measurements within each person is zero. We can compute this using our statistical software, telling it that the data points are paired:

```
##

## Paired t-test

##

## data: BPsys by timepoint

## t = 3, df = 199, p-value = 0.007

## alternative hypothesis: true mean difference is not equal to 0

## 95 percent confidence interval:

## 0.29 1.75

## sample estimates:

## mean difference

## 1
```

With this analyses we see that there is in fact a significant difference between the two measurements. Let's compute the Bayes factor to see how much evidence is provided by the result:

```
## Bayes factor analysis

## --------------

## [1] Alt., r=0.707 : 3 ± 0.01%

##

## Against denominator:

## Null, mu = 0

## ---

## Bayes factor type: BFoneSample, JZS
```

The observed Bayes factor of 2.97 tells us that although the effect was significant in the paired t-test, it actually provides very weak evidence in favor of the alternative hypothesis.

The paired t-test can also be defined in terms of a linear model; see the Appendix for more details on this.

15.6 Comparative analysis of many means

Frequently, we seek to compare multiple methods to ascertain if any of them exhibit significant differences. We are examining data from a clinical trial for hypertension treatment. In the trial, participants are randomly assigned to one of three conditions: Drug 1, Drug 2, or a placebo. Let us produce data and create a plot (refer to Figure 15.4).

15.6.1 Analysis of variance

We would first like to test the null hypothesis that the means of all of the groups are equal - that is, neither of the treatments had any effect compared to placebo. We can do this using a method called analysis of variance (ANOVA). This is one of the most commonly used methods in psychological statistics, and we will only scratch the surface here. The basic idea behind ANOVA is one that we already discussed in the chapter on the general linear model, and in fact ANOVA is just a name for a specific version of such a model.

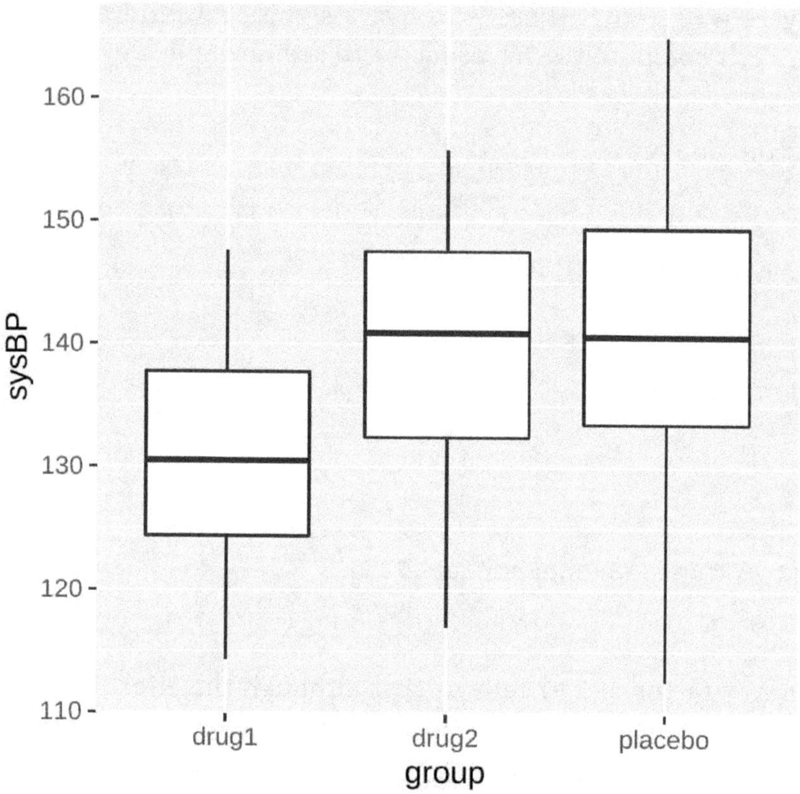

Figure 15.4: Box plots showing blood pressure for three different groups in our clinical trial.

Remember from the last chapter that we can partition the total variance in the data (SS_{total}) into the variance that is explained by the model (SS_{model}) and the variance that is not (SS_{error}). We can then compute a mean square for each of these by dividing them by their degrees of freedom; for the error this is $N - p$ (where p is the number of means that we have computed), and for the model this is $p - 1$:

$$
\begin{aligned}
MS_{\text{model}} &= \frac{SS_{\text{model}}}{df_{\text{model}}} = \frac{SS_{\text{model}}}{p-1} \\
MS_{\text{error}} &= \frac{SS_{\text{error}}}{df_{\text{error}}} = \frac{SS_{\text{error}}}{N-p}
\end{aligned}
$$

With ANOVA, we want to test whether the variance accounted for by the model is greater than what we would expect by chance, under the null hypothesis of no differences between means. Whereas for the t distribution the expected value is zero under the null hypothesis, that's not the case here, since sums of squares are always positive numbers. Fortunately, there is another theoretical distribution that describes how ratios of sums of squares are distributed under the null hypothesis: The *F* distribution (see figure 15.5). This distribution has two degrees of freedom, which correspond to the degrees of freedom for the numerator (which in this case is the model), and the denominator (which in this case is the error).

To create an ANOVA model, we extend the idea of dummy coding that you encountered in the last chapter. Remember that for the t -test comparing two means, we created a single dummy variable that took the value of 1 for one of the conditions and zero for the others. Here we extend that idea by creating two dummy variables, one that codes for the Drug 1 condition and the other that codes for the Drug 2 condition. Just as in the t -test, we will have one condition (in this case, placebo) that doesn't have a dummy variable, and thus represents the baseline against which the others are compared; its mean defines the intercept of the model. Using dummy coding for drugs 1 and 2, we can fit a model using the same approach that we used in the previous chapter:

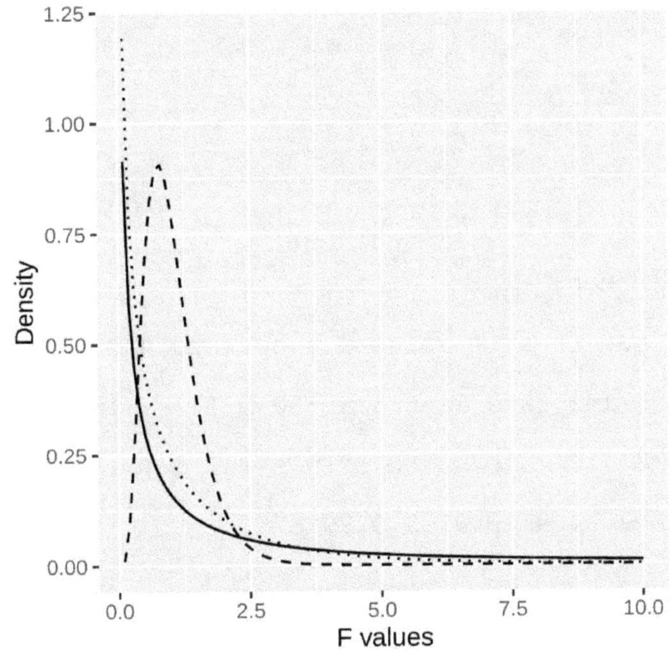

Figure 15.5: F distributions under the null hypothesis, for different values of degrees of freedom.

```
##

## Call:

## lm(formula = sysBP ~ d1 + d2, data = df)


##

## Residuals:


\begin{tabular}{lrrrr}

\#\# & Min & 1Q & Median & 3Q & Max \\

\#\# & -29.084 & -7.745 & -0.098 & 7.687 & 23.431

\end{tabular}

##

## Coefficients:


\begin{tabular}{lrrrr}

\#\# & Estimate Std. Error t value & $\operatorname{Pr}(>|t|)$ & \\

\#\# (Intercept) & 141.60 & 1.66 & 85.50 & $<2 e-16$ & $* * *$ \\

\#\# d1 & -10.24 & 2.34 & -4.37 & $2.9 e-05$ & $* * *$ \\

\#\# d2 & -2.03 & 2.34 & -0.87 & 0.39 &

\end{tabular}

## ---

## Signif. codes: 0 '***' 0.001 '**' 0.01 '*' 0.05 '.' 0.1 ' ' 1

##

## Residual standard error: 9.9 on 105 degrees of freedom

## Multiple R-squared: 0.169, Adjusted R-squared: 0.154
```

```
## F-statistic: 10.7 on 2 and 105 DF, p-value: 5.83e-05
```

This command's output yields two results. The results of a t-test for each dummy variable indicate whether each condition significantly differs from the placebo; Drug 1 shows a significant difference, but Drug 2 does not. It is important to note that interpreting these tests necessitates the adjustment of p-values to accommodate the many hypothesis tests conducted; an example of this process will be presented in the subsequent chapter.

The initial hypothesis we aimed to test was if any differences existed among the circumstances; this is termed an omnibus hypothesis test, which is assessed using the F statistic. The F statistic essentially indicates whether our model outperforms a basic model that solely incorporates an intercept. The F test in this instance is extremely significant, corroborating our observation of differences among the groups, which we are aware of since we generated the data.

15.7 Appendix

15.7.1 The paired t-test as a linear model

We can also define the paired t -test in terms of a general linear model. To do this, we include all of the measurements for each subject as data points (within a tidy data frame). We then include in the model a variable that codes for the identity of each individual (in this case, the ID variable that contains a subject ID for each person). This is known as a mixed model, since it includes effects of independent variables as well as effects of individuals. The standard model fitting procedure lm() can't do this, but we can do it using the lmer() function from a popular R package called lme4, which is specialized for estimating mixed models. The (1 | ID) in the formula tells lmer() to estimate a separate intercept (which is what the 1 refers to) for each value of the ID variable (i.e. for each individual in the dataset), and then estimate a common slope relating timepoint to BP.

```
# compute mixed model for paired test

lmrResult <- lmer(BPsys ~ timepoint + (1 | ID),

        data = NHANES_sample_tidy)

summary(lmrResult)

## Linear mixed model fit by REML. t-tests use Satterthwaite's method [

## lmerModLmerTest]

## Formula: BPsys ~ timepoint + (1 | ID)
```

```
## Data: NHANES_sample_tidy
##
## REML criterion at convergence: 2895
##
```

15.8. APPENDIX261

```
\#\# Scaled residuals:

\begin{tabular}{lrrrrr}
\#\# & Min & 1Q & Median & 3Q & Max \\
\#\# & -2.3843 & -0.4808 & 0.0076 & 0.4221 & 2.1718
\end{tabular}
##
## Random effects:
## Groups Name Variance Std.Dev.
## ID (Intercept) 236.1 15.37
## Residual 13.9 3.73
## Number of obs: 400, groups: ID, 200
##
## Fixed effects:

\begin{tabular}{lrrrrr}
\#\# & Estimate & Std. & Error & df t value & $\operatorname{Pr}(>|\mathrm{t}|)$ & \\
\#\# (Intercept) & 121.370 & & 1.118 & 210.361 & 108.55 & $<2 \mathrm{e}-16$
```

```
\end{tabular}$* * *$
## ---
## Signif. codes: 0 '***' 0.001 '**' 0.01 '*' 0.05 '.' 0.1 ' ' 1
##
## Correlation of Fixed Effects:
## (Intr)
## tmpntBPSys2 -0.167
```

This indicates a p-value that closely aligns with the outcome derived from the paired t-test executed via the t.test() function.

Chapter-16

Multivariate Statistics

Multivariate statistics is a branch of statistics that deals with the analysis of data involving two or more variables simultaneously. Unlike univariate or bivariate analysis, which focus on one or two variables at a time, multivariate techniques allow researchers to understand complex relationships, interactions, and patterns among multiple variables. These methods are essential when variables are interrelated, as they account for correlations and dependencies that might otherwise confound results. Common multivariate techniques include multiple regression, multivariate analysis of variance (MANOVA), principal component analysis (PCA), factor analysis, canonical correlation, and cluster analysis. Multivariate statistics enables dimension reduction, pattern recognition, prediction, and classification, making it widely applicable in fields such as psychology, economics, biology, marketing, and social sciences. It also facilitates the modeling of multiple outcomes simultaneously, improving efficiency and interpretability. Proper application of multivariate methods requires careful attention to assumptions, such as multivariate normality, linearity, homoscedasticity, and independence of observations. Visualization techniques, such as scatterplot matrices, biplots, and heatmaps, help interpret complex multivariate relationships. By capturing the interdependencies among variables, multivariate statistics provides a richer and more comprehensive understanding of data, supporting informed decision-making, hypothesis testing, and predictive modeling.

The term multivariate denotes analyses that encompass many random variables. In prior instances where the model incorporated multiple variables, such as in linear regression, our focus was on elucidating how the variation in a dependent variable could be accounted for by one or more independent variables, typically designated by the experimenter rather than empirically measured. In multivariate analysis, all variables are often regarded as equal, and the objective is to comprehend their interrelationships as a collective entity.

This chapter will concentrate on two principal techniques to multivariate analysis among the various types available. Initially, we want to comprehend and illustrate the structure inherent in the data, namely identifying the relationships among various variables or observations. We often define "related" based on a metric that quantifies the distance between values across variables. A significant technique under this area is referred to as clustering, which seeks to identify groups of variables or observations that exhibit similarity across variables.

Secondly, we may want to condense a multitude of variables into a fewer number while preserving maximal information. This process is known as dimensionality reduction, in which "dimensionality" denotes the quantity of variables inside the dataset. We will examine two techniques frequently employed for dimensionality reduction: principal component analysis and factor analysis.

Clustering and dimensionality reduction are typically categorized as types of unsupervised learning, in contrast to supervised learning shown by models like as linear regression that you have studied thus far. Linear regression is deemed "supervised" since the value of the dependent variable, which we aim to predict, is known, and we seek to identify the model that most accurately forecasts these values. In unsupervised learning, there is no precise value to forecast; rather, the objective is to uncover patterns within the data that may enhance comprehension, necessitating certain assumptions regarding the desired structure to identify.

This chapter reveals that, while supervised learning typically has a definitive "correct" response (once a criterion for the "optimal" model, such as the sum of squared errors, is established), unsupervised learning frequently lacks a universally accepted "correct" solution. Various unsupervised learning techniques can yield markedly divergent results from identical data, and there is typically no definitive means to ascertain which outcome is "correct," as it is contingent upon the analytical objectives and the assumptions one is prepared to accept regarding the underlying mechanisms of the data. Some individuals perceive this as annoying, while others consider it invigorating; it is your responsibility to determine which perspective you align with.

16.1 Illustration of multivariate data

We will examine a dataset gathered by my group and published by Eisenberg et al. as an illustration of multivariate analysis. This dataset is valuable due to its extensive array of intriguing factors gathered from a considerable sample of individuals, and its availability online for independent exploration.

This study was conducted to elucidate the interrelations among many facets of psychological functioning, with a special emphasis on psychological metrics of self-control and associated constructs. Participants engaged in a ten-hour series of cognitive assessments and surveys during a week; this initial example will concentrate on factors pertaining to two particular dimensions of self-control. Response inhibition is characterized as the capacity to promptly cease an action, and in this study, it was assessed by a series of activities referred to as stop-signal tasks. The variable of relevance for these tasks is the estimation of the duration required for an individual to inhibit a response, referred to as the stop-signal reaction time (SSRT), which is represented by four distinct measures in the dataset. Impulsivity is characterized by the inclination to make judgments spontaneously, disregarding probable repercussions and long-term objectives. The study encompassed various surveys evaluating impulsivity; however, we will concentrate on the UPPS-P survey, which measures five distinct dimensions of impulsivity.

Upon calculating these scores for each of the 522 individuals in Eisenberg's study, we obtain 9 numerical values for each individual. Although multivariate data may encompass dozens or even millions of factors, it is beneficial to initially examine the methodologies using a limited number of variables.

16.2 Visualizing multivariate datasets

A fundamental challenge of multivariate data is that the human eye and brain are simply not equipped to visualize data with more than three dimensions. There are various tools that we can use to try to visualize multivariate data, but all of them break down as the number of variables grows. Once the number of variables becomes too large to directly visualize, one approach is to first reduce the number of dimensions (as discussed further below), and then visualize that reduced dataset.

16.2.1 Scatterplot of matrices

One useful way to visualize a small number of variables is to plot each pair of variables against one another, sometimes known as a "scatterplot of matrices"; An example is shown in Figure 16.1. Each row/column in the panel refers to a single variable - in this case one of our psychological variables from the earlier example. The diagonal elements on the plot show the distribution of each variable as a histogram. The elements below the diagonal show a scatterplot for each pair of matrices, overlaid with a regression line describing the relationship between the variables. The elements above the diagonal show the correlation coefficient for each pair of variables. When the number of variables is relatively small (about 10 or less) this can be a useful way to get good insight into a multivariate dataset.

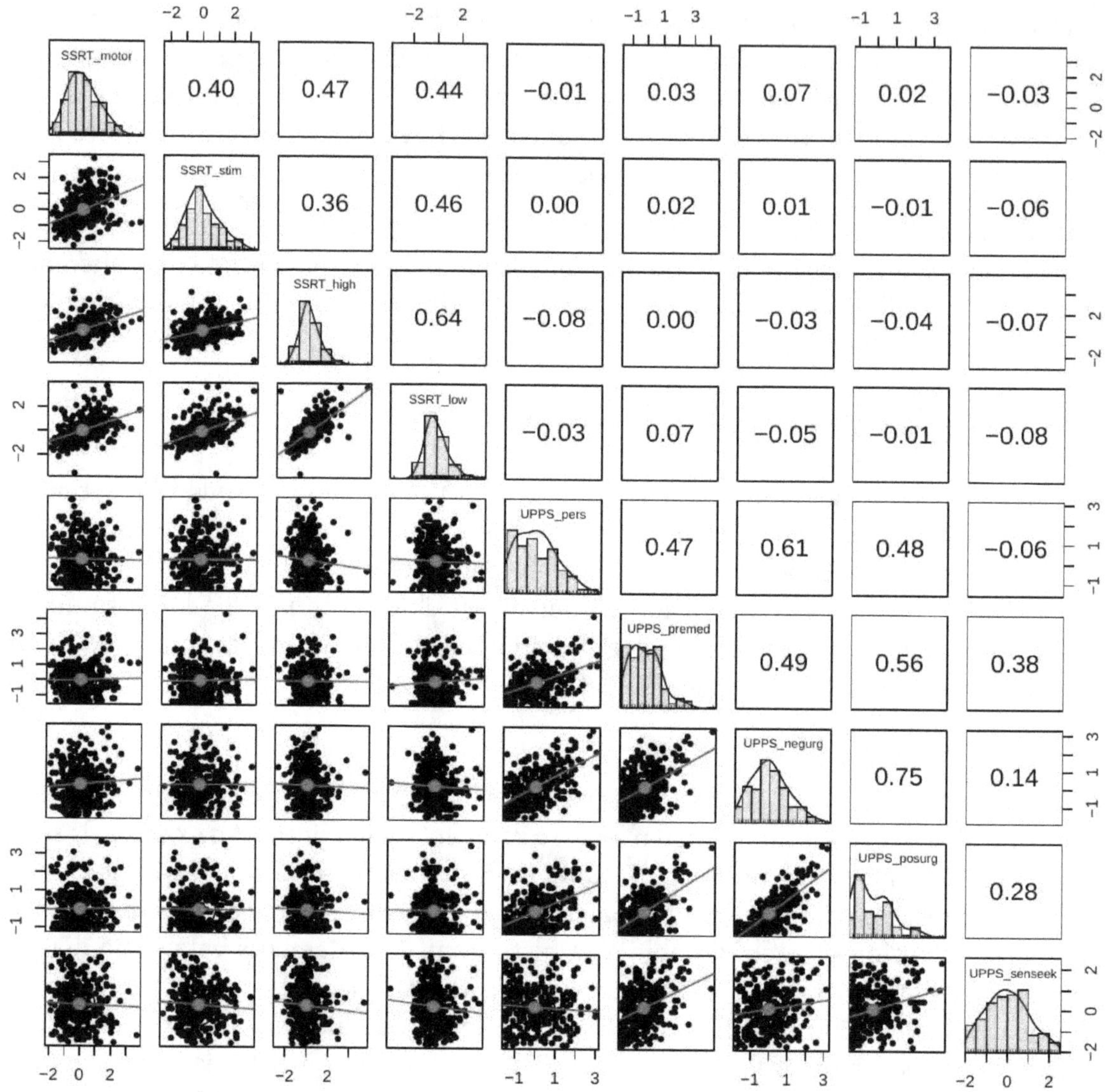

Figure 16.1: Scatterplot of matrices for the nine variables in the self-control dataset. The diagonal elements in the matrix show the histogram for each of the individual variables. The lower left panels show scatterplots of the relationship between each pair of variables, and the upper right panel shows the correlation coefficient for each pair of variables.

16.2.2 Heatmap

In some cases we wish to visualize the relationships between a large number of variables at once, usually focusing on the correlation coefficient. A useful way to do this can be to plot the correlation values as a heatmap, in which the color of the map relates to the value of the correlation. Figure 16.2 shows an example with a relatively small number of variables, using our psychological example from above. In this case, the heatmap helps the structure of the data "pop out" at us; we see that there are strong intercorrelations within the SSRT variables and within the UPPS variables, with relatively little correlation between the two sets of variables.

Heatmaps become particularly useful for visualizing correlations between large numbers of variables. We can use brain imaging data as an example. It is common for neuroscience researchers to collect data about brain function from a large number of locations in the brain using functional magnetic resonance imaging (fMRI), and then to assess the correlation between those locations, to measure "function connectivity" between the regions. For example, Figure 16.3 shows a heatmap for a large correlation matrix, based on activity in over 300 regions in the brain of a single individual (yours truly). The presence of clear structure in the data pops out simply by looking at the heatmap. In particular we see that there are large sets of brain regions whose activity is highly correlated with each other (visible in the large yellow blocks along the diagonal of the correlation matrix), whereas these blocks are also strongly negatively correlated with other blocks (visible in the large blue blocks seen off the diagonal). Heatmaps are a powerful tool for easily visualizing large data matrices.

16.3 Clustering

Clustering refers to a set of methods for identifying groups of related observations or variables within a dataset, based on the similarity of the values of the observations. Usually this similarity will be quantified in terms of some measure of the distance between multivariate values. The clustering method then finds the set of groups that have the lowest distance between their members.

One commonly used measure of distance for clustering is the Euclidean distance, which is basically the length of the line that connects two data points. Figure 16.4 shows an example of a dataset with two data points and two dimensions (X and Y). The Euclidean distance between these two points is the length of the dotted line that connects the points in space.

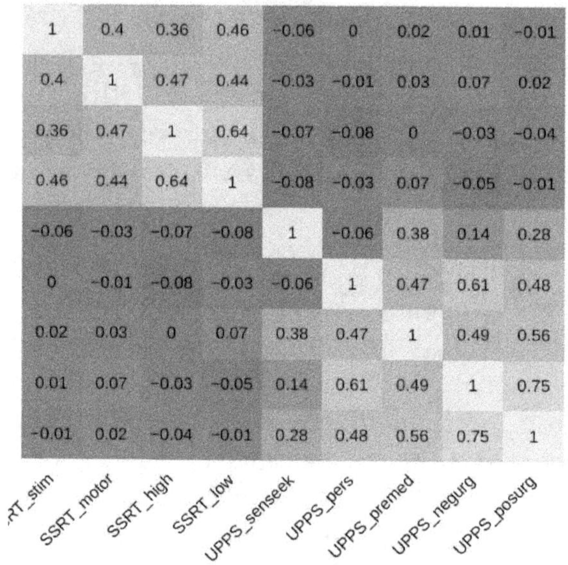

Figure 16.2: Heatmap of the correlation matrix for the nine self-control variables. The brighter yellow areas in the top left and bottom right highlight the higher correlations within the two subsets of variables.

Figure 16.3: A heatmap showing the correlation coefficient of brain activity between 316 regions in the left hemisphere of a single individiual. Cells in yellow reflect strong positive correlation, whereas cells in blue reflect strong negative correlation. The large blocks of positive correlation along the diagonal of the matrix correspond to the major connected networks in the brain

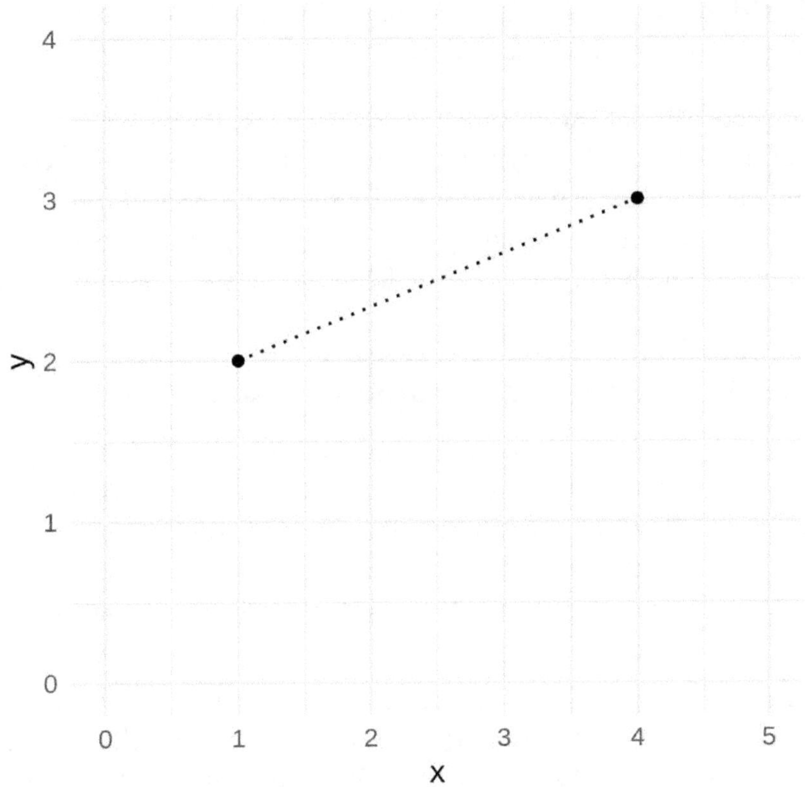

Figure 16.4: A depiction of the Euclidean distance between two points, (1,2) and (4,3). The two points differ by 3 along the X axis and by 1 along the Y axis.

The Euclidean distance is computed by squaring the differences in the locations of the points in each dimension, adding these squared differences, and then taking the square root. When there are two dimensions x and y, this would be computed as:

$$d(x,y) = \sqrt{(x_1 - x_2)^2 + (y_1 - y_2)^2}$$

Plugging in the values from our example data:

$$d(x,y) = \sqrt{(1-4)^2 + (2-3)^2} = 3.16$$

If the formula for Euclidean distance seems slightly familiar, this is because it is identical to the Pythagorean theorem that most of us learned in geometry class, which computes the length of the hypotenuse of a right triangle based on the lengths of the two sides. In this case, the length of the sides of the triangle correspond to the distance between the points along each of the two dimensions. While this example was in two dimensions, we will often work with data that have many more than two dimensions, but the same idea extends to arbitrary numbers of dimensions.

A significant characteristic of the Euclidean distance is its sensitivity to the overall mean and variability of the data. In this regard, it differs from the correlation coefficient, which quantifies the linear association between variables without regard to the overall mean or variability. Consequently, it is customary to standardize the data before calculating the Euclidean distance, which involves transforming each variable into its Z-score representation.

16.3.1 K-means Clustering: Commonly Used Method

A prevalent technique for data grouping is K-means clustering. This method determines a collection of cluster centroids and thereafter allocates each data point to the cluster with the nearest centroid, defined by the minimal Euclidean distance from the data point. For instance, we will utilize the latitude and longitude coordinates of various countries globally as our data points to determine if K-means clustering can accurately classify the continents of the world.

Most statistical software packages include a built-in function for executing K-means clustering with a single command; nonetheless, comprehending the process step by step is beneficial. We must initially determine a specific value for K, the quantity of clusters to be identified in the data. It is essential to note that there is no singular "correct" figure for the number of clusters; multiple methodologies exist to ascertain the "best" solution, although they frequently yield divergent results due to differing assumptions or trade-offs. Clustering techniques, such as K-means, are essential for comprehending the structure of data, particularly in high-dimensional contexts.

After determining the desired number of clusters (K), we must identify K initial locations to serve as our estimates for the cluster centers, as their positions are unknown at the outset. A straightforward method to initiate the process is to randomly select K actual data points to serve as our first centroids. Subsequently, we calculate the Euclidean distance from each data point to every centroid and allocate each point to a cluster according to its nearest centroid. With the updated cluster assignments, we recalculate the centroid of each cluster by averaging the positions of all points allocated to that cluster. This process is subsequently reiterated until a stable solution is attained; we designate this as an iterative process, as it continues to iterate until the result remains constant or until an alternative limit is achieved, such as a maximum number of permissible iterations.

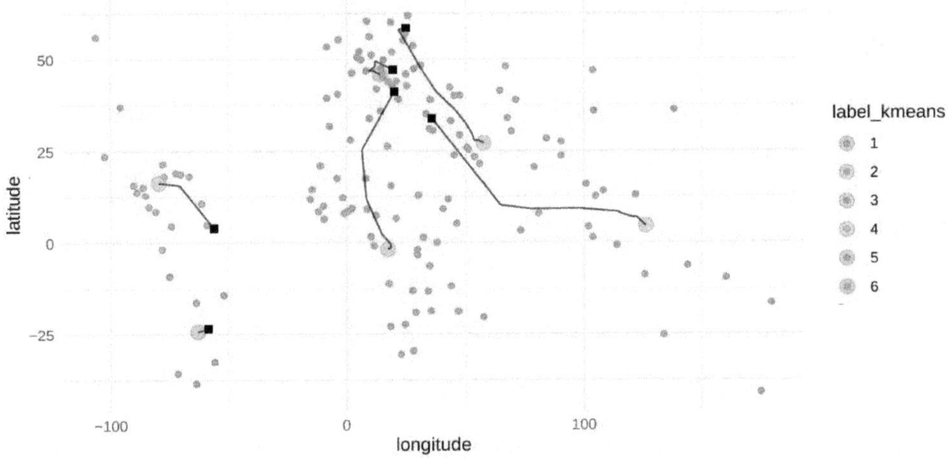

Figure 16.5: A two-dimensional depiction of clustering on the latitude and longitude of countries across the world. The square black symbols show the starting centroids for each cluster, and the lines show the movement of the centroid for that cluster across the iterations of the algorithm.

Applying K-means clustering to the latitude/longitude data (Figure 16.5), we see that there is a reasonable match between the resulting clusters and the continents, though none of the continents is perfectly matched to any of the clusters. We can further examine this by plotting a table that compares the membership of each cluster to the actual continents for each country; this kind of table is often called a confusion matrix.

```
##
## labels AF AS EU NA OC SA
## 1150
## 2 3 24 0 0 0 0
##       3  0  0  0  0  0  7
## }\quad4\mathrm{ 0 }0\mathrm{ 0 15 0 4
## 5 0 10 0 0 6 0
## 635 0 0 0 0 0
```

- Cluster 1 contains all European countries, as well as countries from northern Africa and Asia.
- Cluster 2 contains contains Asian countries as well as several African countries.
- Cluster 3 contains countries from the southern part of South America.
- Cluster 4 contains all of the North American countries as well as northern South American countries.
- Cluster 5 contains Oceania as well as several Asian countries
- Cluster 6 contains all of the remaining African countries.

Although in this example we know the actual clusters (that is, the continents of the world), in general we don't actually know the ground truth for unsupervised learning problems, so we simply have to trust that the clustering method has found useful structure in the data. However, one important point about K-means clustering, and iterative procedures in general, is that they are not guaranteed to give the same answer each time they are run. The use of random numbers to determine the starting points means that the starting points can differ each time, and depending on the data this can sometimes lead to different solutions being found. For this example, K-means clustering will sometimes find a single cluster encompassing both North and South America, and sometimes find two clusters (as it did for the specific choice of random seed used here). Whenever using a method that involves an iterative solution, it is important to rerun the method a number of times using different random seeds, to make sure that the answers don't diverge too greatly between runs. If they do, then one should avoid making strong conclusions based on the unstable results. In fact, it's probably a good idea to avoid strong conclusions on the basis of clustering results more generally; they are primarily useful for getting intuition about the structure that might be present in a dataset.

We can apply K-means clustering to the self-control variables in order to determine which variables are most closely related to one another. For $K = 2$, the K -means algorithm consistently picks out one cluster containing the SSRT variables and one containing the impulsivity variables. With higher values of K, the results are less consistent; for example, with $K = 3$ the algorithm sometimes identifies a third cluster containing only the UPPS sensation seeking variable, whereas in other cases it splits the SSRT variables into two separate clusters.

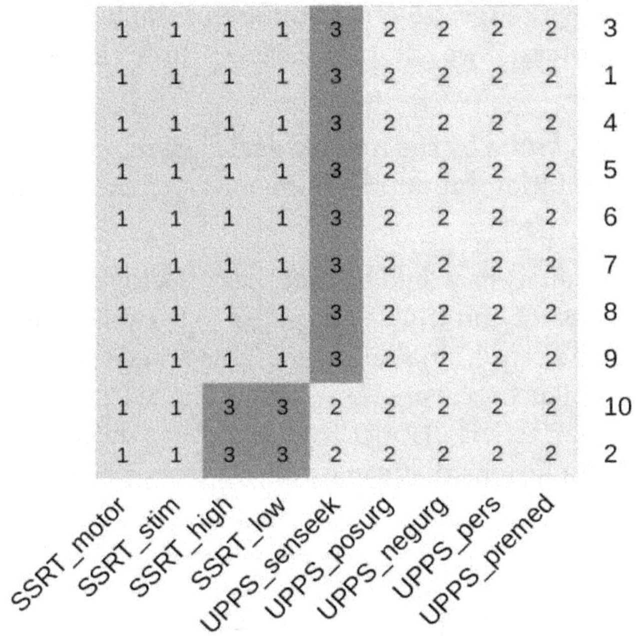

The stability of the clusters with K = 2 suggests that this is probably the most robust clustering for these data, but these results also highlight the importance of running the algorithm multiple times to determine whether any particular clustering result is stable.

16.3.2 Hierarchical clustering

Another useful method for examining the structure of a multivariate dataset is known as hierarchical clustering. This technique also uses the distances between data points to determine clusters, but it also provides a way to visualize the relationships between data points in terms of a tree-like structure known as a dendrogram.

The most commonly used hierarchical clustering procedure is known as agglomerative clustering. This procedure starts by treating each data point as its own cluster, and then progressively creates new clusters by combining the two clusters with the least distance between them. It continues to do this until there is only a single cluster. This requires computing the distance between clusters, and there are numerous ways to do this; in this example we will use the average linkage method, which simply takes the average of all of the distances between each each data point in each of two clusters. As an example, we will examine the relationship between the self-control variables that were described above.

Figure 16.6 shows the dendrogram generated from the self-regulation dataset. Here we see that there is structure in the relationships between variables that can be understood at various levels by "cutting" the tree to create different numbers of clusters: if we cut the tree at 25 , we get two clusters; if we cut it at 20 we get three clusters, and at 19 we get four clusters.

Interestingly, the solution found by the hierarchical clustering analysis of the self-control data is identical to the solution found in the majority of the K -means clustering runs, which is comforting.

Our interpretation of this analysis would be that there is a high degree of similarity within each of the variable sets (SSRT and UPPS) compared to between the sets. Within the UPPS variables, it seems that the sensation seeking variable stands separately from the others, which are much more similar to one another. Within the SSRT variables, it seems that the stimulus selective SSRT variable is distinct from the other three, which are more similar. These are the kinds of conclusions that can be drawn from a clustering analysis.

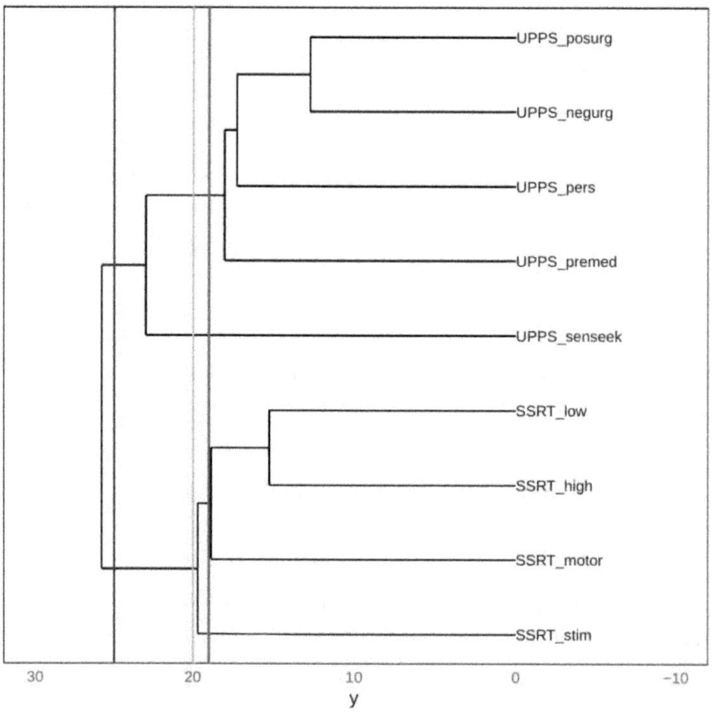

Figure 16.6: A dendrogram depicting the relative similarity of the nine selfcontrol variables. The three colored vertical lines represent three different cutoffs, resulting in either two (blue line), three (green line), or four (red line) clusters.

It is again important to point out that there is no single "right" number of clusters; different methods rely upon different assumptions or heuristics, and can give different results and interpretations. In general, it's good to present the data clustered at several different levels, and make sure that this doesn't drastically change the interpretation of the data.

16.4 Dimensionality reduction

It is often the case with multivariate data that many of the variables will be highly similar to one another, such that they are largely measuring the same thing. One way to think of this is that while the data have a particular number of variables, which we call its dimensionality, in reality there are not as many underlying sources of information as there are variables. The idea behind dimensionality reduction is to reduce the number of variables in order to create composite variables that reflect underlying signals in the data.

16.4.1 Principal component analysis

The idea behind principal component analysis is to find a lower-dimensional description of a set of variables that accounts for the maximum possible amount of information in the full dataset. A deep understanding of principal component analysis requires an understanding of linear algebra, which is beyond the scope of this book; see the resources at the end of this chapter for helpful guides to this topic. In this section I will outline the concept and hopefully whet your appetite to learn more.

We will start with a simple example with just two variables in order to give an intuition for how it works. First we generate some synthetic data for variables X and Y , with a correlation of 0.7 between the two variables. The goal of principal component analysis is to find a linear combination of the observed variables in the dataset that will explain the maximum amount of variance; the idea here is that the variance in the data is a combination of signal and noise, and we want to find the strongest common signal between the variables. The first principal component is the combination that explains the maximum variance. The second component is the the one that explains the maximum remaining variance, while also being uncorrelated with the first component. With more variables we can continue this process to obtain as many components as there are variables (assuming that there are more observations than there are variables), though in practice we usually hope to find a small number of components that can explain a large portion of the variance.

In the case of our two-dimensional example, we can compute the principal components and plot them over the data (Figure 16.7). What we see is that the first principal component (shown in green) follows the direction of the greatest variance. This line is similar, though not identical, to the linear regression line; while the linear regression solution minimizes the distance between each data point and the regression line at the same X value (i.e. the vertical distance), the principal component minimizes the Euclidean distance between the data points and the line representing the component (i.e. the distance perpendicular to the component). The second component points in a direction that is perpendicular to the first component (which is equivalent to being uncorrelated).

It's common to use PCA to reduce the dimensionality of a more complex dataset. For example, let's say that we would like to know whether performance on all four of the stop signal task variables in the earlier dataset are related to the five impulsivity survey variables. We can perform PCA on each of those datasets separately, and examine how much of the variance in the data is accounted for by the first principal component, which will serve as our summary of the data.

We see in Figure 16.8 that for the stop signal variables, the first principal component accounts for about 60% of the variance in the data, whereas for the UPPS it accounts for about 55% of the variance. We can then compute the correlation between the scores obtained using the first principal component from each set of variables, in order to ask whether the there is a relation between the two sets of variables. The correlation of -0.014 between the two summary variables suggests that there is no overall relationship between response inhibition and impulsivity in this dataset.

```
##
## Pearson's product-moment correlation
##
## data: pca_df$SSRT and pca_df$UPPS
## t = -0.3, df = 327, p-value = 0.8
## alternative hypothesis: true correlation is not equal to 0
## 95 percent confidence interval:
```

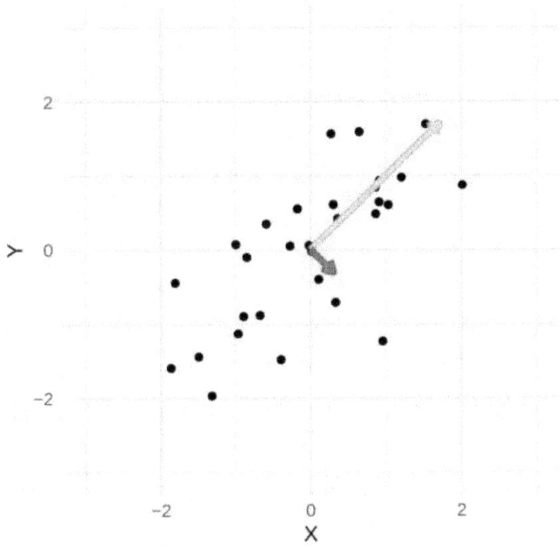

Figure 16.7: A plot of synthetic data, with the first principal component plotted in green and the second in red.

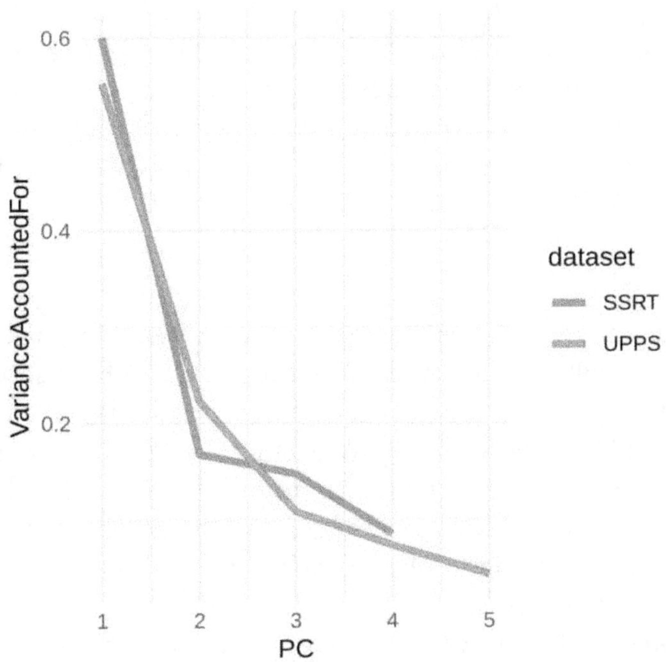

Figure 16.8: A plot of the variance accounted for (or scree plot) for PCA applied separately to the response inhibition and impulsivity variables from the Eisenberg dataset.

```
## -0.123 0.093
## sample estimates:
## cor
## -0.015
```

We could also perform PCA on all of these variables at once. Looking at the plot of variance accounted for (also known as a *scree plot) in Figure 16.6, we can see that the first two components account for a substantial amount of the variance in the data. We can then look at the loadings of each of the individual variables on these two components to understand how each specific variable is associated with the different components.

Doing this for the impulsivity dataset (Figure 16.10), we see that the first component (in the first row of the figure) has nonzero loadings for most of the UPPS variables, and nearly zero loadings for each of the SSRT variables, whereas the opposite is true of the second principal component, which loads primarily on the SSRT variables. This tells us that the first principal component captured mostly variance related to the impulsivity measures, while the second component captured mostly variance related to the response inhibition measures. You might notice that the loadings are actually negative for most of these variables; the sign of the loadings is arbitrary, so we should make sure to look at large positive and negative loadings.

16.4.2 Factor analysis

While principal component analysis can be useful for reducing a dataset to a smaller number of composite variables, the standard methods for PCA have some limitations. Most importantly, it ensures that the components are uncorrelated; while this may sometimes be useful, there are often cases where we want to extract dimensions that may be correlated with one another. A second limitation is that PCA doesn't account for measurement error in the variables that are being analyzed, which can lead to difficult in interpreting the resulting loadings on the components. Although there are modifications of PCA that can address these issues, it is more common in some fields (such as psychology) to use a technique called exploratory factor analysis (or EFA) to reduce the dimensionality of a dataset. [1]

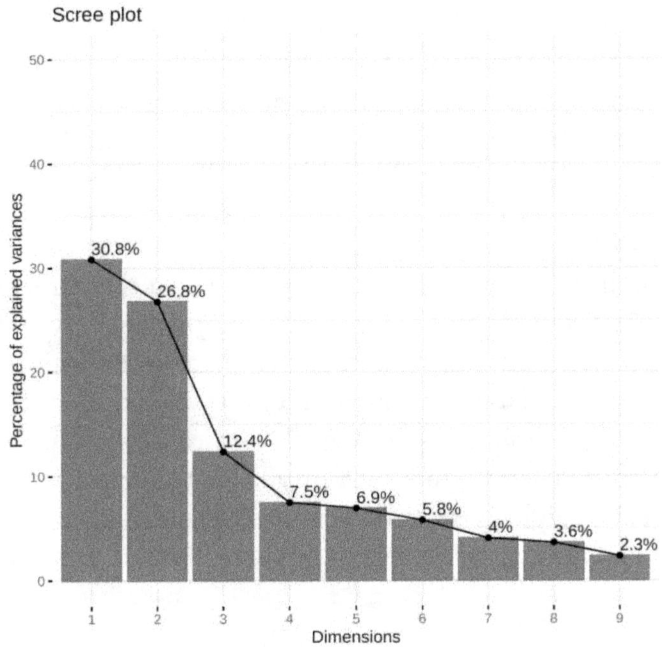

Figure 16.9: (#fig:imp_pc_scree)Plot of variance accounted for by PCA components computed on the full set of self-control variables.

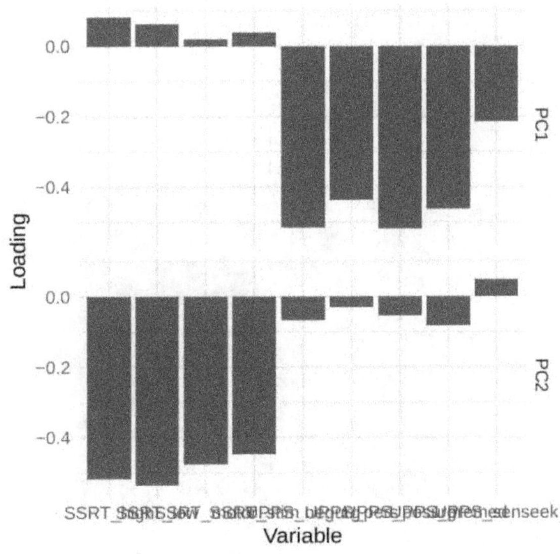

Figure 16.10: Plot of variable loadings in PCA solution including all selfcontrol variables. Each variable is shown in terms of its loadings on each of the two components; reflected in the two rows respectively.

The idea behind EFA is that each observed variable is created through a combination of contributions from a set of latent variables - that is, variables that cannot be observed directly - along with some amount of measurement error for each variable. For this reason, EFA models are often referred to as belonging to a class of statistical models known as latent variable models.

For example, let's say that we want to understand how measures of several different variables relate to the underlying factors that give rise to those measurements. We will first generate a synthetic dataset to show how this might work. We will generate a set of individuals for whom we will pretend that we know the values of several latent psychological variables: impulsivity, working memory capacity, and fluid reasoning We will assume that working memory capacity and fluid reasoning are correlated with one another, but that neither is correlated with impulsivity. From these latent variables we will then generate a set of eight observed variables for each indivdiual, which are simply linear combinations of the latent variables along with random noise added to simulate measurement error.

We can further examine the data by displaying a heatmap of the correlation matrix relating all of these variables (Figure 16.6. We see from this that there are three clusters of variables corresponding to our three latent variables, which is as it should be.

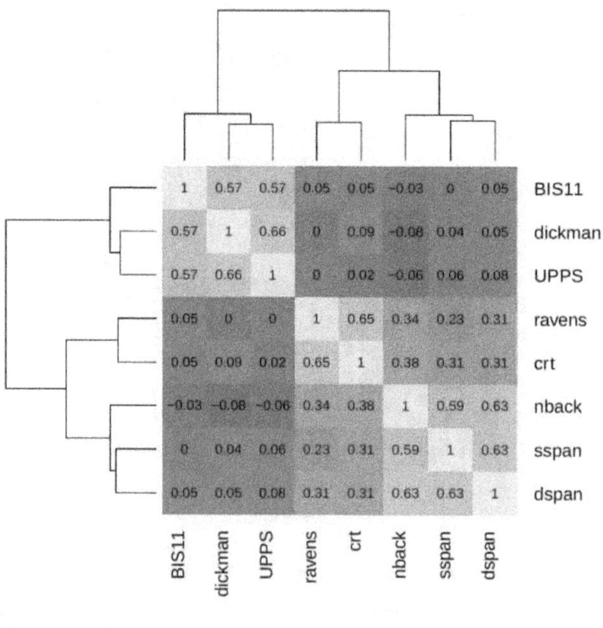

Figure 16.11: (#fig:efa_cor_hmap)A heatmap showing the correlations between the variables generated from the three underlying latent variables.

We can think of EFA as estimating the parameters of a set of linear models all at once, where each model relates each of the observed variables to the latent variables. For our example, these equations would look as follows. In these equations, the β characters have two subscripts, one that refers to the task and the other than refers to the latent variable, and a variable ϵ that refers to the error. Here we will assume that everything has a mean of zero, so that we don't need to include an extra intercept term for each equation.

$$
\begin{aligned}
\text{nback} &= \text{beta}_{[1,1]} * WM + \beta_{[1,2]} * FR + \beta_{[1,3]} * IMP + \epsilon \\
\text{dspan} &= \text{beta}_{[2,1]} * WM + \beta_{[2,2]} * FR + \beta_{[2,3]} * IMP + \epsilon \\
\text{ospan} &= \text{beta}_{[3,1]} * WM + \beta_{[3,2]} * FR + \beta_{[3,3]} * IMP + \epsilon \\
\text{ravens} &= \text{beta}_{[4,1]} * WM + \beta_{[4,2]} * FR + \beta_{[4,3]} * IMP + \epsilon \\
\text{crt} &= \text{beta}_{[5,1]} * WM + \beta_{[5,2]} * FR + \beta_{[5,3]} * IMP + \epsilon \\
\text{UPPS} &= \text{beta}_{[6,1]} * WM + \beta_{[6,2]} * FR + \beta_{[6,3]} * IMP + \epsilon \\
\text{BIS11} &= \text{beta}_{[7,1]} * WM + \beta_{[7,2]} * FR + \beta_{[7,3]} * IMP + \epsilon \\
\text{dickman} &= \text{beta}_{[8,1]} * WM + \beta_{[8,2]} * FR + \beta_{[8,3]} * IMP + \epsilon
\end{aligned}
$$

In effect what we want to do using EFA is to estimate the matrix of coefficients (betas) that map the latent variables into the observed variables. For the data that we are generating, we know that most of the betas in this matrix are zero because we created them that way; for each task, only one of the weights is set to 1 , which means that each task is a noisy measurement of a single latent variable.

We can apply EFA to our synthetic dataset to estimate these parameters. We won't go into the details of how EFA is actually performed, other than to mention one important point. Most of the previous analyses in this book have relied upon methods that try to minimize the difference between the observed data values and the values predicted by the model. The methods that are used to estimate the parameters for EFA instead attempt to minimize the difference between the observed covariances between the observed variables, and the covariances implied by the model parameters. For this reason, these methods are often referred to as covariance structure models.

Let's apply an exploratory factor analysis to our synthetic data. As with clustering methods, we need to first determine how many latent factors we want to include in our model. In this case we know there are three factors, so let's start with that; later on we will examine ways to estimate the number of factors directly from the data. Here is the output from our statistical software for this model:

```
##
## Factor analysis with Call: fa(r = observed_df, nfactors = 3)
##
## Test of the hypothesis that 3 factors are sufficient.
## The degrees of freedom for the model is 7 and the objective function
was
## The number of observations was 200 with Chi Square = 8 with prob <
0.3

##
## The root mean square of the residuals (RMSA) is 0.01
## The df corrected root mean square of the residuals is 0.03
##
## Tucker Lewis Index of factoring reliability = 0.99
## RMSEA index = 0.026 and the 10 % confidence intervals are 0 0.094
## BIC = -29
## With factor correlations of
## MR1 MR2 MR3
## MR1 1.00 0.03 0.47
## MR2 0.03 1.00 0.03
## MR3 0.47 0.03 1.00
```

One question that we would like to ask is how well our model actually fits the data. There is no single way to answer this question; rather, researchers have developed a number of different methods that provide some insight into how well the model fits the data. For example, one commonly used criterion is based on the root mean square error of approximation (RMSEA) statistic, which quantifies how far the predicted covariances are from the actual covariances; a value of RMSEA less than 0.08 is often considered to reflect an adequately fitting model. In the example here, the RMSEA value is 0.026 , which suggests a model that fits quite well.

We can also examine the parameter estimates in order to see whether the model has appropriately identified the structure in the data. It's common to plot this as a graph, with arrows from the latent variables (represented as ellipses) pointing to the observed variables (represented as rectangles), where an arrow represents a substantial loading of the observed variable on the latent variable; this kind of graph is often referred to as a path diagram since it reflects the paths relating the variables. This is shown in Figure 16.12. In this case the EFA procedure correctly identified the structure present in the data, both in terms of which observed variables are related to each of the latent variables, and in terms of the correlations between latent variables.

16.4.3 Determining the number of factors

One of the main challenges in applying EFA is to determine the number of factors. A common way to do this is to examine the fit of the model while varying the number of factors, and then selecting the model that gives the best fit. This is not foolproof, and there are multiple ways to quantify the fit of the model that can sometimes give different answers.

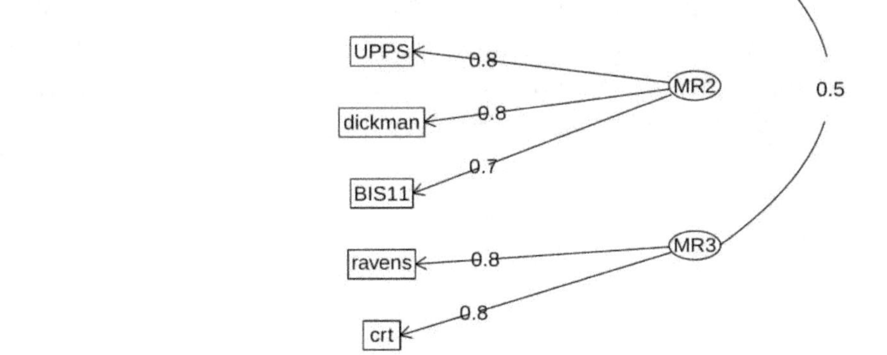

Figure 16.12: Path diagram for the exploratory factor analysis model.

One might think that we could simply look at how well the model fits and pick the number of factors with the best fit, but this won't work, because a more complex model will always fit the data better (as we saw in our earlier discussion of overfitting). For this reason, we need to use a metric of model fit that penalizes for the number of parameters in the model. For the purposes of this example we will select one of the common methods for quantifying model fit, which is known as the sample-size adjusted Bayesian information criterion (or $SABIC$). This measure quantifies how well the model fits the data, while also taking into account the number of parameters in the model (which in this case is related to the number of factors) as well as the sample size. While the absolute value of the SABIC is not interpretable, when using the same data and same kind of model we can compare models using SABIC to determine which is most appropriate for the data. One important thing to know about SABIC and other measures like it (known as information criteria) is that lower values represent better fit of the model, so in this case we want to find the number of factors with the lowest SABIC. In Figure 16.13 we see that the model with the lowest SABIC has three factors, which shows that this approach was able to accurately determine the number of factors used to generate the data.

Now let's see what happens when we apply this model to real data from the Eisenberg et al. dataset, which contains measurements of all of the eight variables that were simulated in the above example. The model with three factors also has the lowest SABIC for these real data.

The path diagram (Figure 16.14) illustrates that the actual data exhibit a factor structure closely resembling that of the simulated data. This is not unexpected, as the simulated data were produced with an understanding of these many activities; yet, it is reassuring to recognize that human behavior is sufficiently systematic to allow for the reliable identification of such correlations. The primary distinction is that the connection between the working memory factor (MR3) and the fluid reasoning factor (MR1) is significantly greater than observed in the simulated data. This outcome is scientifically significant as it demonstrates that, although working memory and fluid reasoning are intricately connected, there is value in modeling them independently.

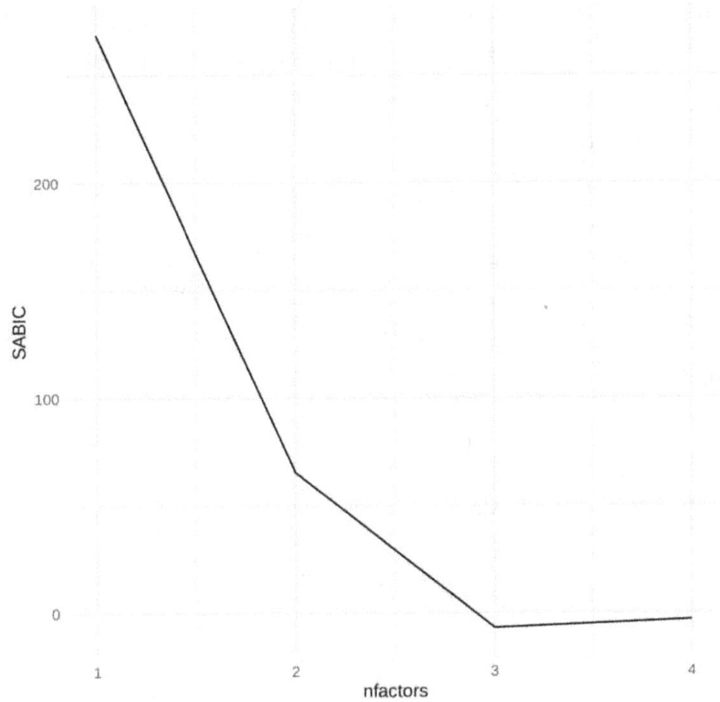

Figure 16.13: Plot of SABIC for varying numbers of factors.

Factor Analysis

Factor analysis is a statistical technique used to explore and identify the underlying structure in a set of observed variables. It aims to reduce a large number of correlated variables into a smaller number of unobserved latent factors that capture the shared variance among the variables. By summarizing information efficiently, factor analysis helps simplify complex datasets, reveal patterns, and uncover the dimensions underlying observed phenomena. This method is widely applied in psychology, social sciences, marketing, and education, where constructs such as intelligence, personality traits, customer preferences, or attitudes are measured indirectly through multiple indicators. Factor analysis can be exploratory (EFA), where the goal is to discover the factor structure without prior assumptions, or confirmatory (CFA), where a hypothesized structure is tested against the data. Key steps in factor analysis include assessing the suitability of data, extracting factors, determining the number of factors, and rotating factors to achieve interpretability. Common extraction methods include principal component analysis and maximum likelihood estimation, while rotation methods such as varimax or oblimin improve the clarity of factor loadings. Factor scores obtained from the analysis can be used in subsequent modeling or for summarizing complex data. Overall, factor analysis provides a powerful tool for dimensionality reduction, data simplification, and uncovering latent constructs that drive observable patterns in multivariate data.

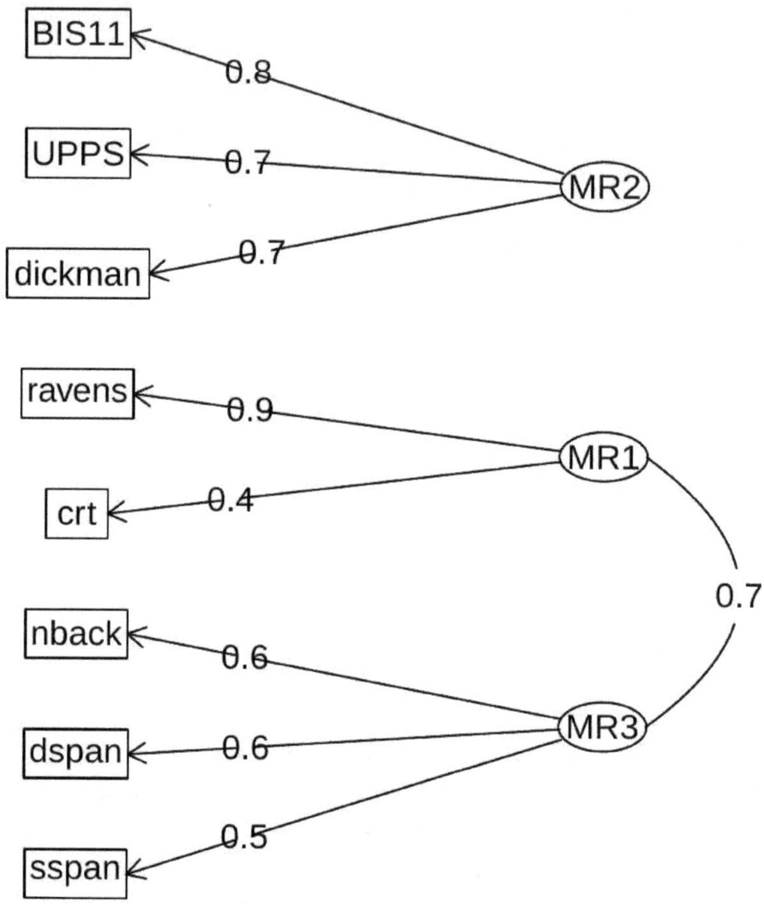

Figure 16.14: Path diagram for the three-factor model on the Eisenberg et al. data.

Chapter-17

Practical Statistical Modeling

Practical statistical modeling involves applying statistical techniques to real-world data in order to understand patterns, relationships, and make predictions. Unlike purely theoretical models, practical modeling focuses on addressing concrete problems and producing actionable insights that inform decision-making. It encompasses a wide range of methods, including regression analysis, generalized linear models, ANOVA, multivariate techniques, and machine learning approaches. A key aspect of practical modeling is the careful consideration of assumptions, data quality, and model diagnostics to ensure valid and reliable results. Visualization, data preprocessing, and exploratory data analysis play crucial roles in identifying trends, detecting outliers, and guiding model selection. Practical statistical modeling also involves evaluating model performance using measures such as goodness-of-fit, accuracy, or predictive error, and refining models iteratively. It is widely applied in fields such as business analytics, healthcare, social sciences, engineering, and finance to inform strategy, optimize processes, and forecast outcomes. By integrating theory with real data, practical statistical modeling provides a systematic framework for translating complex information into meaningful, evidence-based conclusions. In this chapter we will bring together everything that we have learned, by applying our knowledge to a practical example. In 2007, Christopher Gardner and colleagues from Stanford published a study in the Journal of the American Medical Association titled "Comparison of the Atkins, Zone, Ornish, and LEARN Diets for Change in Weight and Related Risk Factors Among Overweight Premenopausal Women - The A TO Z Weight Loss Study: A Randomized Trial" (Gardner et al. 2007). We will use this study to show how one would go about analyzing an experimental dataset from start to finish.

17.1 The procedure of statistical modeling

The procedure of statistical modeling involves a systematic series of steps to build, evaluate, and interpret models that represent real-world phenomena. The process typically begins with defining the research problem and identifying the variables of interest, including the response (dependent) and predictor (independent) variables. The next step is data collection and preparation, which includes gathering relevant data, cleaning it, handling missing values, and transforming variables if necessary. Exploratory data analysis (EDA) follows, where visualizations, summary statistics, and correlation analyses help understand data structure and detect patterns or anomalies. Based on the insights gained, an appropriate statistical model is selected, such as linear regression, logistic regression, ANOVA, or multivariate models, depending on the type of variables and research objectives. The model fitting stage involves estimating parameters and determining the relationship between predictors and the outcome. Model validation and diagnostics are critical steps to assess assumptions, detect outliers or influential points, and evaluate model performance using measures like R^2, residual analysis, or predictive accuracy. If needed, the model is refined or adjusted, including transformations, adding interaction terms, or selecting variables to improve interpretability and predictive power. Finally, the results are interpreted and communicated, often through reports, tables, and visualizations, translating statistical findings into actionable insights. This structured procedure ensures that statistical modeling is rigorous, reproducible, and capable of supporting informed decision-making across diverse applications. There is a set of steps that we generally go through when we want to use our statistical model to test a scientific hypothesis:

1. Specify your question of interest
2. Identify or collect the appropriate data
3. Prepare the data for analysis
4. Determine the appropriate model
5. Fit the model to the data
6. Criticize the model to make sure it fits properly
7. Test hypothesis and quantify effect size

17.1.1 1: Specify your question of interest

According to the authors, the goal of their study was:

To compare 4 weight-loss diets representing a spectrum of low to high carbohydrate intake for effects on weight loss and related metabolic variables.

17.1.2 2: Identify or collect the appropriate data

To answer their question, the investigators randomly assigned each of 311 overweight/obese women to one of four different diets (Atkins, Zone, Ornish, or LEARN), and measured their weight along with many other measures of health over time. The authors recorded a large number of variables, but for the main question of interest let's focus on a single variable: Body Mass Index (BMI). Further, since our goal is to measure lasting changes in BMI, we will only look at the measurement taken at 12 months after onset of the diet.

17.1.3 3: Prepare the data for analysis

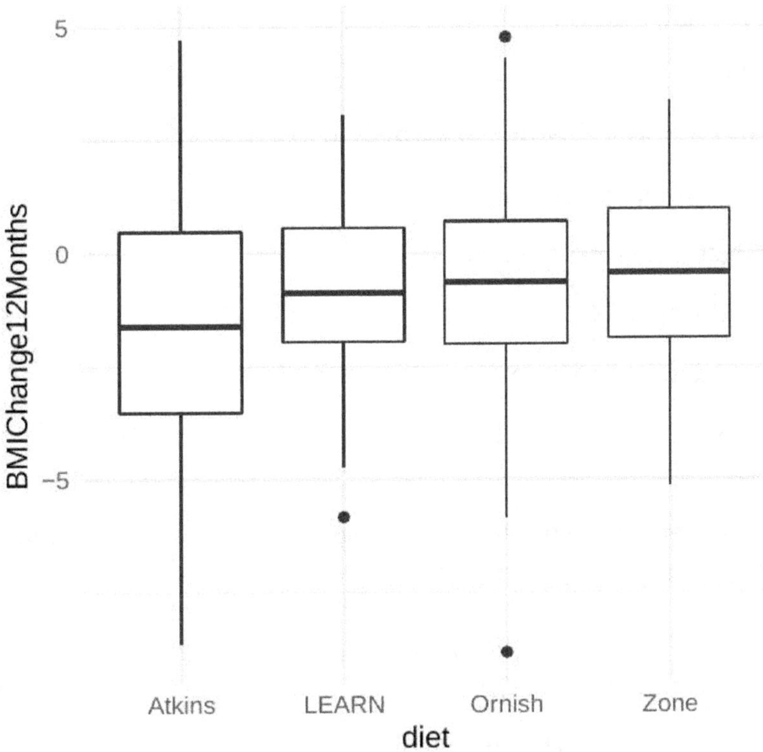

Figure 17.1: Box plots for each condition, with the 50th percentile (i.e the median) shown as a black line for each group.

The actual data from the A to Z study are not publicly available, so we will use the summary data reported in their paper to generate some synthetic data that roughly match the data obtained in their study, with the same means and standard deviations for each group. Once we have the data, we can visualize them to make sure that there are no outliers. Box plots are useful to see the shape of the distributions, as shown in Figure 17.1. Those data look fairly reasonable - there are a couple of outliers within individual groups (denoted by the dots outside of the box plots), but they don't seem to be extreme with regard to the other groups. We can also see that the distributions seem to differ a bit in their variance, with Atkins showing somewhat greater variability than the others. This means that any analyses that assume the variances are equal across groups might be inappropriate. Fortunately, the ANOVA model that we plan to use is fairly robust to this.

17.1.4 4. Determine the appropriate model

There are several questions that we need to ask in order to determine the appropriate statistical model for our analysis.

- What kind of dependent variable?
- BMI: continuous, roughly normally distributed
- What are we comparing?
- mean BMI across four diet groups
- ANOVA is appropriate
- Are observations independent?
- Random assignment should ensure that the assumption of independence is appropriate
- The use of difference scores (in this case the difference between starting weight and weight after 12 months) is somewhat controversial, especially when the starting points differ between the groups. In this case the starting weights are very similar between the groups, so we will use the difference scores, but in general one would want to consult a statistician before applying such a model to real data.

17.1.5 5. Fit the model to the data

Let's run an ANOVA on BMI change to compare it across the four diets. Most statistical software will automatically convert a nominal variable into a set of dummy variables. A common way of specifying a statistical model is using formula notation, in which the model is specified using a formula of the form:

$$dependent\ variable \sim independent\ variables$$

In this case, we want to look at the change in BMI (which is stored in a variable called BMIChange12Months) as a function of diet (which is stored in a variable called *diet), so we use the formula:

BMIChange12Months ~ diet

Most statistical software (including *R*) will automatically create a set of dummy variables when the model includes a nominal variable (such as the diet variable, which contains the name of the diet that each person received). Here are the results from this model fitted to our data:

```
##
## Call:
## lm(formula = BMIChange12Months ~ diet, data = dietDf)
##
## Residuals:

\begin{tabular}{rrrrrr}
\#\# & Min & 1Q & Median & 3Q & Max \\
\#\# & -8.14 & -1.37 & 0.07 & 1.50 & 6.33
\end{tabular}
##
## Coefficients:

\begin{tabular}{lrrrr}
\#\#    &    Estimate    &    Std.    &    Error    t    value    &
$\operatorname{Pr}(>|\mathrm{t}|)$ \\
\#\# (Intercept) & -1.622 & 0.251 & -6.47 & $3.8 \mathrm{e}-10$ \\
\#\# dietLEARN & 0.772 & 0.352 & 2.19 & 0.0292 \\
\#\# dietOrnish & 0.932 & 0.356 & 2.62 & 0.0092
\end{tabular} **
## ---
## Signif. codes: 0 '***' 0.001 '**' 0.01 '*' 0.05 '.' 0.1 ' ' 1
##
```

```
## Residual standard error: 2.2 on 307 degrees of freedom

## Multiple R-squared: 0.0338, Adjusted R-squared: 0.0243

## F-statistic: 3.58 on 3 and 307 DF, p-value: 0.0143
```

Note that the software automatically generated dummy variables that correspond to three of the four diets, leaving the Atkins diet without a dummy variable. This means that the intercept represents the mean of the Atkins diet group, and the other three variables model the difference between the means for each of those diets and the mean for the Atkins diet. Atkins was chosen as the unmodeled baseline variable simply because it is first in alphabetical order.

17.1.6 6. Criticize the model to make sure it fits properly

The first thing we want to do is to critique the model to make sure that it is appropriate. One thing we can do is to look at the residuals from the model. In Figure 17.2, we plot the residuals for each individual grouped by diet. There are no obvious differences in the distributions of residuals across conditions, we can go ahead with the analysis.

Another important assumption of the statistical tests that we apply to linear models is that the residuals from the model are normally distributed. It is a common misconception that linear models require that the data are normally distributed, but this is not the case; the only requirement for the statistics to be correct is that the residual errors are normally distributed. The right panel of Figure 17.3 shows a Q-Q (quantile-quantile) plot, which plots the residuals against their expected values based on their quantiles in the normal distribution. If the residuals are normally distributed then the data points should fall along the dashed line - in this case it looks pretty good, except for a couple of outliers that are apparent at the very bottom Because this model is also relatively robust to violations of normality, and these are fairly small, we will go ahead and use the results.

17.1.7 7. Test hypothesis and quantify effect size

First let's look back at the summary of results from the ANOVA, shown in Step 5 above. The significant F test shows us that there is a significant difference between diets, but we should also note that the model doesn't actually account for much variance in the data; the R -squared value is only 0.03 , showing that the model is only accounting for a few percent of the variance in weight loss. Thus, we would not want to overinterpret this result.

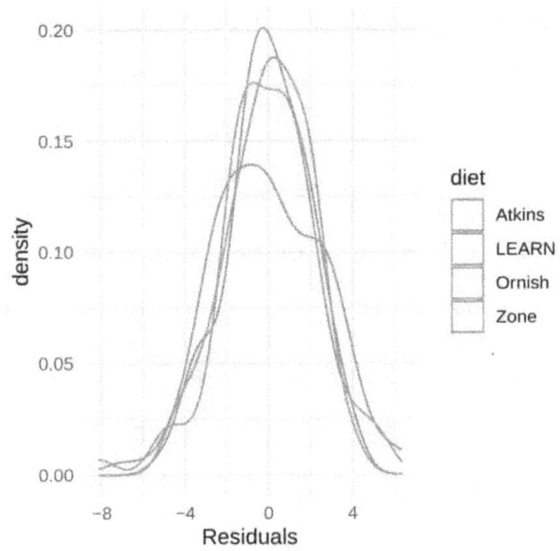

Figure 17.2: Distribution of residuals for for each condition

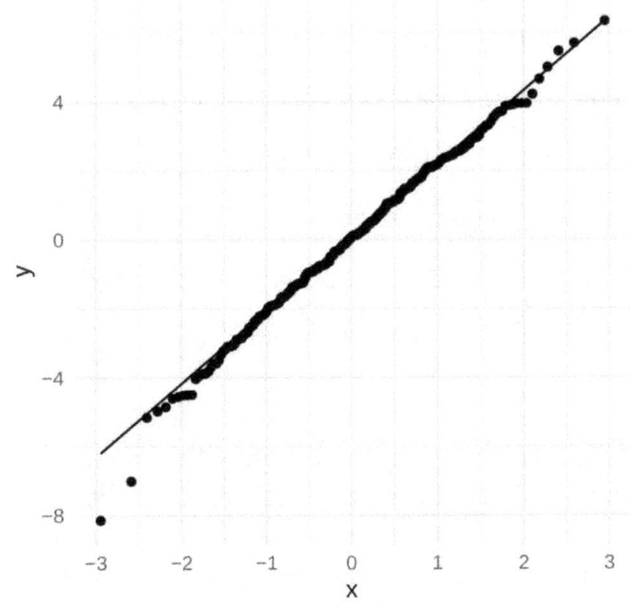

Figure 17.3: Q-Q plot of actual residual values against theoretical residual values

The significant result in the omnibus F test also doesn't tell us which diets differ from which others. We can find out more by comparing means across conditions. Because we are doing several comparisons, we need to correct for those comparisons, which is accomplished using a procedure known as the Tukey method, which is implemented by our statistical software:

```
\begin{tabular}{llrrrrr}
\#\# & diet & emmean & SE & df & lower. CL & upper. CL & .group \\
\#\# & Atkins & -1.62 & 0.251 & 307 & -2.11 & -1.13 & a \\
\#\# & LEARN & -0.85 & 0.247 & 307 & -1.34 & -0.36 & ab \\
\#\# & Ornish & -0.69 & 0.252 & 307 & -1.19 & -0.19 & b \\
\#\# & Zone & -0.57 & 0.247 & 307 & -1.06 & -0.08 & b
\end{tabular}
##
## Confidence level used: 0.95
## P value adjustment: tukey method for comparing a family of 4 estimates
## significance level used: alpha = 0.05
## NOTE: Compact letter displays can be misleading
## because they show NON-findings rather than findings.
## Consider using 'pairs()', 'pwpp()', or 'pwpm()' instead.
```

The letters in the rightmost column show us which of the groups differ from one another, using a method that adjusts for the number of comparisons being performed; conditions that share a letter are not significantly different from one another. This shows that Atkins and LEARN diets don't differ from one another (since they share the letter a), and the LEARN, Ornish, and Zone diets don't differ from one another (since they share the letter b), but the Atkins diet differs from the Ornish and Zone diets (since they share no letters).

17.1.8 What about possible confounds?

If we look more closely at the Gardner paper, we will see that they also report statistics on how many individuals in each group had been diagnosed with metabolic syndrome, which is a syndrome characterized by high blood pressure, high blood glucose, excess body fat around the waist, and abnormal cholesterol levels and is associated with increased risk for cardiovascular problems. The data from the Gardner paper are presented in Table 17.1.

Table 17.1: Presence of metabolic syndrome in each group in the AtoZ study.

Diet	N	P (metabolic syndrome)
Atkins	77	0.29
LEARN	79	0.25
Ornish	76	0.38
Zone	79	0.34

Looking at the data it seems that the rates are slightly different across groups, with more metabolic syndrome cases in the Ornish and Zone diets – which were exactly the diets with poorer outcomes. Let's say that we are interested in testing whether the rate of metabolic syndrome was significantly different between the groups, since this might make us concerned that these differences could have affected the results of the diet outcomes.

17.1.8.1 Determine the appropriate model

- What kind of dependent variable?
- proportions
- What are we comparing?
- proportion with metabolic syndrome across four diet groups
- chi-squared test for goodness of fit is appropriate against null hypothesis of no difference

Let's first compute that statistic, using the chi-squared test function in our statistical software:

```
##
## Pearson's Chi-squared test
##
## data: contTable
## X-squared = 4, df = 3, p-value = 0.3
```

This test shows that there is not a significant difference between means. However, it doesn't tell us how certain we are that there is no difference; remember that under NHST, we are always working under the assumption that the null is true unless the data show us enough evidence to cause us to reject the null hypothesis.

What if we want to quantify the evidence for or against the null? We can do this using the Bayes factor.

```
## Bayes factor analysis
## --------------
## [1] Non-indep.(a=1) : 0.058 ±0%
##
## Against denominator:
## Null, independence, a = 1
## ---
## Bayes factor type: BFcontingencyTable, independent multinomial
```

This shows us that the alternative hypothesis is 0.058 times more likely than the null hypothesis, which means that the null hypothesis is $1/0.058 \sim 17$ times more likely than the alternative hypothesis given these data. This is fairly strong, if not completely overwhelming, evidence in favor of the null hypothesis.

17.2 Getting help

Whenever one is analyzing real data, it's useful to check your analysis plan with a trained statistician, as there are many potential problems that could arise in real data. In fact, it's best to speak to a statistician before you even start the project, as their advice regarding the design or implementation of the study could save you major headaches down the road. Most universities have statistical consulting offices that offer free assistance to members of the university community. Understanding the content of this book won't prevent you from needing their help at some point, but it will help you have a more informed conversation with them and better understand the advice that they offer.

Chapter-18

Conducting Replicable Research

Conducting replicable research is a cornerstone of scientific integrity and credibility, ensuring that findings can be independently verified and reproduced by other researchers. Replicability goes beyond simply repeating an experiment; it involves clearly documenting study design, data collection procedures, analytical methods, and statistical models so that others can follow the same process and obtain consistent results. Key practices include pre-registering hypotheses, using standardized protocols, maintaining transparent and well-organized datasets, and sharing code and materials whenever possible. Careful attention to data quality, measurement validity, and proper statistical analysis reduces errors and increases confidence in the findings. Reporting results with sufficient detail, including effect sizes, confidence intervals, and assumptions, further supports replicability. Replicable research strengthens the cumulative nature of scientific knowledge, enables meta-analyses, and helps identify robust patterns across studies. By emphasizing transparency, methodological rigor, and openness, researchers contribute to a trustworthy and self-correcting scientific community. In fields ranging from medicine and psychology to social sciences and economics, replicable research underpins evidence-based decision-making, policy formulation, and innovation. Ultimately, prioritizing replicability fosters accountability, reduces the likelihood of false discoveries, and ensures that scientific conclusions are both credible and useful for advancing knowledge. Most people think that science is a reliable way to answer questions about the world. When our physician prescribes a treatment, we trust that it has been shown to be effective through research, and we have similar faith that the airplanes that we fly in aren't going to fall from the sky. However, since 2005 there has been an increasing concern that science may not always work as well as we have long thought that it does. In this chapter we will discuss these concerns about reproducibility of scientific research, and outline the steps that one can take to make sure that our statistical results are as reproducible as possible.

18.1 Our perspective on the functioning of science

Our perspective on the functioning of science emphasizes science as a systematic, evidence-based approach to understanding the natural and social world. Science operates through observation, experimentation, and reasoning, seeking to generate knowledge that is reliable, testable, and open to revision. It relies on the formulation of hypotheses, the design of studies to test them, and the use of rigorous methods to analyze data and draw conclusions. Peer review, transparency, and reproducibility are essential mechanisms that ensure scientific findings are credible and verifiable. Science is inherently iterative: new discoveries refine or challenge existing knowledge, leading to cumulative progress over time. Collaboration, critical thinking, and skepticism are fundamental to the scientific process, helping to identify biases, errors, and limitations. Moreover, science functions within a broader social context, influencing and being influenced by culture, technology, and policy. By combining creativity with systematic methodology, science provides a structured way to explain phenomena, predict outcomes, and solve practical problems. This perspective highlights the dynamic, self-correcting, and communal nature of science as a pursuit of knowledge that is both objective and socially relevant. Let's say that we are interested in a research project on how children choose what to eat. This is a question that was asked in a study by the well-known eating researcher Brian Wansink and his colleagues in 2012. The standard (and, as we will see, somewhat naive) view goes something like this:

- You start with a hypothesis
- Branding with popular characters should cause children to choose "healthy" food more often
- You collect some data
- Offer children the choice between a cookie and an apple with either an Elmo-branded sticker or a control sticker, and record what they
- choose
- You do statistics to test the null hypothesis
- "The preplanned comparison shows Elmo-branded apples were associated with an increase in a child's selection of an apple over a cookie, from 20.7% to 33.8% ($\chi^2 = 5.158; P = .02$)" (Wansink, Just, and Payne 2012)
- You make a conclusion based on the data
- "This study suggests that the use of branding or appealing branded characters may benefit healthier foods more than they benefit indulgent, more highly processed foods. Just as attractive names have been shown to increase the selection of healthier foods in school lunchrooms, brands and cartoon characters could do the same with young children." (Wansink, Just, and Payne 2012)

18.2 The operational dynamics of science

Brian Wansink is well known for his books on "Mindless Eating", and his fee for corporate speaking engagements was at one point in the tens of thousands of dollars. In 2017, a set of researchers began to scrutinize some of his published research, starting with a set of papers about how much pizza people ate at a buffet. The researchers asked Wansink to share the data from the studies but he refused, so they dug into his published papers and found a large number of inconsistencies and statistical problems in the papers. The publicity around this analysis led a number of others to dig into Wansink's past, including obtaining emails between Wansink and his collaborators. As reported by Stephanie Lee at Buzzfeed, these emails showed just how far Wansink's actual research practices were from the naive model:

. . . back in September 2008, when Payne was looking over the data soon after it had been collected, he found no strong apples-andElmo link - at least not yet. . . "I have attached some initial results of the kid study to this message for your report," Payne wrote to his collaborators. "Do not despair. It looks like stickers on fruit may work (with a bit more wizardry)." ... Wansink also acknowledged the paper was weak as he was preparing to submit it to journals. The p-value was 0.06 , just shy of the gold standard cutoff of 0.05 . It was a "sticking point," as he put it in a Jan. 7, 2012, email. . . "It seems to me it should be lower," he wrote, attaching a draft. "Do you want to take a look at it and see what you think. If you can get the data, and it needs some tweeking, it would be good to get that one value below . 05. "... Later in 2012, the study appeared in the prestigious JAMA Pediatrics, the 0.06 p-value intact. But in September 2017, it was retracted and replaced with a version that listed a p-value of 0.02 . And a month later, it was retracted yet again for an entirely different reason: Wansink admitted that the experiment had not been done on 8 to 11 - year-olds, as he'd originally claimed, but on preschoolers.

This kind of behavior finally caught up with Wansink; fifteen of his research studies have been retracted and in 2018 he resigned from his faculty position at Cornell University.

18.3 The dilemma of reproducibility in scientific research

While we think that the kind of frauduent behavior seen in Wansink's case is relatively rare, it has become increasingly clear that problems with reproducibility are much more widespread in science than previously thought. This became particularly evident in 2015, when a large group of researchers published a study in the journal Science titled "Estimating the reproducibility of psychological science"(Open Science Collaboration 2015). In this paper, the researchers took 100 published studies in psychology and attempted to reproduce the results originally reported in the papers. Their findings were shocking: Whereas 97% of the original papers had reported statistically significant findings, only 37% of these effects were statistically significant in the replication study. Although these problems in psychology have received a great deal of attention, they seem to be present in nearly every area of science, from cancer biology (Errington et al. 2014) and chemistry (Baker 2017) to economics (Christensen and Miguel 2016) and the social sciences (Camerer et al. 2018).

The reproducibility crisis that surfaced post-2010 was anticipated by John Ioannidis, a Stanford physician who authored a paper in 2005 entitled "Why Most Published Research Findings Are False" (Ioannidis 2005). In this work, Ioannidis contended that the application of null hypothesis statistical testing in contemporary research will inevitably result in elevated rates of false outcomes.

18.3.1 Positive predictive value and statistical significance

Ioannidis' analysis focused on a concept known as the positive predictive value, which is defined as the proportion of positive results (which generally translates to "statistically significant findings") that are true:

$$PPV = \frac{p(\text{ true positive result })}{p(\text{ true positive result }) + p(\text{ false positive result })}$$

Assuming that we know the probability that our hypothesis is true (p(hIsTrue)), then the probability of a true positive result is simply p (hIsTrue) multiplied by the statistical power of the study:

$$p(\text{ true positive result }) = p(\text{ hIsTrue }) * (1 - \beta)$$

were β is the false negative rate. The probability of a false positive result is determined by p (hIsTrue) and the false positive rate α :

$$p(\text{ false positive result }) = (1 - p(\text{ hIsTrue })) * \alpha$$

PPV is then defined as:

$$PPV = \frac{p(\text{ hIsTrue }) * (1 - \beta)}{p(\text{ hIsTrue }) * (1 - \beta) + (1 - p(\text{ hIsTrue })) * \alpha}$$

Let's first take an example where the probability of our hypothesis being true is high, say 0.8 - though note that in general we cannot actually know this probability. Let's say that we perform a study with the standard values of $\alpha = 0.05$ and $\beta = 0.2$. We can compute the PPV as:

$$PPV = \frac{0.8 * (1 - 0.2)}{0.8 * (1 - 0.2) + (1 - 0.8) * 0.05} = 0.98$$

This means that if we find a positive result in a study where the hypothesis is likely to be true and power is high, then its likelihood of being true is high.

Note, however, that a research field where the hypotheses have such a high likelihood of being true is probably not a very interesting field of research; research is most important when it tells us something unexpected!

Let's do the same analysis for a field where $p(hIsTrue) = 0.1$ – that is, most of the hypotheses being tested are false. In this case, PPV is:

$$PPV = \frac{0.1 * (1 - 0.2)}{0.1 * (1 - 0.2) + (1 - 0.1) * 0.05} = 0.307$$

This means that in a field where most of the hypotheses are likely to be wrong (that is, an interesting scientific field where researchers are testing risky hypotheses), even when we find a positive result it is more likely to be false than true! In fact, this is just another example of the base rate effect that we discussed in the context of hypothesis testing - when an outcome is unlikely, then it's almost certain that most positive outcomes will be false positives.

We can simulate this to show how PPV relates to statistical power, as a function of the prior probability of the hypothesis being true (see Figure 18.1)

Unfortunately, statistical power remains low in many areas of science (Smaldino and McElreath 2016), suggesting that many published research findings are false.

An entertaining illustration of this was presented in a study by Jonathan Schoenfeld and John Ioannidis, entitled "Is everything we eat associated with cancer?" A systematic review of cookbooks (Schoenfeld and Ioannidis 2013). The researchers analyzed numerous studies evaluating the correlation between various diets and cancer risk, discovering that 80% of the elements were linked to either an elevated or diminished cancer risk. In the majority of these instances, the statistical evidence was feeble, and when the findings were aggregated across trials, the outcome was null.

18.3.2 The winner's curse

Another kind of error can also occur when statistical power is low: Our estimates of the effect size will be inflated. This phenomenon often goes by the term "winner's curse", which comes from economics, where it refers to the fact that for certain types of auctions (where the value is the same for everyone, like a jar of quarters, and the bids are private), the winner is guaranteed to pay more than the good is worth. In science, the winner's curse refers to the fact that the effect size estimated from a significant result (i.e. a winner) is almost always an overestimate of the true effect size.

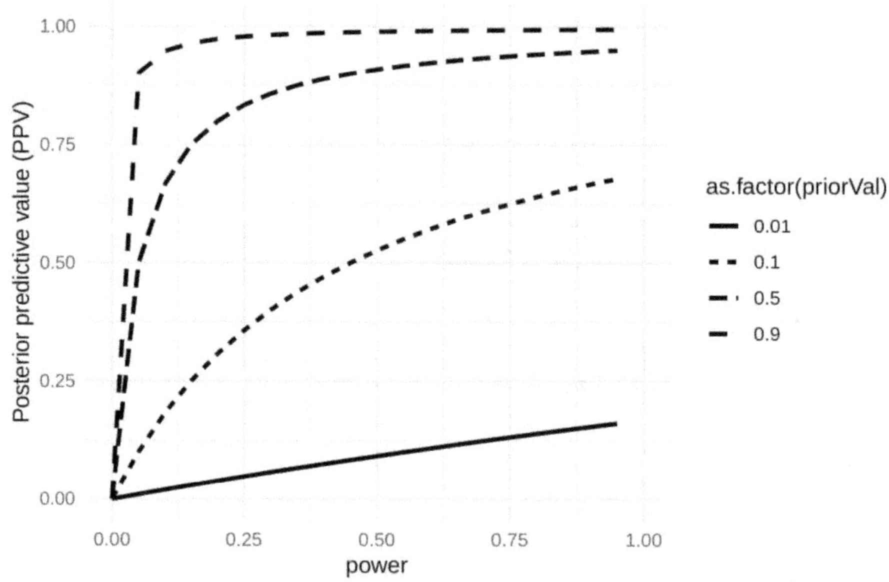

Figure 18.1: A simulation of posterior predictive value as a function of statistical power (plotted on the x axis) and prior probability of the hypothesis being true (plotted as separate lines).

We can simulate this in order to see how the estimated effect size for significant results is related to the actual underlying effect size. Let's generate data for which there is a true effect size of $d = 0.2$, and estimate the effect size for those results where there is a significant effect detected. The left panel of Figure 18.2 shows that when power is low, the estimated effect size for significant results can be highly inflated compared to the actual effect size.

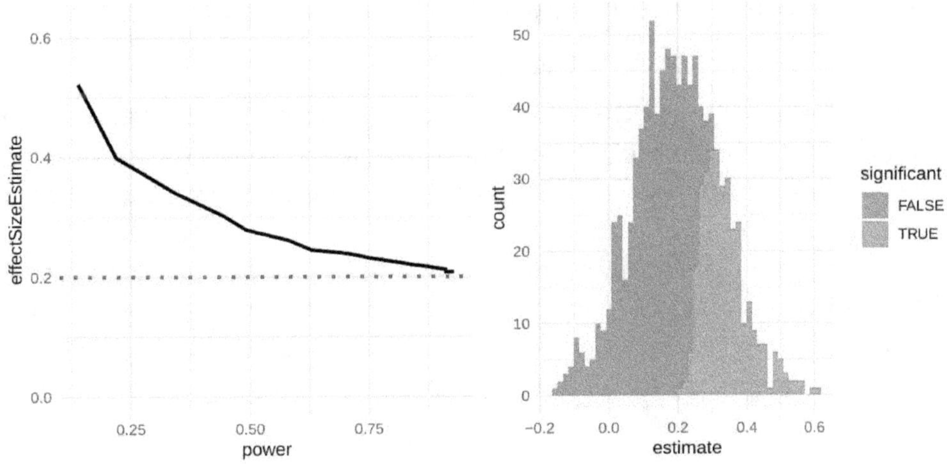

Figure 18.2: Left: A simulation of the winner's curse as a function of statistical power (x axis). The solid line shows the estimated effect size, and the dotted line shows the actual effect size. Right: A histogram showing effect size estimates for a number of samples from a dataset, with significant results shown in blue and non-significant results in red.

We can look at a single simulation to see why this is the case. In the right panel of Figure 18.2, you can see a histogram of the estimated effect sizes for 1000 samples, separated by whether the test was statistically significant. It should be clear from the figure that if we estimate the effect size only based on significant results, then our estimate will be inflated; only when most results are significant (i.e. power is high and the effect is relatively large) will our estimate come near the actual effect size.

18.4 Dubious research methodologies

A popular book entitled "The Compleat Academic: A Career Guide", published by the The American Psychological Association (Darley, Zanna, and Roediger 2004) seeks to offer budding researchers direction for professional development. In a chapter by renowned social psychologist Daryl Bem entitled "Writing the Empirical Journal Article," Bem offers recommendations for composing a research paper. Regrettably, the methodologies he proposes are fundamentally flawed and have been categorized as dubious research practices (QRPs).

Which article ought you to compose? Two potential articles can be composed: (1) the article initially conceived during the study's design or (2) the article that is most logical in light of the observed data. Their congruence is infrequent, and the accurate response is (2).

Bem's suggestion pertains to HARKing (Hypothesizing After the Results are Known) (Kerr 1998). This may appear harmless, although it is problematic as it enables the researcher to reinterpret a post-hoc finding (which should be regarded with skepticism) as an a priori prediction (in which we would have greater confidence). Essentially, it enables the researcher to revise their theory in accordance with the facts, rather than use the theory to formulate predictions and subsequently test them—similar to shifting the goalpost to align with the ball's trajectory. Consequently, it becomes exceedingly challenging to refute erroneous concepts, as the criteria can perpetually be adjusted to align with the data. Bem proceeds:

Data analysis Analyze them from all perspectives. Examine the genders individually. Create new composite indices. If a datum indicates a novel hypothesis, seek additional corroborative evidence within the data. Should you observe faint indications of intriguing patterns, endeavor to restructure the facts to enhance their visibility. Eliminate any participants, trials, observers, or interviewers that yielded unusual results, at least temporarily. Embark on a fishing adventure in search of something intriguing. This is not unethical.

What Bem suggests here is known as p-hacking, which refers to trying many different analyses until one finds a significant result. Bem is correct that if one were to report every analysis done on the data then this approach would not be "immoral". However, it is rare to see a paper discuss all of the analyses that were performed on a dataset; rather, papers often only present the analyses that worked - which usually means that they found a statistically significant result. There are many different ways that one might p-hack:

- Analyze data after every subject, and stop collecting data once $p < .05$
- Analyze many different variables, but only report those with $p < .05$
- Collect many different experimental conditions, but only report those with $p < .05$
- Exclude participants to get $p < .05$
- Transform the data to get $p < .05$

A prominent study by Simmons, Nelson, and Simonsohn (2011) demonstrated that the implementation of such p-hacking techniques could significantly elevate the true false positive rate, leading to an increased incidence of false positive outcomes.

18.4.1 ESP or QRP?

In 2011, that same Daryl Bem published an article (Bem 2011) that claimed to have found scientific evidence for extrasensory perception. The article states:

This article reports 9 experiments, involving more than 1,000 participants, that test for retroactive influence by "time-reversing" well-established psychological effects so that the individual's responses are obtained before the putatively causal stimulus events occur. . . . The mean effect size (d) in psi performance across all 9 experiments was 0.22 , and all but one of the experiments yielded statistically significant results.

As researchers began to examine Bem's article, it became clear that he had engaged in all of the QRPs that he had recommended in the chapter discussed above. As Tal Yarkoni pointed out in a blog post that examined the article:

- Sample sizes varied across studies
- Different studies appear to have been lumped together or split apart
- The studies allow many different hypotheses, and it's not clear which were planned in advance
- Bem used one-tailed tests even when it's not clear that there was a directional prediction (so alpha is really 0.1)
- Most of the p -values are very close to 0.05
- It's not clear how many other studies were run but not reported

18.5 Conducting replicable research

Conducting replicable research is essential for ensuring the reliability and credibility of scientific findings. Replicability means that independent researchers can repeat a study using the same methods and data and obtain consistent results. Achieving this requires careful documentation of study design, data collection procedures, analytical methods, and statistical models. Pre-registration of hypotheses, standardized protocols, and transparent reporting further enhance replicability. Sharing data, code, and materials allows other researchers to verify results and build upon existing work. Attention to data quality, measurement accuracy, and proper statistical analysis reduces errors and strengthens conclusions. Reporting effect sizes, confidence intervals, and assumptions ensures that findings are interpretable and reproducible. By emphasizing methodological rigor, transparency, and openness, replicable research supports the accumulation of robust scientific knowledge. It also fosters accountability, reduces false discoveries, and enhances trust in science. In applied fields, replicable research underpins evidence-based decisions, policies, and innovations. Since the emergence of the reproducibility crisis, a vigorous initiative has been undertaken to create instruments aimed at safeguarding the reproducibility of scientific research.

18.5.1 Pre-registration

One of the most prominent concepts is pre-registration, wherein an individual provides a comprehensive description of a project, including all data analysis, to a reputable repository. Pre-registration enhances confidence that analyses are free from p-hacking and other dubious research methods by requiring detailed specification of goals before data analysis.

The impact of pre-registration in clinical trials within the medical field has been significant. In 2000, the National Heart, Lung, and Blood Institute (NHLBI) mandated the pre-registration of all clinical trials through the ClinicalTrials.gov website. This presents a natural experiment to examine the impacts of study pre-registration. Kaplan and Irvin (2015) discovered that the incidence of favorable results in clinical trials significantly diminished post-2000 relative to the preceding period. Although other potential causes exist, it appears probable that researchers were able to modify their methodologies or ideas prior to study registration to get favorable outcomes, a practice that became increasingly challenging once registration was mandated.

18.5.2 Reproducible practices

The paper by Simmons, Nelson, and Simonsohn (2011) laid out a set of suggested practices for making research more reproducible, all of which should become standard for researchers:

- Authors must decide the rule for terminating data collection before data collection begins and report this rule in the article.
- Authors must collect at least 20 observations per cell or else provide a compelling cost-of-data-collection justification.
- Authors must list all variables collected in a study.
- Authors must report all experimental conditions, including failed manipulations.
- If observations are eliminated, authors must also report what the statistical results are if those observations are included.

- If an analysis includes a covariate, authors must report the statistical results of the analysis without the covariate.

18.5.3 Replication

One of the hallmarks of science is the idea of replication - that is, other researchers should be able to perform the same study and obtain the same result. Unfortunately, as we saw in the outcome of the Replication Project discussed earlier, many findings are not replicable. The best way to ensure replicability of one's research is to first replicate it on your own; for some studies this just won't be possible, but whenever it is possible one should make sure that one's finding holds up in a new sample. That new sample should be sufficiently powered to find the effect size of interest; in many cases, this will actually require a larger sample than the original.

It's important to keep a couple of things in mind with regard to replication. First, the fact that a replication attempt fails does not necessarily mean that the original finding was false; remember that with the standard level of 80% power, there is still a one in five chance that the result will be nonsignificant, even if there is a true effect. For this reason, we generally want to see multiple replications of any important finding before we decide whether or not to believe it. Unfortunately, many fields including psychology have failed to follow this advice in the past, leading to "textbook" findings that turn out to be likely false. With regard to Daryl Bem's studies of ESP, a large replication attempt involving 7 studies failed to replicate his findings (Galak et al. 2012).

Second, remember that the p -value doesn't provide us with a measure of the likelihood of a finding to replicate. As we discussed previously, the p-value is a statement about the likelihood of one's data under a specific null hypothesis;

it doesn't tell us anything about the probability that the finding is actually true (as we learned in the chapter on Bayesian analysis). In order to know the likelihood of replication we need to know the probability that the finding is true, which we generally don't know.

18.6 Doing reproducible data analysis

So far we have focused on the ability to replicate other researchers' findings in new experiments, but another important aspect of reproducibility is to be able to reproduce someone's analyses on their own data, which we refer to a computational reproducibility. This requires that researchers share both their data and their analysis code, so that other researchers can both try to reproduce the result as well as potentially test different analysis methods on the same data. There is an increasing move in psychology towards open sharing of code and data; for example, the journal Psychological Science now provides "badges" to papers that share research materials, data, and code, as well as for pre-registration.

The ability to reproduce analyses is one reason that we strongly advocate for the use of scripted analyses (such as those using R) rather than using a "point-and-click" software package. It's also a reason that we advocate the use of free and open-source software (like R) as opposed to commercial software packages, which would require others to buy the software in order to reproduce any analyses.

There are many ways to share both code and data. A common way to share code is via web sites that support version control for software, such as Github. Small datasets can also be shared via these same sites; larger datasets can be shared through data sharing portals such as Zenodo, or through specialized portals for specific types of data (such as OpenNeuro for neuroimaging data).

18.7 Concise Summary: Enhancing Scientific Practice

Every scientist bears the obligation to enhance their research methodologies to augment the repeatability of their findings. The primary objective of study is not to achieve substantial results, but to pose and address inquiries regarding nature with utmost accuracy. The majority of our hypotheses will likely be incorrect, and we should accept this, so that when we identify one that is accurate, we will possess greater confidence in its validity.

References

Baker, Monya. 2017. "Reproducibility: Check Your Chemistry." Nature 548 (7668): 485-88. https://doi.org/10.1038/548485a.

Bem, Daryl J. 2011. "Feeling the Future: Experimental Evidence for Anomalous Retroactive Influences on Cognition and Affect." J Pers Soc Psychol 100 (3): 407-25. https://doi.org/10.1037/a0021524.

Breiman, Leo. 2001. "Statistical Modeling: The Two Cultures (with Comments and a Rejoinder by the Author)." Statist. Sci. 16 (3): 199-231. https://doi.org/10.1214/ss/1009213726.

Camerer, Colin F., Anna Dreber, Felix Holzmeister, Teck-Hua Ho, Jürgen Huber, Magnus Johannesson, Michael Kirchler, et al. 2018. "Evaluating the Replicability of Social Science Experiments in Nature and Science Between 2010 and 2015." Nature Human Behaviour 2: 637-44.

Christensen, Garret S, and Edward Miguel. 2016. "Transparency, Reproducibility, and the Credibility of Economics Research." Working Paper 22989. Working Paper Series. National Bureau of Economic Research. https://doi.org/10.3386/w22989.

Copas, J. B. 1983. "Regression, Prediction and Shrinkage (with Discussion)." Journal of the Royal Statistical Society, Series B: Methodological 45: 31154.

Darley, John M, Mark P Zanna, and Henry L Roediger. 2004. The Compleat Academic: A Career Guide. 2nd ed. Washington, DC: American Psychological Association. http://www.loc.gov/catdir/toc/fy037/2003041830.ht ml.

Dehghan, Mahshid, Andrew Mente, Xiaohe Zhang, Sumathi Swaminathan,

Wei Li, Viswanathan Mohan, Romaina Iqbal, et al. 2017. "Associations of Fats and Carbohydrate Intake with Cardiovascular Disease and Mortality in 18 Countries from Five Continents (PURE): A Prospective Cohort Study." Lancet 390 (10107): 2050-62. https://doi.org/10.1016/S0140-6736(17)32252-3.

Efron, Bradley. 1998. "R. A. Fisher in the 21st Century (Invited Paper Presented at the 1996 r. A. Fisher Lecture)." Statist. Sci. 13 (2): 95-122. https://doi.org/10.1214/ss/1028905930.

Errington, Timothy M, Elizabeth Iorns, William Gunn, Fraser Elisabeth Tan, Joelle Lomax, and Brian A Nosek. 2014. "An Open Investigation of the Reproducibility of Cancer Biology Research." Elife 3 (December). https://doi.org/10.7554/eLife.04333.

Fisher, R. A. 1925. Statistical Methods for Research Workers. Edinburgh Oliver & Boyd.

Fisher, Ronald Aylmer. 1956. Statistical Methods and Scientific Inference. New York: Hafner Pub. Co.

Galak, Jeff, Robyn A LeBoeuf, Leif D Nelson, and Joseph P Simmons. 2012. "Correcting the Past: Failures to Replicate Psi." J Pers Soc Psychol 103 (6): 933-48. https://doi.org/10.1037/a0029709.

Gardner, Christopher D, Alexandre Kiazand, Sofiya Alhassan, Soowon Kim, Randall S Stafford, Raymond R Balise, Helena C Kraemer, and Abby C King. 2007. "Comparison of the Atkins, Zone, Ornish, and LEARN Diets for Change in Weight and Related Risk Factors Among Overweight Premenopausal Women: The a TO z Weight Loss Study: A Randomized Trial." JAMA 297 (9): 969-77. https://doi.org/10.1001/jama.297.9.969.

Ioannidis, John P A. 2005. "Why Most Published Research Findings Are False." PLoS Med 2 (8): e124. https://doi.org/10.1371/journal.pmed.0020124.

Kaplan, Robert M, and Veronica L Irvin. 2015. "Likelihood of Null Effects of Large NHLBI Clinical Trials Has Increased over Time." PLoS One 10 (8): e0132382. https://doi.org/10.1371/journal.pone. 0132382.

Kerr, N L. 1998. "HARKing: Hypothesizing After the Results Are Known." Pers Soc Psychol Rev 2 (3): 196-217. https://doi.org/10.1207/s1532795 7pspr0203_4.

Neyman, J. 1937. "Outline of a Theory of Statistical Estimation Based on the Classical Theory of Probability." Philosophical Transactions of the Royal Society of London A: Mathematical, Physical and Engineering Sciences 236 (767): 333-80. https://doi.org/10.1098/rsta.1937.0005.

Neyman, J., and K. Pearson. 1933. "On the Problem of the Most Efficient

Tests of Statistical Hypotheses." Philosophical Transactions of the Royal Society of London A: Mathematical, Physical and Engineering Sciences 231 (694-706): 289-337. https://doi.org/10.1098/rsta.1933.0009.

Open Science Collaboration. 2015. "PSYCHOLOGY. Estimating the Reproducibility of Psychological Science." Science 349 (6251): aac4716. https://doi.org/10.1126/science.aac4716.

Pesch, Beate, Benjamin Kendzia, Per Gustavsson, Karl-Heinz Jöckel, Georg Johnen, Hermann Pohlabeln, Ann Olsson, et al. 2012. "Cigarette Smoking and Lung Cancer-Relative Risk Estimates for the Major Histological Types from a Pooled Analysis of Case-Control Studies." Int J Cancer 131 (5): 1210-19. https://doi.org/10.1002/ijc.27339.

Schenker, Nathaniel, and Jane F. Gentleman. 2001. "On Judging the Significance of Differences by Examining the Overlap Between Confidence Intervals." The American Statistician 55 (3): 182-86. http://www.jstor. org/stable/2685796.

Schoenfeld, Jonathan D, and John P A Ioannidis. 2013. "Is Everything We Eat Associated with Cancer? A Systematic Cookbook Review." Am J Clin Nutr 97 (1): 127-34. https://doi.org/10.3945/ajcn.112.047142.

Simmons, Joseph P, Leif D Nelson, and Uri Simonsohn. 2011. "False-Positive Psychology: Undisclosed Flexibility in Data Collection and Analysis Allows Presenting Anything as Significant." Psychol Sci 22 (11): 1359-66. https://doi.org/10.1177/0956797611417632.

Smaldino, Paul E, and Richard McElreath. 2016. "The Natural Selection of Bad Science." R Soc Open Sci 3 (9): 160384. https://doi.org/10.1098/rs os. 160384.

Stigler, Stephen M. 2016. The Seven Pillars of Statistical Wisdom. Harvard University Press.

Sullivan, Gail M, and Richard Feinn. 2012. "Using Effect Size-or Why the p Value Is Not Enough." J Grad Med Educ 4 (3): 279-82. https: //doi.org/10.4300/JGME-D-12-00156.1.

Teicholz, Nina. 2014. The Big Fat Surprise. Simon & Schuster.

Wakefield, A J. 1999. "MMR Vaccination and Autism." Lancet 354 (9182): 949-50. https://doi.org/10.1016/S0140-6736(05)75696-8.

Wansink, Brian, David R Just, and Collin R Payne. 2012. "Can Branding Improve School Lunches?" Arch Pediatr Adolesc Med 166 (10): 1-2. https://doi.org/10.1001/archpediatrics.2012.999.

Index

www.ingramcontent.com/pod-product-compliance
Lightning Source LLC
LaVergne TN
LVHW081938200926
848484LV00009B/2458
* 9 7 8 1 7 8 7 1 5 6 5 4 8 *